SUPERPOWER
EDITED AND DESIGNED BY LARRY SCHREIB

On the cover (left to right): A Gale Banks Engineering turbo-charged 454 inch Chevrolet in full-on trim; Russ Collins' spectacular drag racing Honda, featuring two engines in a V-8 mount with GMC blower; a fine example of the ever-popular early Rochester fuel injector and; (below) John Callies' incredibly detailed and nitrous oxide injected 303 inch Pontiac small block from 303 Enterprises.

SUPER POWER
S-A DESIGN PUBLISHING COMPANY
11801 E. SLAUSON BLVD. BLDG E
SANTA FE SPRINGS, CALIFORNIA
(213) 696-3444   90670

EXHAUST HEADERS

INTAKE RUNNER

INTAKE MANIFOLD

FUEL CONTROL SYSTEM

EXHAUST TURBINE

AIR COMPRESSOR

EXHAUST OUTLET

AIR SENSOR

AIR INTAKE

TABLE OF CONTENTS

TURBO CHARGING

There are few more impressive examples of turbocharging power than the engines in USAC championship cars. These little (159 cid) Ford V-8's and Offy fours put out 800-1000 hp on methanol with 40-60 psi boost and cockpit-controlled wastegates.

WHAT IS
TURBO-SUPERCHARGING

Since the beginning of the automobile, performance enthusiasts have searched for more power from the internal combustion engine. The search has been fueled by the typical American Dream thinking of someday finding the "trick" part that will simply bolt on and produce gobs of elusive horsepower. This book is testament to the varied paths taken to achieve such alchemic results with the good 'ol Otto cycle machine. We think someday is here *now,* and the turbocharger is that device you've been looking for.

Before we get into explaining exactly how this simple-yet-complex device provides its Charles Atlas results on your engine, let's build a hot rod engine, hypothetically. Say we have a maximum budget of $1,000. (this is for a street machine). This would more than cover the cost of a turbocharger and the attendant plumbing and other work required to adapt it to our engine, but what else could we do with this budget? If we were to follow standard hot-rodding practices, we'd blueprint the short block somewhat, balance the reciprocating parts, install heavy-duty bearings, good rings, higher-compression pistons, and a performance camshaft and valvetrain kit. Then, we'd top off this assembly with a three-angle valve job on the heads, an aftermarket intake manifold and performance carburetor, tubular exhaust headers and a good CD ignition system. What would we wind up with? Although this engine sounds like what we'd all like to have in our personal transportation cars, the truth is, it would be a gas hog motor that required constant attention to keep it running

in top shape. It would probably "eat" spark plugs, occasionally overheat in traffic just when we needed to get somewhere, ping, rattle and detonate on even the best available gasoline, and generally exhibit poor driveability in normal driving—unless idled at 1,000 rpm and kept buzzing through the gears by constant shifting and a stiff rear end!

Maybe some of you readers have yet to go through that whole routine, and maybe it's something that you should do to get it out of your system, but in light of the current cost of gasoline, the increasing emphasis on cleaner air, the decreasing quality of "high-octane" premium fuels, the "hopped-up" engine as we used to know it is becoming less and less practical.

It's certain that we can't go down to the local new-car dealership and order ourselves a high-performance car, that kind of dream evaporated years ago due to hot air from Washington and those champions of the Average Man, insurance companies. We're stuck. If you want a high-performance automobile, you're going to have to build it yourself or pay someone to do it for you (in the latter case you have a much higher budget than our $1,000 figure and you probably don't need to read this type of book anyway). Perhaps the neatest device ever created for increasing engine performance is the supercharger.

Since an automobile engine is nothing more than a glorified air pump, it stands to reason that the more air you can get it to pump, the more horsepower it will produce. This has been a fact since the very first racing car builders attached superchargers to their engines. The function of such a device is to pack the engine with more

fuel-bearing air than it can take in by itself. The air around us has a given weight and pressure per square inch (14.76 at sea level) and an engine cannot take in more of this air than is displaced by the cylinders. Your basic passenger-car engine is lucky to boast of even filling the cylinders to within 50% of capacity, or volumetric efficiency. Even the finest all-out racing engine may only achieve 90-95% volumetric efficiency in normally-aspirated form (non-supercharged). Since we know that air is compressible, what is needed for high horsepower output is a method of compressing the air-fuel mixture and cramming it into the intake manifold. This is forced induction and is achieved by a supercharger, which is nothing more than a very efficient air pump to feed our thirsty internal combustion engine. This is usually a separate component, but there have been cases of racing engines where one of the cylinders was used strictly as a supercharger to cram extra air into the other cylinders. Try this on your next Super Stock engine, but if the tech inspectors figure it out, don't tell them where you heard the idea!

Since a supercharger can raise engine power output more than any other modification, what kind should we use? Many supercharger kits have come and gone over the years, from the Latham to the Paxton and McCulloch, and the GMC to the modern turbocharger; but they all fall into two basic types: the positive-displacement type and the centrifugal type. The former is exemplified by the big GMC-type blowers seen on dragsters and funny cars, and the latter are the turbochargers used on Indianapolis cars and the original Cam-Am road racers. If we assumed that the same $1,000 could furnish our street engine with either type of compressor, as opposed to the hot-rod

Turbocharging can add incredible power to small displacement engines. This Rajay kit for the Volkswagen four was one of the earliest kits and is still one of the most effective power improvers.

This Ak Miller cutaway of an AiResearch T04 turbo illustrates the relationship of the two turbine wheels, common shaft and center bearing.

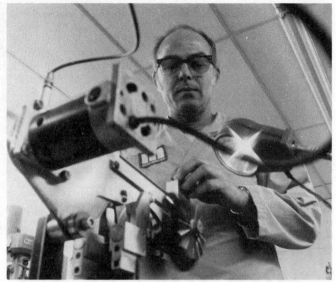

As you can imagine, the shaft, bearing and turbine and compressor wheels must be balanced to extremely-close tolerances.

build-up routine, let's look at these two a little more closely.

The positive-displacement supercharger gulps in air and fuel and crams it into the intake manifold, which is fine, but there has to be a method of powering the supercharger. It is generally driven from the engine crankshaft, either directly (not common any more) or through a chain or belt drive. So we know that in addition to having a special intake manifold on which to bolt this device, we also need special pulleys, belts and idler pulleys to drive it. The turbocharger, on the other hand, is not driven mechanically, but is powered by the flow of exhaust gases out of the engine, and here's where we get into the differences of these two types of blowers. The positive-displacement type, with a direct mechanical link to the crankshaft, takes a certain amount of engine horsepower to drive it, and it places an extra load on the crankshaft. The GMC's (or derivatives thereof) take as much as 100 horsepower to drive at top speed! The turbo is essentially driven by *free power*, like a mill driven by a running stream, and the drive system places no extra loads on the crankshaft.

As engine speed increases, the GMC-type blower compresses more and more air because it, too, is turning faster. If it will provide 5 psi boost at 2,000 rpm, then it will produce 10 psi boost at 4,000 rpm and 15 psi at 6,000. Not bad, except when compared to the centrifugal blower, which can produce boost by a *geometric progression,* or put another way, it will increase boost by the *square* of the rpm increase. This gets touchy quickly! The ideal setup would be a small torque converter to drive the blower, a drive that could take the G-forces of acceleration and deceleration without disintegrating. In

the case of the turbocharger, this is exactly what the flow of exhaust gases from the engine provides.

Being constantly driven by the crankshaft, the positive-displacement blower produces boost at all times, including low-speed operation, at which time it may or may not be desired. Because it relies on a tight seal between the ends of the rotors and the interior of the housing to produce boost, the GMC-type blower is not considered efficient at boost levels above 15 psi, and will always add undesirable heat to the intake charge. It won't help engine emissions or fuel economy either, since it is working all the time. The beauty of the turbo is that it doesn't work all the time. It produces basically a variable-compression-ratio engine, with boost applied only when needed, eliminating

the problems associated with a positive-displacement blower.

What can we expect from our $1,000 if we spend it on a turbo system instead of the usual hot-rod techniques with the disadvantages we have already discussed? In most cases you can *double* the air-pumping ability of an engine with a properly-selected turbocharger. This can translate to an increase in rear-wheel horsepower of 50 to 100%, and a naturally-aspirated engine would have to go some to duplicate those results! Most standard high-performance engine parts increase performance by allowing an engine to turn higher crank speeds, or create the potential for more horsepower when the engine is turned tighter. This whole line of thinking has to be forgotten if we are to continue

Though simple in their operation, turbos must be built to exacting standards to withstand the 100,000 rpm shaft speeds they operate at and maintain their record of reliability. These are computer-controlled machining operations at Roto-Master.

talking about exhaust-driven turbochargers, because all of these tricks become unnecessary. A turbocharged engine doesn't have to turn high crank speeds to produce power—one of the reasons a turbo makes such a superior modification for street machine performance. An 8,000-rpm smallblock Chevy for the street would be a running fool if it was properly built, but the simple addition of a turbocharger kit could give an equivalent power at only 5,000 rpm. *This is with the rest of the engine almost completely stock.* In a typical street turbo application on a stock late-model "smog" motor such as most of us are driving, a small boost of 5-10 psi is enough to make a stock 3,500-lb sedan into a street killer of supercar-era proportions, or make a sluggish RV pickup with ponderous camper, flatten those vacation hills out to level freeways. With just a few changes and a heavier boost load of 10-15 psi, you're ready to take on the baddest big-inch machines in town. One of the beauties of a turbo system is that changing the boost level of your existing setup is no more complicated than changing ratios in a quick-change

rearend. A good system should provide exceptional street performance, combined with reasonable fuel economy, acceptable emissions, excellent driveability, as well as serving occasional warrior duty at the dragstrip on weekends. And, if you sell your car, most of the $1,000 investment in equipment can be saved to reapply to your next machine, something that would be out of the question with normal speed equipment, unless you installed another stock motor in your car before selling it.

SO YOU WANT A TURBO

You've probably heard stories about turbochargers and seen the increasing play that has been given them in the auto press, but their true operation may seem as complicated as the inner workings of an automatic transmission or a Saturn V rocket. Talk is cheap and the drive-ins are full of "experts" who may have given you one reason or another why turbos don't work on the street. Turbochargers have been around for many years, first coming into prominence on World War II piston-driven planes. Today they are used widely on stationary industrial engines and large

commercial trucks, especially diesels. Only in the last ten years or so has much attention been directed toward using them on automobiles. But, for several reasons, progress has been slow. First, the turbocharger manufacturers haven't been interested in the automotive market, the commercial utilizations account for almost all of their lucrative business, and a few automotive applications would seem like small potatoes. Also, to them, the automotive turbo users seem uninformed and fussy. They want everything perfect and often a poor installation of the wrong turbo by a bad mechanic is blamed on the manufacturer when it doesn't live up to expectations. The major manufacturers who deal with steady industrial customers spend money and development time to derive the proper turbo size for each application, therefore they have few problems, despite selling thousands of units. The automotive enthusiast is generally not an engineer and is constantly calling the manufacturer to ask one thing or another about the single turbo he bought. Most of the derogatory stories that circulate about turbos had their beginnings with simi-

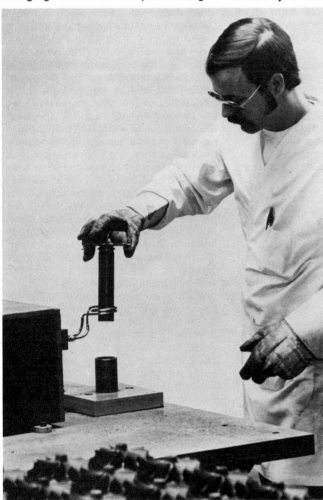

These are Roto-Master wheels and shafts being inspected after undergoing "inertia" welding by the Caterpillar process.

Clean, careful assembly after precise machine work is what makes turbochargers operate as reliably as they do. With a steady supply of oil, they are virtually maintenance-free after installation.

lar scenarios in the 1960's.

Detroit tried, with minor success, to make a production turbo available. Remember the '62-'63 Oldsmobile F-85 with the Jetfire option and the Chevrolet Corvair with the Spyder option? The tubo was a "foreign object" to most mechanics who looked under the hood back then. If something was wrong with the engine the mechanic would blame the turbo unit and advise the owner to get rid of it. A lot of F-85 turbos wound up in the junk piles, and even when they were working, the Oldsmobile engineers had been so conservative with the boost controls that the performance didn't seem to justify learning a new science. When most innovative mechanics and enthusiasts decided that such devices might be a good thing to bolt on their backyard projects, the results weren't spectacular enough to convince anyone that the turbo was to become *the performance device of the future*. Often, the hot rodder would find a turbo unit at a swap meet or in the back of some truck shop, take it home and cobble it onto his engine and expect to take on the world. As you can guess, the turbo was designed for some completely different application and either had the wrong amount of boost or the boost came in at the wrong time. If the boost from the commercial unit was too low, the hot rodder would tell all his buddies that turbos didn't make horsepower. If it was too much he probably flushed his motor on the first pass, allowing everyone to decide for themselves how neat turbos were.

But this was before some of the people who today lead the turbo kit market got involved. People like Ak Miller,

Rigid testing standards after turbos are assembled insure that every unit is ready to go. Large industrial turbo is undergoing a final test at Roto-Master.

Jack Lufkin, Bob Keller, Ted Trevor, George Spears, Hugh MacInnes and Duke Hallock took active interest in the turbocharger and the development of high-performance automotive adaptations of existing turbos. Today we have an ever-increasing variety of commercial turbo kits available that can be installed with sparkling results by any competent mechanic. Naturally, the most popular applications such as the ubiquitous smallblock Chevy V-8 were developed first, but now there is a wide array for almost every make of car, truck, RV, boat, and even motorcycle. Most of the major turbo manufacturers do not make or sell these turbo kits, it is the "distributors" who have put the time and effort into making up common-sense kits with turbochargers matched to the application, so you and I can become modern alchemists to turn our wasted exhaust gases and heat into magical horsepower.

Since we brought up the "magic" of turbo functioning again, let's get a few basics out of the way before we have you turbocharging your car like Foyt and Andretti. The basic turbocharger consists of two housings. Each of these housings contains a turbine wheel, and both of the wheels are connected together by a common shaft, so that when one spins so does the other. We'll call one housing-and-wheel duet the turbine, and the other the compressor. The inlet side of the turbine housing is connected to the exhaust of the engine, allowing hot, rushing exhaust gases to pass over the turbine wheel—making it spin (rapidly). The gas exists through the outlet to the exhaust system. Meanwhile, the shaft, mounted in a bearing between the two housings, is making the compressor wheel spin at the same speed. The compressor half of the turbocharger sucks air or an air-fuel mixture in and blows it through an outlet to the intake side of the engine. You can readily see how the turbo "feeds upon itself"; the more air the compressor packs into the engine, the more exhaust there is to drive the turbine, which spins the compressor wheel faster, and so on. What is interesting is that the normally-aspirated engine loses 35% of its heat energy out the exhaust. With a turbo on the engine some of this energy is recovered and used to increase the en-

Though they have been used for many years, turbochargers are still subjected to extensive research and development. This test cell at Rajay Industries is used for experimental development.

Huge flow-testing facilities are also part of the Rajay Industries testing program. Note here that three flow benches are available in this one test module.

gine power! We've simplified the operation of a turbocharger here, but there's a lot more to be learned. Just picking the proper turbo for a particular application is a science unto itself.

What makes a turbocharger so expensive if it's so simple? The average turbocharger for automotive uses costs from $300 to $400 in bare form, and the average complete kit costs from $500 to $750 (for kits using a single turbo), when all the other pieces are included. The cost of the turbo is easy to understand if we just think about what it is required to do. The turbine, or exhaust-side, has to withstand heat as high as 1800°F. The shaft and both wheels have to stand rotational speeds of 100,000 rpm or more. You can imagine how precisely all of the rotating pieces must be balanced, how perfect the single sleeve bearing has to be, and how precisely these devices have to be assembled. Despite the conditions under which they operate, a modern turbocharger, properly installed and lubricated, can be expected to give incredibly reliable service with little or no attention. The cost of a turbo kit is easy to understand when you realize how many pieces the kit manufacturer has to fabricate for each specific kit, not to mention the development time spent finding exactly the proper turbo for a given use. When compared to any other kind of modification, there are no performance avenues open to the enthusiast that can promise as carefully planned a "package" approach as a good turbo kit.

We'll assume at this point that you'd like to have something in common with A.J. Foyt and Mario Andretti, and your friends would be impressed to know

your Nova shares some of the mystique of the $28,000 Porsche Turbo-Carrera. You'd like to have an exhaust-driven supercharger on your street machine, but before you send off a check for the only piece of NASA-quality equipment your car is ever likely to see, there are still more basics to be discussed.

What type of engine is best-suited to a turbocharger? There are kits available now for just about everything from minicars to motorcycles and from large marine engines to monstrous Allison aircraft engines. It can be said without fear of contradiction that any engine can be turbocharged, but some are

more suitable by design than others. One of the primary considerations would be the compression ratio. The higher the stock compression ratio of an engine, the less boost can be applied before encountering detonation. Most turbo manufacturers recommend a static compression ratio of around 8:1, for street use. One of the major reasons turbos were not practical for street applications during the 1960's was the high factory compression ratios. Since the average Detroit compression was around 10:1 and many performance-optional engines had even higher numbers, a turbo installer would have to rebuild his entire engine in order to install a set of custom-made, low-compression pistons. But we all know what has happened to factory compression ratios since 1970. Due to ever-constricting emission laws, the average Detroit compression ratio in the past several years has been reduced to about 8:1. Now isn't that number familiar? It's true, despite what we may think about the effect of clean air legislation on automobile performance, one of the effects has been to make the average Detroit engine the perfect candidate for turbocharging. In stock form, it has all the requirements, a low static compression ratio and anemic performance that fairly cries out to be improved upon.

As we stated earlier, if you've been around standard hot-rodding practices for some time, you're going to have to start with a clean slate when dealing with turbochargers. Forget 90% of what you've learned is "trick" performance. Most of the blueprinting, wild cams, lightweight valvetrain equipment, special manifolding and exotic headwork

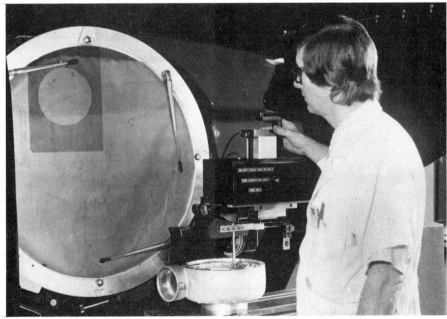

Manufacturing tolerances and testing are very important. Here at Garrett Corporation's AiResearch Industrial Division a turbo compressor housing is being checked with a contour comparator.

9

Matching the turbo to the engine-application is the key to top notch performance. Expertise and experience are required for the best results as there is a wide variety of turbos on the market to select from. This sampling from AiResearch includes (left to right): a T04B (frequently used in automotive kit applications), a TV61, a TV71, a TV81 and a T18A.

is an unnecessary waste of money on a turbocharged street engine. In terms of which, stock motors are best for a turbo. Consider the factors that would make an engine attractive as a basis for any buildup. Look for an engine with a good reputation for durability. Additionally, strong bottom end and good cylinder-head-to-block attachment are primary considerations. The more boost you plan to run, the more such factors affect engine suitability. The average Detroit engine can withstand 7-10 psi boost (given the proper fuel to avoid detonation) without affecting the reliability. In fact, the turbocharged engine will probably last much longer at a given level of horsepower than a hot-rodded engine, since the turbo engine doesn't have to rev high to produce power and because the turbo is only working during a portion of the engine operating time.

In a discussion among hot rodders about the best engines made, the fa-

vorites usually are the four-bolt-main smallblock Chevy, the big-block Chevy, the Boss Ford engines, and Chrysler 340, 440 and 426 Hemi. When talking about suitability for a turbocharger, some of the engines you would not normally consider are every bit as practical and some more so. For instance, any of the 400-inch smog motors take just as well to the air machine as those we have just mentioned, yet they are seldom thought of as suitable for performance. When street boost levels are employed, an American Motors 304 or a 345-inch International Harvester motor can be just as desirable as a four-bolt-main 350 Chevy. Any engine that has proven to be durable in other applications will operate successfully with a turbo, and conversely, if an engine is known to be unreliable even when stock, then expect it to be even more self-destructive when, if you'll excuse the pun, the pressure is on.

Among those engines we summarily

dismiss when discussing high-performance work are inline engines and truck motors. Shocking as the concept may be to all but the already dyed-in-the-wool inline freak, these are some of the best candidates for an exhaust-driven blower. Not only do they usually need the power, but they usually have plenty of engine compartment room around them for the special plumbing attendant to a turbo installation. Truck engines are often built with heavier blocks, heads, and beefier lower end components, which means they can often stand more boost than an equivalent passenger-car engine. A cross-flow cylinder head on an inline engine is generally thought to be desirable for performance use, but the mundane inline with both intake and exhaust systems on the same side is preferred for turbocharging because the intake charge and exhaust gases can be channeled directly to the turbo. The turbo exhaust housing can be

An AiResearch T3 turbo with built-in wastegate.

A TurboSonic turbo assembly from Roto Master.

A Rajay 801F80 turbo assembly.

easily adapted to the stock exhaust system and the compressor side can be directed easily to the intake manifold.

Another reason truck and inline engines are perfect for a turbocharger adaptation is their inherent low-end torque. If you plan to run a normal amount of street boost (5-10 psi) and your system is designed for the turbo to work on a demand basis (boost does not occur until the engine speed reaches 2500-3000 rpm, so that you're not using boost all the time), then you will have some turbo lag. This is a slight delay between the time you floor the throttle and the time you feel the boost. A turbo system can be designed for greater performance without turbo lag, which we'll discuss later, but some lag is inherent in a typical low-boost application. What makes the truck V-8 or six-cylinder engine attractive for this type of setup is that they are usually designed for low-end torque, with maximum torque being realized at 2500 rpm or less. In other words, when one of these engines has reached peak torque and starts going "down the other side" (of the torque curve), the turbo takes over and keeps building torque. With a properly-engineered setup, there can be a smooth transition from the normally-aspirated conditions to boost conditions.

A final consideration, though it sounds drastically simple, is that the engine must be in prime condition. It should go without saying that satisfactory results are not going to be realized with an engine that suffers from worn rings, sloppy bearings, or burned valves; but some rodders never take engine condition into consideration. As often the case when the engine starts to lose its edge, some "backyard mechanic"

decides that the addition of a new manifold or other "go-fast goodie" is going to stop the aging process and bring the engine back to life. This type of thinking can be especially dangerous with a piece of equipment that makes horsepower easily, such as a supercharger or exotic fuel. We remember when nitromethane first became popular at the dragstrip. Those who had formerly built high-horsepower gas dragster engines and switched to nitro found they could get away with cutting corners in engine building. While they had previously taken great pains in assembly and parts-selection for their gas engines, in order to extract that last drop of power, they found that this new go-juice made things simpler. They didn't have to be so fastidious in assembly because if the engine didn't put out as much power as the tires could stand, they just "tipped the can" a little more and the higher nitro percentages made up for it, at least for a while. When one of these $75 "junkyard specials" would blow up, they would grab another from their tow-truck. This system sometimes got them through a weekend of racing! Fortunately, this practice has faded from drag racing, but the philosophy that you can make up for any engine deficiency by tipping the can a little further is not altogether gone from the automotive scene. Today a turbocharger provides the same kind of horsepower improvement that nitro did back then, and successful long-term results (horsepower that lasts) still depends on a strong engine in prime condition.

WHAT IS BOOST

We have discussed, in general terms,

the theory of turbocharging, but before we go any further we should discuss what makes this wonderous engine power—the magical and mysterious world of *boost*. Turbo kit manufacturers and installers tell us that the most frequently asked questions concern boost; questions like: what is it, how much can be used, when does it "come in," and many other questions you may be asking yourself at this point.

Boost is simply the amount of pressure the turbocharger is blowing into the intake system. This is sometimes expressed in inches of mercury or water (the amount of pressure needed to raise a column of mercury or water the designated height—in inches or fractions thereof—above the height established by standard atmospheric pressure), but we'll use the more common measurement of *pounds* (pounds of pressure per square inch—expressed as psi). Just remember that when you hear about USAC championship cars running 80-100 inches of boost (how else do you think they get 1,000 hp from 160 c.i.), two inches pressure (water) equals one pound boost. The amount of boost a turbo system develops and the engine speed range over which this boost is produced, depends on a number of interrelated factors; such as—engine size, turbo size, intake and exhaust restrictions. Smaller engines can be built with a single turbo, but some large V-8 engines will require two turbos for really high performance use.

The choice of the turbo size and the relationship of the turbine wheel and turbine housing have everything to do with the boost developed. There is an entire science to picking the right turbo

It's not a good idea to purchase a used turbo unless you know it's exactly right for your installation. This T05 AiResearch unit was used on the original Olds Jetfire, but one you find in your local wrecking yard may be worthless if you can't get replacement parts for it today.

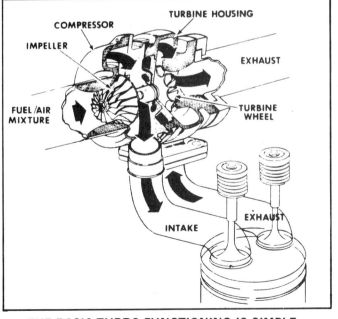

THE BASIC TURBO FUNCTIONING IS SIMPLE

for a specific application, and even after using a ream of scratch paper and two sets of batteries in your pocket calculator, the model that "the numbers" say is perfect for your use may work differently when you actually fire the engine. Let the experts pick the turbo for your use. Even after the basic size of turbo is selected, there are other factors which affect the boost level; what you might call the "fine-tuning" after the initial installation. The relationship of the turbine wheel to the housing, usually termed the *A/R ratio,* can be adjusted to arrive at the desired boost. A turbine with smaller clearance between the wheel and housing will put out more boost and start boosting sooner than one with more clearance. The turbine housing is easily changed to a larger or smaller one to adjust your boost level. Since all of the currently available turbochargers used for automotive applications have more than enough potential to blow your engine to bits, no matter if you have a blueprinted 454 or a stock 327, you have to exercise some caution in this business of picking a turbine housing size. If you think you want lots of boost at low engine speeds and you pick a small housing, the boost at higher speeds may exceed the design limits of your engine, as good as it may be. Just as it is better to start off with your carburetion rich and dial down, it's also wise to start with a larger turbine housing—to see exactly how the boost works in your vehicle—before experimenting with higher pressures.

The basic idea in building a high-performance street engine with a turbocharger is maximum performance with a measure of reliability. This, in some cases, means using a turbine housing which might be too small (too high boosting) for high engine speeds and just right for low and medium speeds; but which makes boost "early" in the speed range. This is one of the methods for avoiding the turbocharger lag you've heard so much about (usually from enthusiasts who are still fans of the mechanically-driven supercharger). Yet, if we pick a turbo that produces boost at lower engine speeds, we have to limit the amount of boost that it puts out at higher speeds or we buy stock in TRW and lay in a good supply of short blocks. However, there are a number of ways to limit this boost level; some excellent, some good, and some are little more than adequate compromises. The three basic means are: *restrictions, controllers, and wastegates.* All three have their advantages and disadvantages, but let's look at them more closely.

It is possible to select a turbocharger size and turbine A/R ratio that on a certain engine will not produce more than the desired boost, simply because ei-

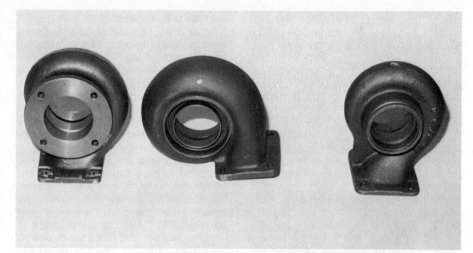

In addition to there being many sizes of exhaust housings for the same turbo, there are also different shapes. Depending on the room available in your application, you may want an on-center housing such as at left, or an off-center housing (center). At right is an on-center with a clamp-type outlet instead of the four-bolt flange.

ther the carburetion is restrictive, the turbo is not spinning fast enough (due to engine size and exhaust system design), or the exhaust system out of the turbo creates back pressure that keeps the turbo under control. These kinds of restrictions aren't the best way to control boost, but we've seen some street setups for maximum power wherein the engine would not make more than 20 psi boost, no matter what was done. Since 20 psi gave more than enough power, the owners were satisfied and saved the money they otherwise might have spent on a controller or waste gate. It's when you get a little more reasonable about maximum boost levels, more in the realm of 8-15 psi, and still want it to come in at lower engine speeds, that some type of control is helpful. Restrictions in the intake or exhaust system may work in some instances, but it may take some experimentation to arrive at the best setup. Even then, a change to an unusual load condition, such as a long

climb up a steep grade, may cause the turbo to put out more boost than normally experienced in level driving.

For most of us, another type of control, one that is easily adjusted for a particular engine-car use, is required. A method that has been successful in street applications is a controller on the compressor side of the system. Many kit manufacturers use such a device, e.g., the Roto-Master Turbosonic control and the IMPCO TC-2 controller used by Ak Miller, Spearco and others. These devices sense intake manifold pressure through a hose connecting them to the intake manifold. When boost reaches the limit desired, they throttle down the compressor-to-engine tract and reduce the flow, at the same time causing less exhaust gas flow to be produced. This slows the turbo to below the maximum boost level. Such controllers can be adjusted to do this at different boost pressures, so that, unlike restriction controls, they can be used even if the basic

Ak Miller and Gale Banks make available these heat shields for turbine housings. Made of stainless steel, they will keep more heat in the turbo, keep heat off your other components, and besides, they look better than a rusty old turbine housing! As you will find, no paint will last on a turbo.

You say you need a little power Bunkie! Well, this Gale Banks turbocharged 454-inch Chevy pumps out a cement-shaking 1000 lb/ft torque (uncorrected) at 6500 rpm.

Inline engines are particularly suited to turbocharging because of the underhood room around them. This Ak Miller installation on a California Highway truck uses propane fuel for clean emission and a clean engine. Note the large air cleaner at right.

turbo size is changed or another turbine housing is installed. They are extremely simple, with few moving parts, and, because they are on the intake system and not the exhaust system, they can be built of cheaper materials than an exhaust control.

The IMPCO TC-2 uses a spring-loaded piston assembly. When boost pressure on the engine side of the compressor is too high, it overcomes the pressure of the spring and pushes the piston back—partially closing down the tract to cut flow to the engine. Various springs can be easily substituted to achieve different boost levels. The Turbosonic control uses a piston and cylinder which is not within the inlet tract, but which connects through a linkage rod to a butterfly plate that is in the compressor-to-engine path. When boost approaches the

desirable limit, the piston pushes the linkage to close the inlet butterfly, and the induction boost is restricted. On some kits this is a predetermined "street level," but an adjustable control is also available.

The other type of boost control is the well-known exhaust wastegate. This is also a form of spring-loaded valve—connected to the exhaust system before the turbo—that dumps or releases excess exhaust pressure when the predetermined boost level is attained (thus slowing down the turbine and reducing boost). A simple poppet-valve won't do the job because it will just rattle around on the seat. The wastegate has to be controlled by something other than just the amount of exhaust pressure. This calls for some sophistication and a variety of methods have been used to control the

opening time of the wastegate. The most common is to use the boost pressure present in the intake manifold to act against the spring pressure. In other words, the spring is constantly trying to keep the valve seated against the exhaust pressure; but a line is connected to the wastegate (below the diaphragm at the top of the valve stem) providing intake manifold pressure to the backside of the diaphragm. When boost reaches a predetermined level, say 10 psi, this pressure on the diaphragm (plus the exhaust pressure working against the valve head), is enough to overcome the spring and open the valve. By having a threaded bolt above the spring, boost is adjustable. Turning the bolt down will effectively increase the spring resistance and make it open only at a higher boost level. Racers affectionately refer to this

You can lay awake nights thinking about what kind of ride this must be. A full-on turbocharged Chevy (again a Banks Engineering job) with wastegate and intercooler.

Boost-control devices are important for certain applications but when the turbo units can be matched to the engine-application needs they may not be necessary.

as the "horsepower screw", and on most Champ cars it is adjustable from within the cockpit. Extreme boost is used only when necessary, conserving fuel in the long race.

Because the wastegate must work under conditions of extreme heat, it must be precisely made, of super materials. This makes them expensive to manufacture, and, in the past, they have been hard for the average guy to buy. Indy engine builders don't have trouble getting them, but wastegates are expensive and aren't always suitable for street use. The AiResearch and Schwitzer units seen on most of the Indy cars are made for extremely high boost levels, and the valve size and spring pressure normally used make them slightly impractical. While they are adjustable, they often don't react quickly to control boost in the relatively low pressures a street application requires. A difference of a few pounds opening pressure on an engine running alcohol fuel and 45 or 50 psi boost isn't critical; but it would be a big difference on your motorhome, because a few pounds could be the difference between survival and detonation.

John Anderson, one of the kit manufacturers, has available a wastegate of his own design, which costs only $195, and has a small valve that is responsive down to as low as 5 psi boost. Yet it has the capacity to handle engines up to 500 cubic inches when a single turbo is used. It's small, lightweight, and if a dual-turbo V-8 is planned, two of these wastegates can be used.

The disadvantage of a wastegate is largely its cost, but intake controllers have their drawbacks, too. When they throttle down the intake path, the engine power drops, and it's enough that you can feel it in the seat of your pants. With a wastegate the engine reaches a certain power level and boost level and it just stays there as long as you keep your foot in it. Another problem with controllers is that they can sometimes cause the turbo to overspeed, bringing it close to a dangerous surge condition. However, this would be rare and those kit manufacturers who utilize them have picked the proper turbo exhaust housing for their kits to avoid this. An exhaust wastegate doesn't allow the turbo to spin any faster than is necessary to achieve the preset boost level. From this it would seem that wastegates are the ideal boost control system, but it must be said that relatively inexpensive controllers like the IMPCO have been successfully used in hundreds of installations too.

A final word about wastegates, they must be operated regularly. The valve and valve guide used in them (indeed,

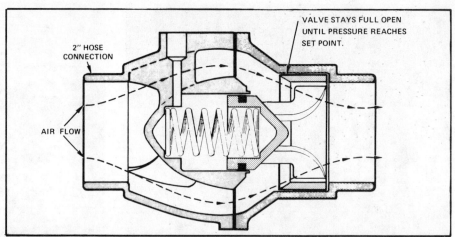

One of the more inexpensive methods of boost control is with an intake controller such as the IMPCO TC-2. This aluminum unit is just the right size (2-in) to plumb into your turbo-to-intake-manifold line.

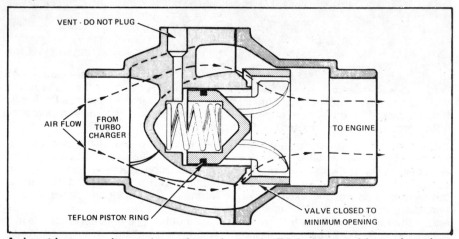

As boost increases, it overcomes the spring on the TC-2 piston and forces it to close down the internal passage, which cuts the boost going to the engine. Springs are available in 3, 5, 7, 9, 11 and 15 psi. Changing a spring is a five-minute job.

In this blow-through application, a TC-2 is used for each turbo and the vent merely passes dry air when controlling boost.

14

Here's a TC-2 used on a twin-turbo big-block Chevy. The aluminum boost controller is welded directly to the air box over the intake manifold. In this type of draw-through installation, the vent from the TC-2 releases fuel-air and must be plumbed back to the air cleaner. Rotating the compressor housing relative to the exhaust turbine here will make a straight line from turbo to the TC-2.

One of the best ways to control boost is with an exhaust wastegate, but they aren't cheap. This AiResearch unit with adapter body and modifications by Ak Miller costs more than a turbocharger! As modified by Miller, that knob at the top provides precise click-stop boost adjustments in one-psi increments.

all the parts of a wastegate) are subject to very high prolonged temperatures and to the corrosive effects of heat and condensation moisture. As a result, some light corrosion buildup can take place on the valve stem, which would make the wastegate sluggish or sticky. This generally only happens if the system is set for a high level of boost and the car is driven for several weeks at a time without reaching this level and moving the valve. Just hitting the activating boost level once a week, even if only for a few seconds, will move the valve and prevent corrosion from accumulating on the valve stem. Once you've felt the surge of power that a "whoosh-maker" provides your

engine, we're certain that your problem will be one of not watching your speed limits rather than not putting your foot in it occasionally!

DESIGNING YOUR TURBO SYSTEM

There are six basic connections from a turbocharger to an engine. These are: exhaust flow into the turbine, exhaust flow out of the turbine, air flow into the compressor, air flow out of the compressor, and oil flow into and out of the central bearing. How these connections are routed will determine the efficiency and success of your installation. There are right and wrong methods for every one of these con-

nections, and what looks like the "trick" or "cleanest" setup isn't always the most effective. Let's first examine the exhaust system, because this is of basic importance to the work that a turbocharger does, and there aren't too many choices of how to plumb it properly.

EXHAUST PLUMBING

For years, the biggest selling performance item in speed shops (not counting appearance items like aluminum wheels) has been exhaust headers. Back in the '50's when custom-built tube headers were expensive and hard to buy, the first performance improvement a hot rodder would make would

John Anderson makes his own wastegates that are compact and relatively inexpensive. Turning the horsepower screw inward increases the spring pressure and makes the valve open only at a higher pressure or boost level.

The Anderson wastegate disassembled. A boost line from the intake manifold is plumbed into the wastegate below the diaphragm and spring, so that when boost reaches a certain level, the pressure can overcome the spring and open the valve. This slows down the turbo without killing engine power, as a restriction would.

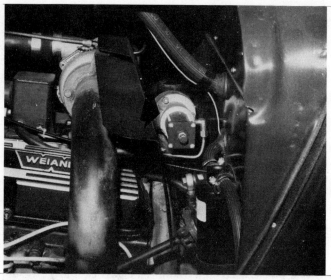

The Anderson wastegate is here mounted with its "dump" hole pointing down to vent the excess exhaust gasses. Note the large oil drainback line, free of restrictions.

On Anderson's '34 Ford coupe, wastegate is mounted at the rear of the engine, where the two exhaust systems join together (this is a single-turbo installation) just before turbo.

be to install dual exhausts and glasspack mufflers, then a larger carburetor. But, because of the dual benefits of improved performance and better fuel economy, headers have become incredibly popular, with dozens of companies churning out reasonably-priced jig-built sets for every popular engine chassis combination. We see them today on just about every street machine, street rod, or van, and thousands of otherwise-stock grocery getters.

Today's enthusiast may be dismayed to find that he won't be able to use these racy-looking tubes on his turbo car. Headers, with individual pipes for each exhaust port and tuned tube and collector lengths, account for improved engine performance on a non-turbo engine because they reduce back-pressure and can even create a scavenging or siphoning effect on the cylinders if they are tuned properly. This effect aids the induction system in filling the cylinder on the intake stroke.

In a turbocharged application, the least of our worries is trying to accomplish extra cylinder filling; a single turbo, small as it may appear, has the potential to blow your engine right into the old parts bin. What we're after is an exhaust system that provides the most direct route to the turbine and retains as much of the exhaust heat, pressure, and velocity, as possible.

In most applications, you'll be using modified stock exhaust manifolds, which may not appear very glamorous, but cast iron manifolds retain the heat and headers do not. Also, the high exhaust temperatures created in a turbo system will tend to shorten the life of exhaust system material adjacent to the turbo. With high boost, the turbine and part of the manifold can get red hot, and the thin-wall tubing normally used for exhaust headers would burn up quickly unless there were sufficient air flowing over the pipes to dissipate the heat. If you're building an unusual installation where a stock manifold won't

work (even in modified form) or engine compartment limitations make it impractical, it is possible to construct a suitable tubing setup using thick-wall tubing and a very thick flange plate. The flange plates with starter tubes that many header companies sell for do-it-yourselfers are not thick enough for turbo use. You'll have to flamecut some new flanges of at least ⅜-in steel. A thinner flange may warp and allow a leak to develop. The headers you build should be as short and direct as possible. You can make a set of tubing pipes retain heat pretty well if you insulate them with asbestos tape and metal foil, but this will also burn them up faster. Another solution, used primarily on race-car applications, is to build the headers of stainless steel tubing instead of normal "muffler-moly." You can imagine how expensive such a set of headers would be, though.

Assuming that you are going to use some form of cast iron manifold, how can you hook up the turbo? You'll have

Some turbos are available with three- or four-bolt exhaust outlet flanges that require only welding a similar flange on your exhaust pipe. Others have a clamping rim. Ak Miller sells the rings (center) to weld onto your pipe so that a V-band clamp can be used to hook pipe-to-turbo.

A simple flange like this Ak Miller unit can often be welded directly to your stock manifold to provide turbo mounting.

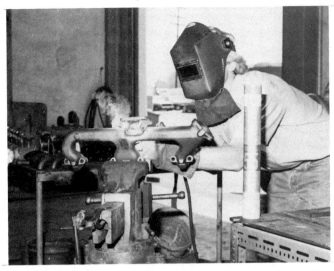

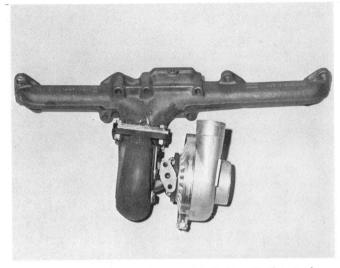

Cast iron exhaust manifolds work best because they retain the heat and don't burn out. Flanges can easily be welded on using arc-welding with special Ni-Rod rods.

Inline engines are the easiest to plumb. Usually the stock exhaust manifold can be modified to mount the turbo directly to it.

to cut off the stock pipe flange and weld on a new flange that matches your turbo. Cast iron cuts and grinds easily and the new flange can be successfully mounted by arc-welding with a rod made specifically for cast iron, such as *Ni-Rod*. The turbo flanges themselves are available from some of the kit manufacturers, or you can make your own by taking a pattern to your local welding shop and having one flamecut from ⅜-in, or thicker, plate. If your engine-turbo combination is one of the more popular ones, the kit manufacturers may have a special cast iron manifold available to accept a turbocharger, saving a lot of trouble. If you weld up a system, the job must be a good one with absolutely no leaks, so make a few extra passes with the arc welder to build a very solid joint.

If you're building a V-8 engine, you're going to have to connect both exhaust

manifolds somehow, whether you plan to use a single turbo or one on each bank. When using one turbo, you mount the turbo on one exhaust manifold as outlined above but leave the stock pipe flange intact. You weld your turbo flange on the topside of the stock exhaust manifold. The exhaust from the manifold on the other side of the engine is routed to the turbo side with an under-the-engine crossover pipe. Then, the flow of gases from both manifolds will go through the new flange into the turbine. Even with a turbo on each side of a V-8, you need a crossover tube to balance the boost between the turbos. The stock exhaust-heat crossover in the intake manifold is adequate, but if you don't have one there, you'll have to make one of tubing.

If you're not using one of the commercial turbo kits, you'll have to fabricate the rest of the exhaust system,

from the turbo(s) through the mufflers and tailpipes. The turbine outlet is usually larger than standard exhaust pipe, so you'll probably have to use 2½-in tubing and flamecut a flange to match the turbine outlet. *Take the routing of this pipe into consideration when planning the turbo mount.* Leave room between the firewall and the turbo for the exhaust pipe, remembering it is difficult to make tight bends in large-diameter tubing. However, having an unrestricted flow of exhaust out of the turbine is extremely important for engine response. A system with a minimum of bends and restrictions will have better throttle response and quicker boost buildup than one with the same large-size tubing but with sharp bends. The size of this system is also critical to the performance. Many turbos can get by with a 2½-in system from the turbo on back, but the same engine with a 3-in system all the way

For most popular V-8's, special cast manifolds are available for turbos. This is an Ak Miller unit for big-block Chevys using twin turbochargers. Note oil drain extension pipe from the turbo to the oil pan.

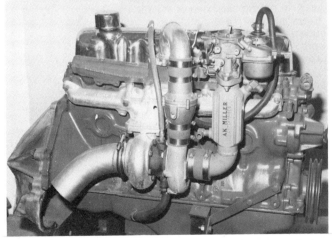

The exhaust outlet tubing from the turbo is extremely important. It should be large in diameter and free of sharp bends. The larger the outlet tubing, the more boost you can get and quicker engine response. Note also the IMPCO boost controller, Ak Miller carb adapter and the turbo oil-return line.

Single-turbo installations on V-8's require a crossover system of some kind. Expansion in that long crossover tube requires a slip-joint (arrow).

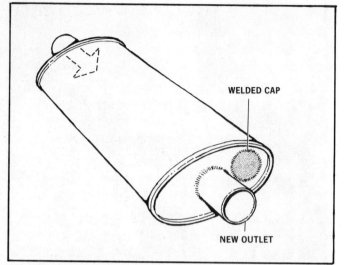

WELDED CAP

NEW OUTLET

The exhaust system from the turbo on back must be low in restriction, and that includes the muffler. Most systems have a 2½-inch pipe leading back to a Corvair turbo muffler, with a 2½-inch core. The Corvair unit can be made even less restrictive by capping the outlet and welding on a new one in the center.

back would have even quicker boost response. For dual-turbo setups on large V-8's, the 2½-in system is fine, because each turbo is only doing half the work and you have a separate pipe for each turbo. If a 3-in exhaust is impractical for your installation, then split it just after the turbo and use two 2½-in pipes and low-restriction mufflers instead of just one.

With the exhaust routed under the car and all the way back to the rear bumper, most turbos are deceptively quiet, even without a muffler. We'd suggest, however, in face of increasing state and federal noise legislation, that you install a muffler of the "turbo" type. We've seen a dozen copies of the original GM muffler designed for the turbocharged Corvair Spyder, and some of the companies take great license in calling their cheap imitation a "turbo muffler", even making it look outwardly similar. The original mufflers were one of the best Detroit compromises between low restriction and low noise, with 2½-in inlet, core passage, and outlet. On a real turbocharged car, there's no room for inefficient look-a-likes. The Walker version of the Corvair muffler is among the best we've seen. Most of the typical "hot-rod" mufflers aren't very good for a turbo setup, no matter how neat they sound on a normally-aspirated engine. The turbo muffler can even be improved. Originally, it had the inlet coming into the center of the core, and the outlet coming out the back, off to one side of the core. Slightly less restriction can be achieved by capping off that outlet, and cutting a new outlet at the center of the rear, making the design completely straight through. If you can't find a good Corvair-type muffler

or can't fit one in your application (the turbo mufflers are oval instead of round), then look for a glasspack with the same large inlet and outlet, as well as a "saw-core" construction (the inside passage has saw cuts through the metal, instead of the tiny louvers used inside many glasspacks).

As important as a leak-free exhaust manifold is in a turbo setup, you should also pay some attention to the mating between the manifold and cylinder head ports. Check the surfaces of the exhaust ports with a straightedge to be certain there is no warpage there. If you make up a special set of exhaust headers or modify your stock manifolds, they should be machined flat at their mating surfaces to correct any warpage resulting from the welding operations. On those inline engines

where the exhaust manifold and the intake manifold are on the same side of the head and retained by the same set of bolts, you may also have to machine the flange of the intake manifold to keep the manifold flange thickness the same on both (for proper gasket sealing). Even with this attention to the exhaust manifold flanges, you should use a gasket between the heads and the manifolds for a good seal, despite the fact that your engine may not have had gaskets there when it was stock. Some exhaust gaskets will blow out under the increased backpressure of a turbo, so use only those gaskets that are asbestos, sandwiched in metal. If you really want to play it safe, you could cut O-ring grooves in both the port flanges and the manifolds and use copper wire for the O-rings. The same

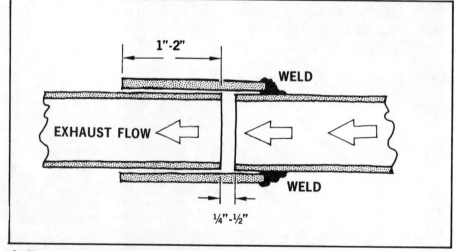

1"-2"

WELD

EXHAUST FLOW

WELD

¼"-½"

A slip or expansion joint can be made simply, using a short length of tubing that is just slightly larger in diameter than your crossover tubing. For a quieter and more leak-proof joint, you could cover the joint with a flexible metal bellows and weld it to each of the crossover halves.

The one important thing to remember in the turbo oil system is to provide a steady supply of cool oil and to provide a large-diameter return line to the pump in order to allow sufficient oil flow capacity through the entire system.

could be done at the mating between the manifold and the turbine inlet flange.

Because the pipes in your setup will be running much hotter than in normally-aspirated form, they will expand much more. The longer the pipe, the more it will tend to grow. This is especially a problem on V-8 installation using a single turbo. That long crossover pipe under the engine will need a slip-joint of some kind to allow for the growth. Not having a slip-joint is acceptable if you never plan to remove the crossover pipe. It will survive the installation, but later you'd have to pry it off, and then it would never go back on again. While we're still talking about expansion under heat, a word should be said about turbo mounting bolts. Ak Miller has found that most hot rodders doing their first turbo setup will invariably attach the turbine inlet flange to the exhaust manifold flange with some kind of trick aircraft bolt of grade eight or better because it would appear to be in keeping with the advanced technology of the turbo. Such super bolts are actually too hard and brittle; they tend to break when the flanges expand. Common hardware store bolts are more elastic and won't snap.

One final note on the exhaust systems, watch the proximity of the turbine exhaust pipe to other components in the engine compartment. This pipe will radiate tremendous heat due to its surface area. Reroute any

wiring that is close by and don't get the pipe too close to parts that would be affected by the heat (that, in effect, includes nearly everything in there). On many installations where the turbo is on the right side of a V-8, the pipe passes near the starter motor and you may want to build a metal and asbestos heat shield (14 or 16 gauge steel) for the starter. If so, make one such that air can flow around both sides of the shield. Since the pipe will increase underhood temperatures, you may also want to insulate it with asbestos and foil wrapping.

THE OILING SYSTEM

It's been said by every turbo expert that a modern turbocharger will last virtually forever, "given a steady supply of clean oil." Ensuring that kind of reliability won't take any major redesigning of the oiling system on your engine. Stock oil pumps are perfectly adequate with 30 psi or better, so forget the trick pump or the high-pressure relief spring. Full engine oil pressure should be available at the turbocharger bearing, which in most cases means you should tap into the engine lubrication system at an unrestricted point. Near the oil filter or the idiot light sending unit is usually a convenient place to mount a T-fitting for the turbo oil feed and a sending unit for an oil-pressure gauge. The gauge sending unit should be in the same location so that we can always moni-

tor the oil pressure available to the turbo. The turbo manufacturer may have specific recommendations, but the oil line is usually ¼-in or 5/16-in. Since rubber hose may be damaged by the heat near the turbo, this is one place where you can go trick and use some aircraft braided line. The bolt-on oil flanges usually supplied with the turbo can be drilled and tapped for the AN fitting needed to attach the oil-feed line to the bearing housing of the turbo.

The drainback is another matter. The inside diameter of the oil outlet from the turbo must be considerably larger than the oil inlet. Ak Miller and most other installers recommend that the inside diameter be at least ⅝-in for best results because of the aeration and foaming that take place as the oil passes through the high-speed bearing. It's vital that the drainback system from the turbo to the oil pan be completely free of kinks, sharp bends or other restrictions so that oil backpressure in the line can't spoil the flow of fresh oil coming into the unit. Obviously, the point at which you dump this drain line into the oil pan should be above the pan static oil level or there will be backpressure.

Connecting this oil drainback line to the oil pan is occasionally a problem. Removing the pan completely is the best way. Getting the pan off the engine in some cars requires unbolting the mounts, and jacking the engine up so the pan will clear the front crossmember is recommended. But, many installers do not remove the pan to mount the fitting. They cut a hole in the side of the pan and epoxy the fitting in place, draining the oil before starting the engine to remove any chips developed when cutting the hole. Certainly a magnetic drain plug would be an asset here. Some turbo installers, to avoid the metal chip problem, simply punch the hole in the pan, and then use a thread-tap on the folded-inward metal to mount a screw-in type fitting. When mounting your fitting to the pan, remember that it should enter the side of the pan at a slight downward angle, having it enter straight could cause a slight restriction to the flow. If you want to avoid either removing the pan or worrying about metal chips, you could plumb the drainback to some other point on the engine, such as the rocker covers, valley cover or tappet cover (on the side of most inline motors), but the point at which you return this aerated oil must be capable of handling the flow without backpressure and, of course, must be lower than the turbo itself.

A dry (unlubricated) start with an engine can damage the rings or bearings, but to a turbocharger bearing spinning 100,000 rpm or more, it is certain disaster. When your entire installation is complete and you're ready to fire the engine, disconnect the oil inlet line from the turbo temporarily and squirt a generous portion of motor oil into the turbo bearing. This is a procedure recommended by all turbo manufacturers. Also, before reconnecting the oil line, pull out the ignition coil wire and turn the engine over until a good supply of oil is coming out of the turbo end of the pressure line. You can catch this oil in a coffee can and return it to the engine later or just hold the end of the oil line over the oil filler hole in your valve cover while building up pressure. Even better, and especially important for an engine that has never been fired, is to use an auxiliary oil pump driver such as racing-engine builders use. Get a length of material that fits your oil-pump drive and weld it onto a length of steel rod that will fit the chuck of an electric drill. Pull the distributor out, insert the driver, and spin it with the drill until the oil pressure gauge shows plenty of pressure (remember, if yours is an electric gauge, the ignition key must be on to get a reading). On Ford engines, the oil pump is driven by a hexagonal rod. You can make a "pre-oiler" from an old distributor drive or from a length of the correct size Allen wrench welded to a rod. On most GM and other engines that have a slot in the oil pump driveshaft, a driver can be made from an old distributor shaft, but it needs to have the plastic sleeve over the end to keep the tool in the slot while the drill is running. A precaution that can be taken in future cold starts (when the engine sits idle for a long period, the long oil supply line may drain back into the pan) is to rig a toggle switch in your coil wire line so the engine can be turned over a few times to get oil into the line before the switch is thrown and the engine fired.

Since the turbocharger is a heat pump, and the bearing is both cooled and lubricated by engine oil, the addition of a turbo to your engine is certain to increase engine oil temperature, especially under boost conditions, when the normal oil temperature may be increased by 50° or more after passing through the turbocharger. The use of an oil temperature gauge is important on any RV or performance engine, and turbocharged engines in particular. If you really want to know what is happening with your oil temperature (and you have enough brass fittings in your parts bin), you should measure the temperature at various points around the engine. We're not suggesting that you hook up 13 temperature gauges and senders all at one time, but you can switch the location of your sender. Try this at the sump of the pan, at the oil filter, at the point where oil is

supplied to the turbo, and where the oil leaves the turbo. In the latter case, do not mount the sending unit in such a manner that it will restrict the flow of drainback oil. After measuring various locations under different engine conditions (idle, heavy load and heavy boost), you should have a pretty good "map" of oil temperature conditions, and, in particular, how much heat the turbo is adding to the system. If you find that engine oil temp under boost is up to the dangerous 250°F and above range, then you should add an oil cooler. A mild case of oil overheating can be inexpensively cured by running the oil line to the turbo through a small finned cooler, such as used on some power-steering systems.

INDUCTION SYSTEM

This is one of the most important facets of turbocharging. Here you can make or break your installation. How you plumb air in and out of the compressor side of the turbo and the carburetion you select can determine whether you wind up with a hot-blooded street stomper or a cold-blooded turkey. Many of the negative rumors about turbocharged setups have been created because of a poorly-designed induction system. A question that is often asked by the novice about forced-induction systems is "Where should I mount the carburetor(s), before or after the compressor?" In simpler terms, should the turbo draw the air-fuel mixture from the carburetor and blow this mix into the intake manifold, or should the turbo just induct air which it then blows into the top of the carburetor? In almost all cases the

most efficient method will be the former, which we'll call the "draw-through" method of induction.

BLOW-THROUGH SYSTEMS

The "blow-through" method is actually the easiest system to build. You need only direct the compressor outlet air into the top of the carburetor, which remains in its stock location on the intake manifold. If your engine had good cylinder-to-cylinder fuel distribution in stock form, then it will work just as well in a blow-through setup. All the stock connections for fuel lines, manifold heat, choke, and throttle linkage can be left as they are, but, and this is a big but, there are some definite problems, requiring a number of modifications to the fuel supply system and the carburetor itself.

Most carburetors do an acceptable job of metering fuel to an engine under normal conditions. They have an idle circuit, a cruise circuit, a choke for cold starts, and a system of enriching the mixture for acceleration, with a float to control the level of fuel in the bowl. All of these systems work fine when the carburetor is subject to the normal engine vacuum on one side and 14.7 psi atmospheric pressure on the other, but with a supercharger blowing into the top, everything changes. First of all, the standard thin brass float may collapse, so it must be replaced with a solid float, such as the foam *Nitrofil* type, or the brass float can be drilled and filled with quick-setting foam (gas resistant). All of the areas of a standard carburetor that have an air connection to the throttle body will have to

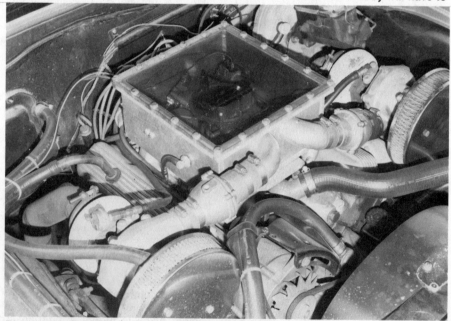

Blow-through applications generally have the least plumbing work, but require serious carb modifications. This street machine uses two turbos blowing into a homemade box around an 850-cfm Holley. Using a box means the carb doesn't need extra mods, but working on the carb can be a tedious proposition.

20

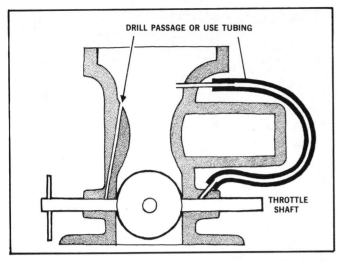

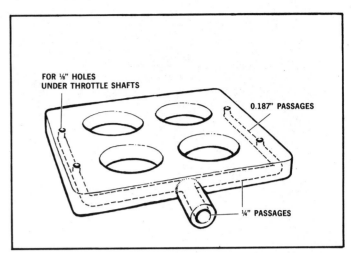

Another blow-through problem can be boost leaks in the carburetor, especially at the throttle shafts. This can be fixed by plumbing dry (before the fuel is added) air under boost to the throttle shaft boss, either by a drilled passage or tubing.

If drilling from above proves to be impractical with your carburetor, you can drill up into the throttle shaft bosses from below and use a drilled base plate under the carburetor. Again, dry boost air is plumbed to the base plate to prevent wet-fuel leaks.

be sealed or modified, since they will leak pressure under boost. This can be dangerous, if the leak is below the portion of the carburetor where the fuel is added to the airstream, as it would emit flammable fuel-air mixture—to say nothing of the performance loss the leak would create. After plugging the obvious vacuum connections on the carburetor, you also have to seal the drillings where the throttle shaft comes through the carb body. This has been successfully done by drilling a small hole through the casting into each end of the throttle shaft area, epoxying in a short length of brass tubing, and plumbing this with rubber hose to an area of the carburetor above the venturi. In this way, plain air (without fuel) is directed to the throttle shaft bosses to overcome the reduced pressure there, preventing a leak. If there is linkage connected to only one side of the carburetor, you may have to do this on only that side, since the shaft can be shortened on the other side and leaks prevented there by plugging the end of the boss. If your carburetor would be difficult to drill into (at the throttle shaft bosses) from the top, you can drill up from the bottom into the shaft bosses. Then, you must make an adapter to go under the carburetor base that has holes to correspond with the newly-drilled boss holes and which can be then be plumbed to the above-the-venturi connection.

Another potential source of trouble, if you have one of the smog-era vehicles, is the charcoal vapor can that collects fuel bowl vapors and returns them to the gas tank. Since there will be boost pressure in the fuel bowl, pressure could leak to the cannister and from there into the fuel tank. If you want to keep the cannister hooked up in a blow-through system, you'll have to put a check-valve in the line to the cannister and plumb the bypass back to the air cleaner. Any fuel that enters the system through this bypass line to the air cleaner will simply cool off the intake charge a little (not a bad idea considering how much a supercharger heats up the incoming air).

Under boost conditions, as a supercharged engine requires more fuel than a comparable normally-aspirated engine. A supercharged engine at about 15 psi boost (15 lb above standard atmospheric pressure) requires roughly twice as much fuel, since the engine receives two "atmospheres" of air—twice the volume. This is a somewhat unique problem, requiring something other than a simple high-pressure supply pump. On a turbocharged engine the boost is a function of load more than rpm, therefore the fuel supply must be varied according to the engine load or boost requirement rather than varying strictly according to engine speed (as do all mechanical pumps). In a blow-through application, the fuel pump pressure must be variable, not only to keep the float bowl full when you've got your right foot stuffed into it, but also there must be enough pressure to overcome the boost pressure created in the top of the float bowl by the incoming "supercharged" air. Some diaphragm-type mechanical fuel pumps can be modified by plumbing boost pressure into the air chamber above the pump diaphragm. This effectively increases the spring pressure and makes the pump work harder under boost conditions, raising the supply volume. Some fuel pump designs will not allow this modification but it is suitable, wherever practical, on low-boost systems.

Another setup that may work is a combination of the engine mechanical pump and an auxiliary electric pump.

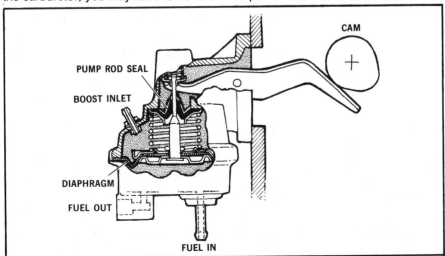

A problem with a blow-through setup when a box isn't used around the carburetor is getting enough fuel pressure in the float bowls to overcome the boost pressure. You can use an auxiliary electric pump, or put a boost line into your mechanical fuel pump if it has a sealed rod. Boost above the diaphragm will increase fuel pressure.

A draw-through installation is preferred by most turbo installers when there is hood height to allow it. This Ak Miller kit on a Capri V-6 sets the custom air cleaner no higher than it was in stock form, and the carburetor is left untouched, but for a jet change.

A draw-through setup that uses a long intake pipe, such as on a cross-flow head like the Pinto, may require the addition of some exhaust or engine water heat to prevent wet fuel puddling in the plumbing.

The electric pump can be hooked to a pressure switch on the intake manifold, so that when boost exists the pressure switch turns on the electric pump (through a relay) to provide the extra fuel pressure required. The purpose of the extra pump is to overcome the boost pressure; the stock mechanical pump is then doing the work to fill the fuel bowl. Since the biggest of aftermarket electric pumps like the Stewart-Warner 240A or the Holley P-6230 only develop a maximum of 12-15 psi (after being adjusted to the max pressure), this setup is only good on turbocharged systems where the boost also does not exceed 12-15 psi.

To get back to some other disadvantages of the blow-through approach, consider the vacuum and smog control hookups to the carburetor. What would be the effect on them if they were under pressure instead of vacuum? Your positive crankcase ventilation system (PCV) for one isn't going to go for it. The PCV valve is designed to prevent an occasional back-

fire in the intake manifold from pressurizing or igniting the oil vapors in the valve cover or crankcase. If the valve plumbing remains as stock, under prolonged steady boost the PCV valve would stay shut and allow crankcase vapor pressure to build up unless the breather cap is vented back to atmospheric (preferably inside the air cleaner). In a blow-through system, it is best to reroute the manifold end of the PCV line to dump into the compressor inlet, where there will be a relatively stable vacuum source. The other crankcase vent line should also be relocated to connect with the air cleaner, which will now be upstream of the turbo.

If your hot-rodding trivia goes back far enough, you may remember the Paxton and McCulloch superchargers that were popular back in the late fifties and early sixties. They were briefly available as original equipment on some rare two-seater Thunderbirds and some even-rarer 312 Fords for drag and NASCAR racing (Ford's answer to the

limited-production '57 Chevy passenger cars with Rochester fuel injection). These belt-driven mechanical superchargers were designed for a blow-through system, but some of the above-described problems were avoided by putting a box (pressure chamber) around the carburetor. The supercharger was ducted to the box, placing the carburetor under boost both inside and out. This eases some of the float and fuel pressure problems, but the carburetor linkage still must somehow exit through the box. This is difficult to do without some leakage, even with modern cable throttle linkage, and every time you need to work on the carburetor, even for a minor adjustment, you have to take the lid off the pressure chamber, make your change and then seal it up again. You can imagine how frustrating this could be, although many hot rodders have put up with these inconveniences in their thirst for more performance.

An interesting solution to the problems of the blow-through installation is

The plenum on John Anderson's '29 is actually in two halves, the front half mounts the carburetors and feeds the turbos, while the turbos blow the mixture into the rear half. With two turbos, you should run two wastegates, and they should be close to the turbines.

Other side of Anderson's '34 shows the water-heated carb base, Weiand air cleaner turned sideways for clearance, cable type throttle linkage, boxy plenum over the intake manifold to promote turbulence, and the washer bottle at left for water injection.

Inline sizes are particularly suited to both the blow-through and draw-through methods, since most have the exhaust and intake on the same side of the head, like this 300-cid Ford. This keeps plumbing to a minimum with either system.

A variety of carburetor-to-turbo adapters are available for plumbing draw-through setups for any popular carburetor. For driveability, most draw-through adapters have provisions for hot water to circulate under the plenum.

to convert the engine to run on LPG fuel (propane or butane) instead of gasoline. These liquid petroleum gases vaporize into their gaseous state before they reach the engine, therefore, the special carburetors used on such installations have little in common with gasoline carburetors—including the problems we've mentioned about blow-through applications. Propane has other advantages over gasoline, especially on turbocharged engines, and we'll discuss these later on.

DRAW-THROUGH SYSTEMS

Despite the advantages of simplified plumbing that the blow-through method has, its disadvantages stack up a lot quicker than for the more common draw-through type. In this system, the carburetor is mounted out in front of the compressor inlet of the turbo, so that the turbocharger draws air and fuel through the carburetor and

blows it through the compressor outlet into the intake manifold. Because the carburetor isn't under pressure, it acts as if it is on a normally-aspirated engine. All of the stock vacuum and PCV connections can be retained, though they may have to be lengthened depending on how far the carb is relocated from the original location. The vapor cannister can likewise be left attached in a stock manner. The carb will not have to be modified to allow for pressurization, and the fuel pump pressure requirement isn't much different than for any other high-performance street engine. The stock fuel pump is generally adequate for a moderate-boost system, although if you're building a super-screamer you may want to opt for one of the high-volume performance mechanical pumps (TRW, Holley, Carter, etc.) that are direct replacements for the stock pump.

Depending on the type of carburetor

selected and the mounting location of the turbo itself, underhood clearance can be considered and a system designed which doesn't require a hood bubble; even the stock air cleaner can often be reused.

Naturally, there are also some drawbacks to the draw-through approach; everything mechanical is, to some extent, a trade-off of one kind or another. Plumbing is the biggest problem. Mounting the carburetor to the turbocharger isn't difficult unless you have a really unusual layout. The commercial kit manufacturers list quite a few different carburetor adapters in their catalogs, allowing you to use just about any popular two-barrel or four-barrel carburetor. For something unusual like a side-draft Weber, you'll have to make your own adapter. These adapters can be made of steel or aluminum, most of the commercial ones are cast aluminum, and it should

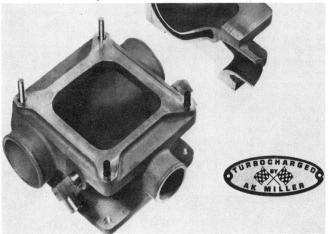

Some of the turbo kit companies have these adapters to mount the carburetor in the stock location except several inches higher, when you want a draw-through setup but don't have room to mount the carb to one side. The turbo draws through the top one-half of the adapter, then blows the mix through the bottom half. This Ak Miller unit has provision for hot water.

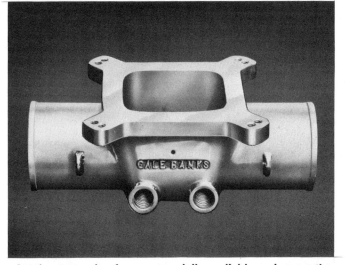

Another example of a commercially-available carb mounting box is this aluminum casting from Gale Banks Engineering. All internal surfaces are designed for maximum mixture control and provisions are built into the floor for hot water pre-heating of the mixture.

23

provide a plenum under the carburetor with a round outlet tube at one side. This outlet tube should be the same diameter as the compressor inlet and is usually connected to the turbo by means of a short length of reinforced hose and some clamps. Since the weight of the carburetor, air cleaner and adapter can be quite heavy—you should build a metal support bracket to anchor the adapter firmly to the engine. The commercial adapters usually have threaded mounting bosses for this purpose.

Driveability should always be a concern, even for a high-performance car, and there's no reason a turbocharged engine should be hard to start or suffer from air-fuel mixture problems. A difficulty with draw-through turbocharging is that the carburetor must be removed from the normal location on the intake manifold; thus, the manifold heat passage will not keep the carburetor warm and aid vaporization of the fuel. To compound the problem, the velocity of the air passing through the carburetor will be so high during boost operation that it is possible for the carburetor to "ice up"; and the cold temperatures will create puddles of unwanted unvaporized fuel throughout the adapter, compressor and inlet track. To avoid this, the bottom of the adapter plenum should be heated. The easiest method is to build a passage under the plenum for hot engine water to pass through. This water chamber can be spliced into the normal heater hose circuit to supply it with hot engine coolant. You'd be surprised how quickly engine water is heated. This approach has proven successful in numerous applications. Spearco, Ak Miller Enterprises, John Anderson and other kit manufacturers use this type of heating for good carburetor performance. Ducting exhaust gases under the plenum might provide a quicker-acting source of heat, but the heater-hose approach is easier to build. And water, with the proper 50% dilution of anti-freeze, is less corrosive than exhaust gas.

Building the plumbing from the compressor outlet to the intake manifold isn't a serious proposition. The compressor discharge on most commonly-used turbos is a round outlet about two inches in diameter, which can easily be coupled to a two-inch tube by using clamps and cloth-reinforced silicone hose (to resist heat). Naturally, you should avoid sharp bends in this pipe, but bends here are less detrimental to performance than they are on the exhaust side. The other end of this pipe is going to be mounted to the carburetor flange on the intake manifold. You should build a small plenum here, too. Resist the temptation to build a trick, super-flow piece and make your

plenum square. The air-fuel mixture coming out of the compressor needs to have something to break up the flow and promote turbulence, *otherwise some cylinders will run lean and others rich.* This can lead to exhaust valve problems, at the least, and blow holes in an otherwise-healthy set of pistons. In some cases, further breakup of the mixture is required and can be accomplished simply by adding a screen or plate drilled with many small holes. Install the plate inside the plenum box or between the plenum box and the intake manifold. You can readily determine if you have a mixture-distribution problem by comparing the spark plug readings from the various cylinders or by using an inexpensive pyrometer to read the exhaust gas temperature from each exhaust port (more on this later). This is the easiest and cheapest approach to sorting out distribution problems and is the method used by many engine dyno technicians and intake manifold designers.

Even with good distribution in the intake manifold, good turbulence, and water-passage heat under the carburetor plenum, a draw-through installation may still have some problems with fuel puddling. This is most

often noticed in cold starts; when the engine will start, run very roughly for a few minutes, and finally spit a gob of black smoke from the exhaust when the puddling clears up. After the engine warms up this shouldn't be a problem. This trouble is inherent whenever the carburetor is remote from the engine and the intake passage has areas that can cool off rapidly after the engine is shut off. You can minimize such puddling by keeping the intake plumbing as short as practicable and as devoid of bends and low pockets (places where fuel can drop out of the airstream and collect) as possible.

The choice of carburetor that you hang out in front of the compressor will have a definite effect on the overall performance of a turbocharged engine. We've already indicated that a turbocharged engine will require more air and fuel during "boost"; but the choice of how big or small a carburetor you use must be ruled by the engine size, the amount of boost you'll be running, and the type of vehicle usage. Are you after ultimate performance, or is fuel economy also to be considered? Obviously, the bigger the engine displacement, the more flow capacity the carburetor must have, and the more

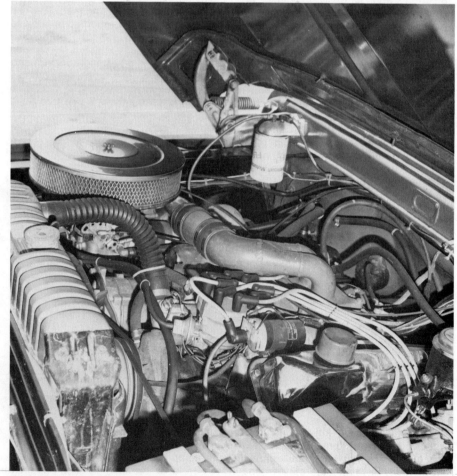

Draw-through systems can sometimes make for a crowded engine compartment. Note on this late Ford, however, that a large free-flowing air filter has been retained on the relocated carburetor.

boost employed, the more the carburetor will have to flow to feed the same engine. When the carburetor is much too small, it acts like a restriction on the turbo, cutting down the potential boost. The right carburetor is usually larger than you think. On small four-cylinder inline engines, the original carburetor, in modified form, may be adequate at low-boost levels, but above approximately 6 psi you'll have to step up to a two-barrel carb from a larger engine or a small four-barrel. Holley has a 390-cfm four-barrel and Carter a 400-cfm four-barrel that are perfect for such an application. On six-cylinder inline engines up to 250 cubic inches a very large two-barrel or a small four-barrel would be adequate at low levels of boost. For higher boost, a small four-barrel of about 650-cfm capacity would be better. Engines of 300-350 cubic inches can use a 650-cfm four-barrel for low boost and up to 850-cfm for higher boost. On larger V-8's the carburetor choice would have to be correspondingly larger. On large-displacement engines or small V-8's used for all-out performance, you may be using two turbochargers instead of one. In this case you can use a small four-barrel carb at each turbo. All of these rough recommendations may sound a little large for the applications suggested, but remember that the carburetion has to exhibit a dual personality to work properly on a turbocharged engine. Under normal driving conditions, when the engine is running on vacuum, the carburetor has to provide good driveability (and fuel economy if that is one of your considerations), and yet when under boost it has to flow perhaps twice what it does for the normally-aspirated mode. If it doesn't, the specter of detonation will haunt you. For this reason, spreadbore four-barrels that have small primary venturis for good low-speed driveability and large secondaries for WOT (wide open throttle) performance are excellent choices for a turbocharged engine. For good fuel economy and to maintain engine flexibility, vacuum-operated secondaries are recommended. The biggest problem with progressive carburetors (two-stage two barrels such as the Pinto/Vega Holley-Weber and all four barrels) is to get the proper transition from the primary mode (under vacuum conditions) to the opening of the secondaries in the boost mode. Carefully selecting the spring force in the diaphragm of a vacuum-operated secondary can usually eliminate the problem, but this will require considerable testing. Fortunately, Holley carburetors have a wide range of springs (with different colors to designate each level of tension), allowing considerable latitude of adjustment. If your engine bogs as the secondary circuit tips in, switch to a heavier spring to delay secondary action. If the engine seems to run too lean during this transition, use a lighter spring to make them come in sooner. On a draw-through installation, this aspect of carburetor modification isn't much different than tuning a normally-aspirated engine.

When you take the carburetor out of the box, you should increase the size of both primary and secondary jets; or on some carbs you will have to modify the metering rod tips to increase fuel flow (it's better to start out too rich and dial backwards than to start out too lean and flush the engine on the first hard pass). On carburetors that have power valves (low-vacuum enrichment), you can also juggle the power valve signal point (this applies primarily to Holley carbs). If the engine is lean when going into boost, then maybe a power valve that opens (enrichening the fuel supply) at a higher vacuum reading would do the trick, or vice-versa. Enlarging the feed passages in the power valve circuit will also increase the volume of fuel delivery, but you should consult with a carb expert before drilling passages in the Holley metering blocks or main body. Low-vacuum enrichment can be accomplished in Carter carbs, which do not have diaphragm-operated power valves, by altering the diameter of the mixture enrichment rods and the tension of the mixture enrichment control spring. In most low-boost (streetable) systems carburetor driveability will not be a problem, so most of this work can be eliminated if the right carb is selected. Those who fully understand the operation of a specific carburetor and who desire to tailor delivery curves for a particular engine and loading circumstance will find an exhaust gas temperature gauge helpful to map the cylinder heat response, i.e., fuel requirement, under various speed-load conditions.

AIR CLEANERS

What you put on top of your carburetor after the installation is completed is important. A good air cleaner is a must, though limited underhood room in some installations may necessitate a smaller air cleaner than you might like. The right filter is important for two reasons: it must keep the air going through the turbo clean, and too small an air cleaner may restrict engine breathing. Remember that at 15 psi boost you're flowing twice the air your engine would in normally-aspirated form. If your stock air cleaner was barely adequate before, it certainly won't do the trick with a turbo. Fortunately, most engines come with a large enough air cleaner. Custom air cleaners usually are smaller than stock, but the range of diameters gives you some choices for tight spots. In cases where a small-diameter (less than 10-

Late-model trucks are ideal prospects for turbocharging. This '77 Chevy has a Roto-Master TurboSonic kit, yet it retains most of the stock components including the stock air cleaner.

inch) custom air cleaner must be used due to space limitations, additional filtering can be gained by stacking two or more elements. Custom cleaners usually have a simple carb adapter plate, a throwaway pleated paper element and a chromed sheetmetal lid. By using a longer air cleaner stud in the carburetor, it's possible (where diameter is limited but height is not a problem) to stack two or more of the paper elements between the base and the lid. You can glue the two rubber-flanged paper elements together with epoxy or silicone sealer.

Mounting a remote air cleaner near the carburetor is sometimes the only answer to full filtration when space is very limited. You can mount a stock or custom air cleaner right behind the grille, beside the radiator, on the radiator support sheetmetal. The connection from the carburetor airhorn to the base of the air cleaner can be made with an elbow plenum on the carburetor (such as is found in some aftermarket cold-air induction packages) and some large-diameter flexible ducting (like clothes-dryer hose). Since the space between the radiator support and the grille shell is shallow on most cars, you'll probably have to mount the air cleaner vertically.

If your turbo vehicle is going to be used for off-roading or in exceptionally dusty conditions, you may be interested in some of the cannister-type air cleaners used by the off-road racing buggies. These are smaller versions of the huge cans you see on the hoods of turbocharged 18-wheelers. You may be able to find a spot to mount one on the fenderwell opposite the turbo plumbing.

THROTTLE LINKAGE

Throttle linkages require some reworking in a draw-through installation, of course, but this represents only a minor problem for a good "kluger." If you're good with geometry and physics, you can use a mechanical linkage even when the carb is located far from the original position. Most of the hot-rod intake manifold companies list universal linkages and parts in their catalogs. Adjustable bellcranks can be useful to change the direction of travel (such as when you substitute a carburetor that requires a "pull" action when your stock one was a "push" type) or to achieve a different leverage for best pedal feel. With late-model vehicles, cable-operated throttles are common. This is by far the easiest system to adapt. The carburetor may be a long distance from the intake manifold on some installations, and on inline engines with crossflow heads, such as the Pinto and Colt, the carburetor will be on the opposite side of the engine than when it was stock. By shopping the

parts books you may be able to find a stock vehicle, which has a cable of just the right length for your setup, or you can splice into your own cable. In older vehicles this means swapping to a late-model pedal bracket which has the arm to pull back on the cable. Bulk cable suitable for automotive uses can also be found at an industrial supply house or surplus store. You just cut off the amount you need to splice into your cable, clip the outside cable at the ends and mate the inside cable to the stub of your stock cable by crimping the cables together with a solderless butt connector.

At the carburetor, the cable can also be crimped into a solderless terminal; usually a flat, round-hole terminal will hold the cable and attach it to the carburetor throttle arm without binding during linkage travel. Adjust the linkage to give full-throttle action at the carburetor, but only just as the pedal is bottoming out on the firewall. Having a turbocharger on your engine will tempt you, regardless of your personal integrity and law-abiding nature, to stomp the throttle on occasion; and if you allow full throttle to be reached before the pedal is at full travel you may bend the linkages or throttle shaft(s) when you succumb to the passions of acceleration.

DETONATION CURES

When you take a recent Detroit automobile (one designed for unleaded fuel or regular fuel) and start up a hill or freeway ramp with your right foot on the wall, you may hear a death-rattle "pinging" sound inside the engine. This is detonation, or preignition, and is

caused by a combination of factors. That sound you hear is the pistons being battered by preignited gases hitting the piston before it rocks over top dead center between the ignition and power strokes. High temperatures, in the engine cooling system, combustion chamber, intake mixture and exhaust gases, can contribute to detonation, but it is also brought on by too much ignition advance, low-octane fuel, too much compression, carbon deposits in the combustion chamber and on top of the pistons, and lean air-fuel mixtures. Any or all of these will be a problem in a turbocharged installation, but there are proven methods of dealing with this engine killer.

The choice of fuel is of primary importance. *Under no circumstances will a low-octane fuel be acceptable,* use the highest octane available. It's been said by some turbo installers that in their experience you must raise the octane number of your fuel by one point for each pound of boost that you turbocharge the engine with. If you're running 89-octane regular in your car now and you plan to boost it with 6 psi, then you'll have to use at least 95-octane premium. We've all seen the octane ratings of gasoline decline in recent years, and it's one reason so many cars today have detonation and run-on ("dieseling" after the key is shut off). The high-temp thermostats (for smog control) just add to the problem. Can you remember when Sunoco 280 and 260 used to be the hot setup for street machines? Those days are gone, and with a few exceptions such as hard-to-find aviation fuel and equally rare Union 76 "racing gas," most turbo users

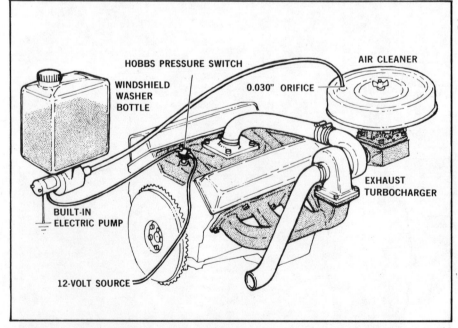

Detonation control can be as near as your wrecking yard. Find a windshield washer tank, a Hobbs pressure switch to activate it under manifold boost, and plumb the water to an orifice or jet in the air cleaner.

are going to wind up with less octane than they should have, and some other steps will have to be taken to remedy the detonation.

A rich fuel mixture under boost conditions is helpful, almost necessary. We've already discussed the advantages of progressive-type carburetors with rich secondaries that open only during the boost phase. Another remedy could be the use of an octane-improver added to the fuel. Drag racers have been feeling the lack of high-octane fuel for several years now, and some enterprising individuals have come up with "secret sauce" to beef up standard gas. When your drag engine has a static compression of 13:1, you just don't get by on 95 octane, and a turbocharged engine is even more particular about its fuel diet. The makers are understandably secretive about the makeup of their gasoline additive, but there are several common substances that work as well. Alcohol (methanol) is one, and another is plain old acetone, like you buy at the paint store to clean fiberglass resin off your hands. Both substances are relatively inexpensive, and have been used for years by Southern California off-roaders who venture into Mexico, where only low-octane gasoline is available. Alcohol should run through your system without trouble, but acetone can cause problems. If you have plastic components in your carburetor or fuel tank, acetone may "eat" some of these pieces. Several years ago Edelbrock Company was doing chassis dyno research on a variety of late-model cars, and using acetone as an octane improver in the gasoline. Some of the cars developed fuel delivery problems that defied detection. After considerable teardown time and head-scratching, it was discovered that these cars had plastic screens on the fuel tank pickups and the acetone had melted them and cut off half of the fuel supply! Those who have used it successfully tell us that a ratio of about one ounce of acetone to each gallon of gasoline works fine. At that rate you won't go broke, but adding it each time you fill up can get "old" after awhile.

WATER INJECTION SYSTEMS

Even a good fuel, administered to the turbocharged engine in rich mixtures for the boosted mode, may not be enough to stave off "death rattle." One of the problems that makes this happen is the high intake air temperature of a supercharged engine. We all know by now how high underhood temperatures can get, and we've seen enough race cars and street machines with a cold-air ram induction system to the air cleaner to know that cool air means more power. Ever notice how your car feels a little bit stronger at night, when you've just pulled out of the driveway with a cold engine and you stab the throttle? When the old Lions drag strip in Wilmington, California, was in operation, racers used to love the night racing there because of the cool, dense ocean air. As a general rule, horsepower rises about 1% for every ten degrees (F) that you can drop the intake air temperature, and conversely power drops when temperatures go up. If your engine compartment air was at 150°F and you switched to a cold-air induction system, picking up air at the base of the windshield or at the grille (say at 70°F), the 80° drop in intake air temperature could net you an 8% increase in power. That's the good news. The bad news is that superchargers make the incoming air even hotter. When you compress air, it heats up, and the friction from a hot supercharger adds more heat. The more boost and the tighter the turbo, the hotter it will make the incoming air. With the 75% efficiency of most turbos, your incoming air could be heated to as much as 250°F under maximum boost! You can readily see how detonation can be a major stumbling block to a turbocharged street machine (one that has to run on gasoline; the methanol used on the USAC champ cars creates less of a problem) when the air-fuel mixture is this hot. You can find some comfort in the fact that air is heated to an even higher degree with the lower efficiency and higher internal friction of a mechanical GMC-type supercharger.

Obviously there is an answer to the detonation problem, or we wouldn't be able to devote a chapter of this book to practical turbocharging for the street. The answer is water injection. It's been around in various forms since the 1930's and was used extensively on military aircraft in World War II or whenever available fuel has had less octane than desired. The energy crunch brought a lot of new gimmick-type devices onto the market, and some not so very new. All were designed to save precious fuel, from the "atomic ignition intensifier" that use to be sold at county fairs to so-called water injectors. Most of these water-adding devices are technically not injectors but controlled air leaks that draw water vapors from a tank and allow these cooler vapors to mix with the fuel-air at the carburetor base or intake manifold. We won't delve into the merits or demerits of these devices here, suffice it to say that since they work only with engine vacuum, they are not what we're after for a turbocharged engine at all.

A true water injector forces liquid into the engine, and not at all times (or we'd have to have a water tank as big as our gas tank). The injection operates only when it's needed. In our case, that would mean only when the engine is under boost and in danger of detonation. When a controlled amount of water is injected into the induction of a turbocharged engine, it has the effect of cooling off the charge substantially. The water absorbs the heat and turns to steam, which has a secondary benefit of keeping the combustion chamber and spark plugs clean. Sort of a steam-clean-as-you-drive kind of operation.

It's also quite simple to build a pressure-motivated system, where the boost pressure itself pumps the water. Obviously, the more boost, the more water injected.

What we need is a compact water tank that can be kept under hood and a system of extracting water from it when the engine is in the boost mode. A number of basic variations exist, and ingenious hot rodders are forever coming up with new approaches. One of the simplest systems uses the manifold boost pressure to power the water injection. The water tank must be made of metal or other strong material to withstand the pressure (it would have to stand your maximum boost pressure at least). A line from the intake manifold carries boost pressure to the sealed tank (a screw-on lid is mandatory for a boost-applied system). Two other hoses are connected to the tank. At the turbo end, both of these hoses open ahead of the compressor. At the tank end, one of these hoses fits on a tube that reaches almost to the bottom of the water tank (like a fuel pickup in a gas tank). The other fits on a short tube soldered to the lid, that opens above the water level of the tank.

The line above the water is a vent line, while the other functions as the water supply to the engine. When in the boost mode, pressure comes through the line from the intake manifold and forces water through the pickup tube and into the airstream, ahead of the turbo. By placing a restriction orifice in the bottom of the vent line, you can delay the injection starting time until after a certain level of boost is reached. Using a jet drilled to about 0.030-0.040-inch seems to work in most cases. You'll also have to install a one-way check valve in the boost line, or when the manifold is under vacuum instead of boost you will have a vacuum leak. At this time, air will pass through the vent line and back into the manifold through the boost line, bypassing the carburetor entirely. Even if it picked up water vapors as the air passed over the surface of the water, you would have a lean condition until boost came in. Useful one-way check valves can be found in surplus stores or in some of the emissions hoses on late-model cars.

Another simple method for injecting water under boost is the one preferred by Ak Miller and many other turbo installers. All you need is a windshield washer tank and a pressure switch. Most windshield washer bottles have a small, built-in electric pump; this is the type of tank you want. From this tank you plumb a hose to the air cleaner, where it fits over a tube that directs the water spray directly into the carb throats. The pump inside the tank is wired to an adjustable pressure switch threaded to the intake manifold (or other convenient source of boost pressure). These pressure switches can be purchased at some auto parts houses or from most of the turbo kit companies. A 12-volt source line connects to one side of the switch, the other

Spearco's Injectronic water injector is designed for normally-aspirated engines but works well with turbos, too. The mini computer senses manifold vacuum and engine rpm to determine when to inject water.

side of the switch connects to the washer pump. The only simpler wiring job you'll ever have is hooking up your Xmas tree lights. When boost pressures reach a certain level, the switch closes and turns on the pump, which injects water into the air cleaner-carburetor. Some guys run two extra wires from the pump to the dash for a small red light that tells them whenever the water injection is turned on. You may still want to put some kind of restrictor jet in the water line at the air-cleaner end, and it seems that the same range of 0.030-0.040-inch works in most cases. You don't want to flood your combustion chambers, just cool them off. You can adjust the pressure switch to have the water inject at any boost level you specify. If you really want to conserve water, you could only have it come on just before the engine would otherwise reach the detonation point, but most installers figure any boost over 5-6 psi is a good starting point.

Within the last two years, another type of electric water injection has come along. It is marketed by Spearco Performance, and is called the Injectronic system. This device uses a standard electric windshield-washer bottle with built-in pump, but it has a different control mechanism. The Injectronic utilizes a small electronic computer module to turn the pump on and off. It is connected to your intake manifold with a vacuum line and to the negative post of the coil. It "reads" the engine rpm and vacuum to determine when the engine is under enough load to need the benefits of some water, which may not be just in the boost mode. The system was designed for

late-model normally-aspirated cars that often suffer from preignition, and for older high-compression cars that don't like low-octane fuels. It also happens to work quite well on turbocharged engines. All the fittings are included, along with a selection of orifices for the water line and orifice recommendations for various displacement engines. The bigger the engine, the more water it will need to cool off the mixture, so Spearco offers the Injectronic with a choice of two fluid reservoirs, a half-gallon tank for engines up to 250 c.i. and a gallon tank for larger ones.

The amount of water you'll use per miles driven will vary from one engine and driving style to another, just like fuel economy. Whatever water injection system you use, you'll want a tank big enough to hold water to last as long as a full tank of gasoline. This way you won't have to be constantly checking the water level under the hood, just remember to fill up the injector tank every time you fill your gas tank.

Some of the vapor injectors you may have seen advertised in auto magazines specify that you only use their special-formula "elixir" in their water tanks. In our case, plain tap water is fine. Those commercial concentrates are mostly acetone and methanol, which just makes the solution (you mix these concentrates with water) more of an anti-detonant. The water injector for a turbo motor can use plain water (you don't even need to go to the hassle of distilled water). Racers have sometimes used a solution of methanol mixed in with the water because it creates a little more power, but it creates

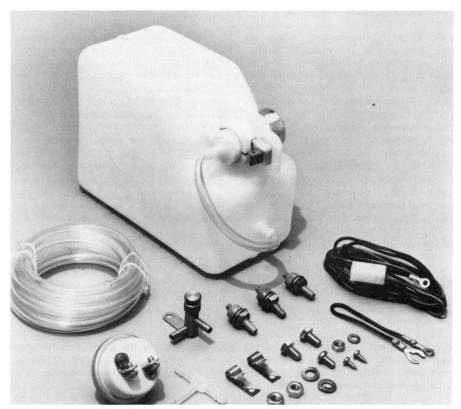

Roto-Master's TurboSonic kit for water injection features all the pieces you'll need. This type of Hobbs switch can be reset to start the injection at any boost level you want, but come adjusted to start pumping water at the 2 psi level.

an extra hassle at every fillup. If you operate your turbo-car in winter weather conditions, you'll have to add some methanol to keep the water tank from freezing, but whether you're adding it for power or for antifreeze protection, you'll never need to use more than a 50-50 ratio of water and alcohol.

TURBOCHARGING AND PROPANE

An approach that can pay off with many more benefits than just avoiding detonation is to convert your vehicle to LPG fuel. Liquid petroleum gas (propane or butane) has an octane rating of about 105, higher even than so-called racing gasoline. Several pages of this book could be devoted to propane installations, but we'll briefly outline some of the advantages of this fuel.

Propane or LPG is a by-product of the same refining process that makes gasoline from crude oil, so it is not the answer to our energy shortage in that respect. It doesn't just come up out of the ground; that fuel is natural gas. Years ago, refineries didn't know what to do with propane so they just burned it off into the atmosphere, but somebody finally figured out that farmers could use it in huge gas dryers used to dry feed grains. LPG has been used for motor fuel in limited applications since the early '50's, but only in the last ten years has it been widely available. In rural areas without natural gas supply lines,

it is used for home heating and cooking, and now it is often seen at regular gas stations, thanks to the explosion of interest in motorhomes and recreational vehicles. Campers use LPG for their stoves, heaters, and gas refrigerators. If you do any traveling at all, you know how numerous these vehicles are. They always seem to be doing 45 mph in front of you when you're on a two-lane country road, which is about the time you wished they also had a turbocharger!

Propane is gaseous at standard pressure and temperature, but is transported and sold in highly-condensed, pressurized liquid form. On an LPG-equipped vehicle, it is stored in cylindrical tanks of various sizes (these tanks don't have to be long and skinny like welding bottles) under about 200 psi pressure. Other than the tank, there are three major differences in the fuel system of a propane engine as compared to a gasoline engine. A high-pressure hose carries the liquified propane from the tank to a combination filter and safety shutoff device, which is operated either electrically or by vacuum—preventing propane flow unless the engine is turning over. From this unit, the still-liquified gas is plumbed to another device, which functions as both a pressure reducer and vaporizer. Hot water from the engine block is plumbed through the bottom section. All it takes is about 40° F

to fully vaporize the propane into the gaseous state. From the vaporizer, which also regulates the pressure down to a lower pressure, the gas flows through a larger-diameter hose to the propane version of a carburetor. Actually, it is more correctly called an air valve, because all it is is a chamber with a throttle butterfly that mixes propane and air for the engine. Propane carburetors also function as an additional safety device, since they are controlled by the engine airflow and shut off the gas if the engine stops. That's about all there is to the propane conversion, except for installing a lower heat range spark plug, a low-temp thermostat, and a good high-voltage ignition system.

The advantages of LPG fuels are considerable. Because it is a gas when it reaches your engine, it mixes readily with air and causes none of the usual vaporization or mixture problems we normally associate with carbureted gasoline engines. There is no liquid to break up into air-born particles, no wet-fuel separation inside manifold or ports, no vapor lock, and, since we're talking about a closed system, there is no vapor loss to the atmosphere through float bowl vents. Another important benefit of the fuel is that carbon deposits don't form in your engine because of the more complete and even combustion. Consequently, there is very little engine wear caused by residual abrasives, and no "washdown" of the cylinder walls as there is with gasoline. The engine oil doesn't get thinner as you drive, it gets slightly thicker and stays clean two or three times longer than it would in a gas engine. Additionally, the spark plugs will last much longer.

The emissions from a propane engine are incredibly low, even with no other emissions controls. Ak Miller, a proponent of propane and turbocharging since long before it became popular, delights in telling a story about the first time his blown and "gased" Pinto was routinely pulled into a roadside check by the California Highway Patrol. It seemed that before they opened the hood, the officers checked the tailpipe emission. When they couldn't get a reading, they spent considerable time and effort recalibrating their machine in an effort to get some sort of indication. Finally Ak (who has a well-known wry wit and little tolerance for harassment) had them pounding and kicking this $4,000 infrared machine like it was a used TV set!

With the low emissions, high octane, and lack of mixture problems that propane offers, it's a natural fuel for turbocharged installations, and as you can see the increased boost range (detonation limit) is not the only benefit. It does have a few drawbacks, of course, that we'll discuss briefly. Like some of the unleaded fuels we're burning now, LPG has little lubricating quality. Therefore, your valves will have a tendency to wear on the streets and actually recede into the heads. Late-model engines designed for unleaded fuels are not only perfect for turbocharging because of their comparatively low static compression ratios, but suitable because they feature induction-hardened valve seats and valve rotators. On older engines, you'll have to have a machine shop install hard-stellite seats and do a good concentric valve job.

When first apprised of propane advantages, most drivers worry about the availability of fuel, the same question that confronts buyers when they purchase a diesel-powered automobile. These fuels are obviously not on every street corner, but when you are aware of these fuels and keep a sharp eye out while driving, you begin to notice the places that sell it. Most propane users go a little larger in fuel tank capacity when they switch to propane, for extended range, and the major propane distributing companies, like Petrolane, publish free booklets listing all of their dealers in every state. As you'll find out, many independent gas stations are also carrying LPG now, because of the rise in business from RV's when they offer it. Propane, sold as camper fuel for appliances, sells for about 55-60¢ per gallon because of the service hassle of setting up to fill what is usually only a five-gallon tank, but many dealers have a different rate for propane as a motor fuel, as low as 45¢, which is cheaper than even the lowest-grade gasolines, let alone one with 105 octane.

Due to lower energy (by volume, not by weight) and lower volatility of propane, compared to gasoline, you may suffer a slight loss of power with propane, but you can make up for that (on a normally-aspirated engine) by increasing the compression ratio and using an efficient CD ignition. Just because many modern engines run so ragged on gasoline with all their stop-gap, add-on emission equipment, the switch to propane seems to give more power than gas, and even better fuel economy. It's especially suitable for in-line engines because the propane smooths out a lot of the inherent vibrations. Four-bangers run like rotaries, and sixes at idle feel like pre-emissions V-8's. Many fleet car and truck operations run propane exclusively, using their own refueling stations. The results in terms of lower engine maintenance and fuel costs, especially for vehicles that have to idle for long periods of time, more than make up for the cost of conversions. It's especially attractive to those companies that like

the additional benefit of good public relations that clean-air fuels represent.

On a recent trip to Las Vegas, we were told that all the taxicabs in that city use gaseous fuels. Most of the installations we saw were of the dual-fuel nature, and we'll touch on those briefly. In a dual-fuel conversion, the engine is equipped to run on either the gaseous fuel or gasoline. This sounds like having your cake and eating it too, at least if you worry about running out of propane in Resume Speed, Nebraska. The drawback to such systems is that the propane is plumbed into a special can atop the stock gasoline carburetor. Going through the standard carburetor like this restricts the flow and results in a less-than-totally-efficient setup, though switching fuels from a dash knob is a convenience. If you're really worried about running out of propane, carry a small spare tank with you. You can get a 5-gallon camper tank quite cheaply; just keep it filled and carry it in your trunk with you. If you run out, you just switch the supply hose from your main tank to the spare. Besides, in your turbo installation you'll probably have your boost level up to take advantage of the propane octane; if you switch over to gasoline without changing your controls, you'll have a detonation problem.

THE IGNITION SYSTEM

The ignition system on a blown engine is no more difficult to set up than it is for any high-performance engine. You want to eliminate high-speed point bounce and create a "hot" spark. The timing does differ because of the detonation danger (always a threat).

On most stock engines there are both vacuum and mechanical advance systems. The vacuum system provides advance at the times when it can contribute most to performance and economy, at part throttle and cruise. The mechanical advance is controlled by centrifugal weights that automatically give more spark lead as engine speed increases, so you have the right amount of advance for acceleration and top speed. The engine needs the more advance at higher speeds because there is less time between strokes for the mixture to burn. Your standard distributor does an admirable job of fulfilling these functions, but the problem is that the amount of advance that would suit a normally-aspirated engine at 5000 rpm could be enough to cause detonation with a turbocharged application. Total advance with a turbo should be around 10° less than the best total advance for the same engine, normally-aspirated. A lot will de-

Another detonation control, with extra benefits, is running on 105-octane propane. Besides the special fuel tank, there are three components needed, A) is a special fuel filter and safety shutoff, B) is the water-heated vaporizer and regulator, and C) is the propane "carburetor".

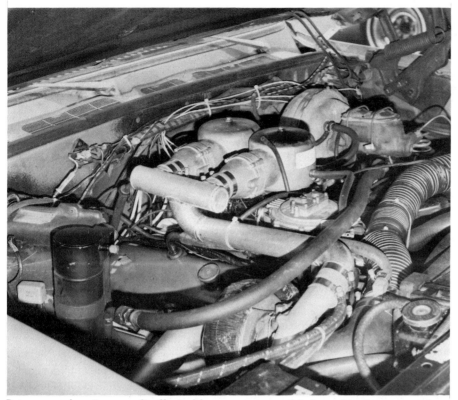

Propane carburetors aren't affected by pressure, so this is an ideal way to go for a blow-through application such as on this camper. Large AiResearch turbo feeds through two boost controllers to two large propane carburetors. With only 5 psi boost, driver hardly knows he's towing a 27-foot trailer.

pend on how close the engine is to detonation -- as dictated by the boost and octane requirement. The following recommendations have been successfully used by many turbo-engine builders. Set the distributor curve up on a Sun machine to give fairly rapid advance with full mechanical advance of 18-24° by 2000-2700 rpm. Initial crankshaft timing of about 10° is a good place to start. This provides a total advance of 28-34°. So much depends on the peculiarities of each setup that it's hard to prescribe the perfect curve for every street machine. This is something you'll have to work out on your own.

Unless you have a mechanical-advance-only distributor, you can modify your vacuum advance for better operation on a turbocharged motor. The turbocharged Corvair Spyders had a very healthy initial advance of over 20°, for good performance and economy in the normally-aspirated mode, and used a pressure-retard diaphragm instead of a vacuum advance unit. This retarded the timing during the boost mode to avoid detonation. A turbocharged street machine will spend only a small portion of time in the boosted mode, and the rest of the time it is usually in no danger of pinging. By running a low compression ratio and a good fuel, the engine can use more advance (during non-boost operation) than the average engine, but there must be a method of

retarding the ignition when the boost arrives.

Some late-model smog motors have a dual-diaphragm vacuum unit on the distributor. These are used mostly on Ford products, and they're easy to recognize because they have two hose connections instead of one. When the engine is idling, manifold vacuum connected to one side of the diaphragm pulls back the advance plate to retard timing. The hose that is outboard from the distributor body is the advance line, which is connected to ported vacuum (above the throttle plates in the carburetor) so that the distributor advances at cruise load conditions, to give proper economy and performance. This is a case where the smog engineers unknowingly did something to make late-model engines more suitable for turbocharging. This system can be modified as follows. Leave the inner (retard) hose off the unit, and connect the outer hose to straight manifold vacuum. When the engine is in the unboosted phase, vacuum will operate the advance unit normally, but because these diaphragms can move both ways against spring pressure, when there is pressure in the intake manifold, the unit will retard. By simply switching one hose, you've turned your Ford distributor into a turbo unit. In case you're dealing with an older Ford engine that doesn't feature the dual-diaphragm, you can ei-

ther buy a new late-model distributor or swap with a guy that has a later engine and wants the pre-emission type. You each get a fair trade! We haven't seen a successful adaptation of the dual-diaphragm advance unit to an early distributor, but you could possibly save money by trying.

The GM engines are not without a pressure-retard method. It's just a little harder to find. Other than the Corvair advance unit, the only such GM diaphragm was the '67 Pontiac. It is available in auto parts stores under Filko number VC189X, and is the unit sold by most of the turbo kit manufacturers for this purpose. It fits most other GM distributors without modification except the newer High Energy Ignition (HEI) models. For those cars, with the huge distributor head, you'll have to change the length of the arm on the Pontiac advance-retard unit. They are usually too long, and by carefully measuring the length of the old advance rod, you can cut and braze the Pontiac rod and bracket to match. Just don't get too much brass on the joint in the rod or it may bind as it travels within the close-fitting bracket. It is possible to check the retard mechanism on a distributor machine with a substitute pressure source to see how much the timing will retard before you actually run the distributor in the car. Most of the GM units we've seen retard a total of about 8-10°, and retard at the rate of about 1° for each pound of boost.

A hot spark is a must for a turbo engine, just as it is for a propane-burning engine. The use of a high energy coil is recommended for this reason, unless you have the Delco HEI system which already has a 35,000-volt spark. We've seen equally successful results obtained with both the Accel Supercoil and the Mallory Voltmaster Mark II. Depending on how much money you have to spend, you may also want to make other modifications to the ignition system. For increased dwell and no chance of point bounce, Ford has an excellent dual-point kit (Autolite part #DOAZ-12A132-B) that fits all late Fords and is inexpensive. GM cars can take advantage of an HEI system out of a wrecking yard, or one of the earlier transistorized setups used on production muscle cars. The perfect update for a Mopar distributor is to switch to a complete electronic setup such as has been standard on Mopars since 1973. The basic kit (Mopar #P3690428) only lists for about $60 and includes a new breakerless distributor, cap, rotor, wiring and electronic box. For higher output and a tach-drive connection on the distributor body, you Mopar fans can have the same unit used by the Pettys and the top Pro-Stocks for about $90 (Mopar #P3690424). Of course,

The Rotor-Master kit fits nicely inside this late-model Chevrolet El Camino engine compartment. Well-designed kits can be installed by the amateur mechanic in 35-40 hours, provided he has a modicum of mechanical skills. No special tools are required other than a welding torch, required to hook the turbo exhaust to the stock muffler system. This can usually be accomplished by the local muffler shop.

there are also a lot of excellent aftermarket breakerless ignitions as well. Even if you don't go the pointless route on your turbo machine, a good capacitive discharge (CD) unit can really fire that compressed mixture.

The plug wires are not to be forgotten either. If you are using a hotter coil or CD system, your stock secondary wires aren't likely to enjoy it for long, unless you have a '76-'77 engine with the new factory silicone-jacketed wires and silicone boots. Steel-core wires have always been the best bet for off-road performance and racing, but a nuisance on the street. The electrical radiation can interfere with your car radio, but you can almost use the radio static hum as a tachometer! If you think it's OK because your super-macho machine doesn't have a radio, wait till the 250-lb beer drinker next door comes over after discovering that your car is interfering with his TV baseball game (a rare, but possible, occurrence). The types of wire marked *TVR* are usually not rugged enough for use with a hot secondary

system, so your best bet is to get some of the aftermarket silicone-jacketed wires that are marked as *magnetic-suppression* like the Delco orange wire.

With the rest of the ignition system taken care of, we're down to the spark plugs where all of this energy is released. Your stock plugs are probably going to be one range too hot for your turbo application, but you can't go too cold either or they'll carbon up. Everyone has their own preference for spark plug brands, but we've found that Autolite plugs last about the longest in high-compression or turbocharged applications. Whatever brand you use, you might investigate some of the commercial plugs available, they usually have much beefier electrodes. Speaking of electrodes, you should close down the plug gap somewhat from a normally-aspirated setting. The extra-dense mixture induced during the boost mode is harder for the spark to ionize, so set the gap to about 0.010-inch smaller than the stock setting. On '75-'77 cars with electronic ignitions and resistor plugs set at .050-.060-inch, you can drop the gap about .015-inch. You can expect normal plug life, given a reasonable driving style, and with the water injection they should last even longer than on a stock engine.

TURBOCHARGER KITS

You may be wondering at this point when we're going to start getting technical on you, and describe exactly how to choose a particular model of a such-and-such turbocharger for your specific case. Indeed, we could fill quite a few pages with charts, tables, flow maps and the like, interspersed with a heavy dose of formulae. Maybe, if

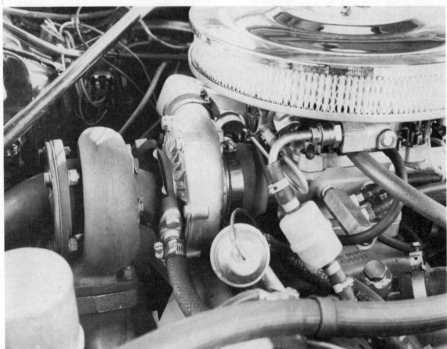

The Roto-Master turbo fits neatly on the right side of this small Chevy. The oil drain was routed into the top of the intake manifold for return to the pan via the lifter galley.

you're fresh out of school you could follow it all and , a ream of scrap paper later, you and your pocket calculator would know the best "theoretical" turbo to use. But a turbocharger is an expensive piece of equipment (even though it is relatively cheap from a horsepower-per-dollar standpoint), and making the wrong choice could be very disappointing. There is some math involved in selecting the proper unit, and the best exhaust housing, but even then, when it comes down to a real-life installation, the "book" answer is often just a good starting point. There's really no need for you to go through all this, when the work has been done for you by experts with considerable experience. If you have any of the currently-popular performance engines, rest assured that there is more than one kit out there for your engine, and both the theoretical and practical work in selecting the proper pieces has already been done for you. There are new companies starting up all the time to produce kits for an increasing variety of domestic and foreign engines, and even the marine, tractor-pulling, aircraft, and motorcycle contingents are being catered to by enterprising manufacturers. Even if you don't run the ubiquitous smallblock Chevrolet and your taste runs to four-bangers or flathead Hudsons, these same kit manufacturers can help you design a system based on the simple information you give them on your engine specs and proposed vehicle use. If you're the do-it-yourself type and have access to welding equipment and basic home shop tools, you can purchase the turbocharger and a few accessories from one of these companies, grab a few tubing U-bends and

The turbocharger driven element and housing is on the left. Supported by the special cast iron manifold (supplied), it will withstand temperatures near red hot and speeds approaching 100,000 rpm. Under these unearthly operating conditions, the oil supply is the life line of the turbo (oil inlet indicated by arrow). If lube is stopped, even for a second or two, you can expect a large "doctor bill."

whack out your own system with the savings applied to something else like a new set of rear tires with twice the traction of your old ones. Building the installation, if you go by some of the guidelines we've described, is no more complicated than many of the projects that hot rodders tackle as a matter of course.

There are only four major manufacturers of turbochargers in this country: the AiResearch division of Garrett Industries; Rajay Corp.; Roto-Master Inc., a division of the Echlin Co.; and the Schwitzer Division of the

Wallace-Murray Corp. All of the kits you will find available for automotive use will employ one of these units, and if you design a system yourself, you'll have to get your turbo from one of their representatives. But before you whip off a letter to one of the addresses listed at the end of this chapter, you should know that there are differences in turbos. All of the above companies have a reputation for consistent quality, but the design of their units could have an effect on how you build your system.

The type of oil seal, for instance, is

The carburetor sits on top of the Rotor-Master priority valve assembly. The water injection nozzle is indicated by the arrow, and such a system is the best method to make the turbo really practical on the street.

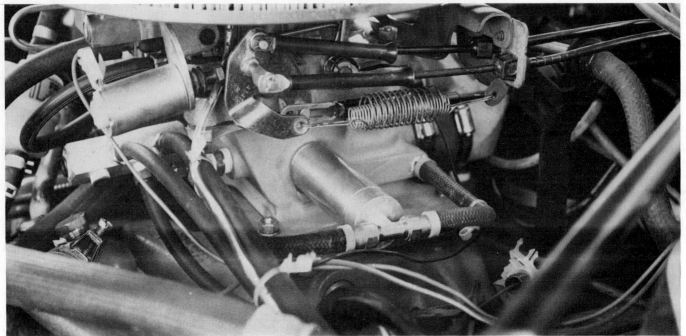

The Roto-Master turbo kit uses a unique air piston and valve assembly to control boost. As the boost level reaches maximum, the piston is pushed against a spring in this cylinder (arrow). By connection through a short link-rod, the piston closes a valve causing a restriction on the turbo inlet and thereby limiting the boost level. The hose on the right is connected to the intake manifold and senses the boost level, while the left connection goes to a bleed-off valve that allows the user to dial in the desired boost pressure. Truly a simple, reliable, inexpensive, and easily-adjustable system.

important to consider. We talked earlier about draw-through and blow-through applications, and a certain type of oil seal on the turbo is required in order to mount the carburetor ahead of the compressor. The first three companies mentioned use a carbon-face seal in their turbochargers, which is what you need if the engine is to draw fuel and air both. The Schwitzer turbos have a piston-ring type seal which won't work in a draw-through application because the fuel can get past these seals and wipe out the high-speed bearing in a hurry. However, being relegated to a blow-through application isn't as bad as it sounds. Crane (the cam people) have done a lot of work with the Schwitzer turbos, and there is much to commend their approach. When the turbo is blowing only dry air (no fuel), compressor-side boost control becomes more practical. With the carburetor in the original location on the stock intake manifold, you don't have any problems with fuel puddling in the intake tract of the turbo and boost plumbing. Also, and even more importantly from an emission standpoint, the cold-start emissions problem with a turbocharged engine (one of the reasons a gasoline turbo setup is not legal in California, unless it is an original equipment setup) is considerably less with a blow-through installation. Having the carburetor a long distance from the manifold, as it would be in a draw-through system, can cause some problems with cold-start emissions because of the wet fuel that collects along the intake tract. There

may also be a problem with delayed throttle response when the carburetor butterflies are so far from the intake valves (although selecting the proper exhaust housing can cure the "lag"). *So there is no one type of turbo, to the exclusion of all others, that is perfect for every application.* If you have to spend ten dollars or so in catalogs from everyone to get the facts before you buy, it's worth it to know the advantages and disadvantages of the different types.

Inherent in every listing of anything is incompleteness. There are many more manufacturers of turbo conversions for marine, cycle, industrial and other uses that we won't be discussing here. What we'd like to point out are the biggest of the kit manufacturers, who have the experience and right components for efficient street turbocharging for performance and RV work.

JOHN ANDERSON TURBOCHARGING

Ten years ago, John Anderson, a die-hard hot rodder of the old school, was in the same boat that you are in today. He had heard about turbochargers, and after years of campaigning conventional street-driven hot rods and dragstrip winners of one kind or another, he thought he'd see what all this incredible "free horsepower" stuff was about. After wading through whatever misinformation he could find about them, and after burning down a few turbos and several motors, he found out what made them tick. Since then he's

turbocharged his own cars, campaigned a blown alcohol dragster with a potent turbocharged Rat, and done custom turbo installations on everything from inline "econo" motors to four-wheel-drives, street Mustangs and Camaros, even a few exotic numbers such as Panteras and a Lamborghini. He faces every new job as a challenge, and just enjoys making mud-turtles into asphalt streakers. None of the conversions he's done have been namby-pamby; he reasons that if you're spending the money for a turbocharging system you should get as much performance as can be reliably obtained from your engine.

None of the applications he covers are available in off-the-shelf "kit" form; he deals with every customer on an individual basis, even as far away as England, Canada and Australia. Once he's got the technical facts on your vehicle and engine, he'll make up the pieces for your conversion or just ship you the basic turbo with the necessary tubing bends, fitting, carb adapter, etc., that you'll need to finish your own. Because of the variety of optional engine equipment, such as smog pumps, air conditioning, and power steering, he'd rather sell you a custom-designed setup than ship you something off the shelf that needs to be modified to fit your particular car or truck.

In addition to the custom Rajay turbo conversions he does in his Napa Valley, California, shop, Anderson also distributes water injection units, pressure-retard distributor advance units, turbo instruments, and makes his own

John Anderson obviously likes turbos! Both of his personal street rods are blown, this '29 roadster featuring two Rajay turbos sucking through two sidedraft Webers.

carb adapters and waste gates. The wastegates utilize cast-iron bases, lids and seamless moly tubing bodies, and are responsive at boost levels as low as five pounds. The Westach line of "Turbo-Test" instruments he distributes are also worth your attention (more about instruments later on). Call or write for further information on your specific needs, or if you find yourself in the vicinity of the famous Northern California wine country, stop by and take a convincing test ride in one of his turbo'd street rods and have a sip of his special "turbo" wine!

GALE BANKS ENGINEERING

Building racing engines for a living gives you a certain perspective on how to gain horsepower from a street engine. Gale Banks has been doing high-quality turbocharging on marine engines for some years, and one of his dual-turbo big-block Chevys has set class records in several competition boat events. Recently he has entered the automotive market, and will have a variety of kits for popular engines before long. His first kit, now available, is for the Chevrolet Vega four-cylinder, and it has some interesting differences from other aftermarket kits.

The Banks Vega kit uses a short header system to plumb the exhaust to the turbine. Built of heavy-wall tubing

to retain the heat, it couples the turbine flange with a V-band clamp, with a bellows unit to allow for expansion of the system under heat. Banks uses AiResearch or Rajay turbochargers on his engines, and his kits show the marks of engineering learned through race-car and race-boat experience. A sheetmetal heat shield fits closely over

the turbine housing, to retain heat and protect components under the hood, while the carburetion (draw-through) is provided by a modified 46-mm Hitachi. This Japanese copy of a British SU has just the right throat diameter to adapt to the turbo compressor inlet and uses a piston dampener as a power enrichment circuit. The SU-types are also considered very easy to tune.

Two components that are part of the "deluxe" Banks Vega kit are racing-derived, a wastegate and an intercooler device. The AiResearch wastegate features a 1⅝-inch valve head and is adjustable for any boost level. Using a wastegate for control allows using an exhaust housing for the turbo that produces good boost and quick response. The intercooler, Bank's own design, is an optional part of the kit and an interesting item not found on any other automotive street system we've seen. An aluminum housing bolts to the intake manifold and houses a small-but-efficient water-type radiator. The air-fuel mixture coming from the compressor outlet is plumbed through this radiator and housing before it enters the intake manifold. The radiator is connected by hoses to another radiator mounted in the car fenderwell. To lower intake charge temperatures to make more power without detonation, a pressure switch on the intake manifold turns on an electric water pump whenever boost exceeds 1-2 psi. The water pump circulates the cooling medium through the intercooler radiator (where it extracts heat from the intake charge) to the second radiator, where an electric fan cools off the medium.

Banks ran a modified Vega engine on a dyno as a prototype of his kit and came up with some startling numbers.

Gale Banks Engineering is one of the largest suppliers of turbocharged engines to the marine market. Custom-ordered turbocharged engines are available from 750- to 1500-horsepower levels.

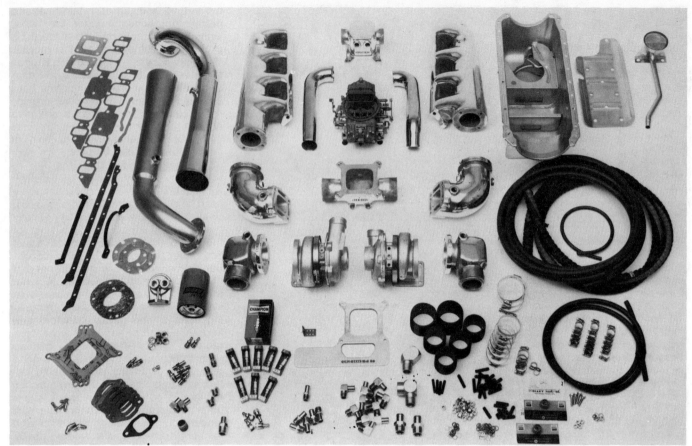

Gale Banks also offers a complete do-it-yourself bolt-on kit for big and smallblock Chevys, 460 Fords and 455 Olds marine engines. These kits include every part required to perform the conversion.

With everything hooked up and the wastegate adjusted up to 20 psi boost, the little four-in-a-row produced a whopping 309 hp at 6000 rpm! That's not bad from a 140-ci engine, and even with a more streetable 15 psi blow-off point, 260 hp was achieved at 5800 rpm. Without the optional intercooler, and with just 10 psi boost, the engine still developed 226 hp at 5800 rpm. This engine was blueprinted, but certainly similar results would be obtained with any good engine.

With such optional equipment as AiResearch wastegates and his own neatly-turned-out aluminum intercoolers, other Gale Banks kits now in the works should provide just as formidable power improvements for street machines as his 1500-hp racing engines have done for his marine customers.

CROWN MANUFACTURING CO.

Crown and the turbocharger have been closely associated since the first Corvair Spyders appeared on the automotive scene almost 15 years ago. What started out as a dune buggy equipment company soon turned into a high-performance outlet for Corvair goodies, from engine swap kits to turbochargers, even a competition kit to garner increased boost from the stock Spyder. Founder Ted Trevor advanced into making turbocharger

kits for other cars, including the Datsun 240Z and 260Z, and the 1600 and 1800 Datsun passenger car engines. Quite a few of these conversions have been on the streets for several years, demonstrating the reliability and punch of a turbo setup on a stock engine. Today, under new ownership, Crown is still involved in high performance turbocharging, with new kits for the Porsche 914 flat-4 engine, and others in the works.

All of the Crown kits contain detailed and well-planned instructions, designed for the average enthusiast so that a conversion can be completed in a weekend's time. The Crown kit for the Datsun 510 sedan, for instance, has 11 pages of instructions and six full-page illustrations, detailing everything from the retention of stock emission controls to hookup of the choke, throttle, oil lines, exhaust system, and even tuning instructions. With a copy of the factory shop manual (Datsun, Porsche or whatever you're converting) and these instructions, you should have no problems getting back on the road. The Datsun Z-car kit instructions have step-by-step photos of exactly how the conversion goes together. In most of these Crown conversions, the boost is set for a street level of 7-12 psi and comes in at about 2500-2700 rpm (when you tromp it). A test of a turbo 240Z indicated a 30% rear wheel horsepower

increase at 2500 rpm (50 bhp vs 38 bhp) and a whopping 140% increase at 5000 rpm with 12 psi boost (190 rear wheel horsepower compared to 78 bhp stock)! And all this is done using only one of the two Hitachi (Japanese version of the British SU) carburetors that the Z-car comes with.

In addition to their line of turbocharger kits, Crown also offers some of the accessories needed for installations, such as a water injection kit and a hot CD ignition.

CRANE CAMS, INC.

A name familiar to performance enthusiasts for cylinder heads and valve train equipment, Crane has recently extended into the turbocharging field, becoming the major distributor for the Schwitzer turbocharger. Schwitzer formerly produced their own turbo kits for 1500 and 1600 cc Volkswagen engines, and Crane now distributes these plus their own kit for the Chevrolet Vega four-cylinder engine. A 140 ci Vega four with the Crane-Schwitzer kit produced some 150 bhp on an engine dyno, which is exactly double the horsepower of a stock one-barrel Vega. Because the Schwitzer turbo utilizes a piston-ring-type seal on the ends of the sleeve bearing, it isn't suited for draw-through applications. Most of the production Schwitzers are used on diesel applications (boats, buses, trucks, farm equipment) where a blow-through is desired because the fuel is injected at the ports. The company has also been involved in turbocharging some of the top Indianapolis USAC cars for the past eight or nine years, so they're not strangers to the high-performance world. The 1600cc Volkswagen kit uses mild boost to almost double the horsepower from the original 45 bhp, and still achieves 25 mpg fuel economy with complete reliability.

Crane, of course, is also a major aftermarket camshaft manufacturer, and it has some recommendations in that area. Crane is one of the few cam grinders to offer camshafts specifically ground for turbocharged applications. It has a full selection, regardless of what application or make of turbo you're using. It has a tech sheet you can fill out to get an expert suggestion for a cam if you aren't sure which of its catalog-listed items applies.

Crane's Don Hubbard has written an excellent basic booklet on turbocharging, with complete listings of which Schwitzer turbos should be used for certain engines and uses, which camshafts to use, and a complete repair and overhaul section for the Schwitzer 3LD turbocharger. Crane also sells "a short kit" for building your own single or dual-turbo setup, which includes the gaskets, oil system parts, V-clamp for the exhaust, an exhaust stub (for exhaust out), an exhaust flange (for exhaust in), a compressor inlet strainer bonnet, and a Holley high-performance electric fuel pump and pressure regulator. The Crane manual makes some excellent points about the benefits of blow-through application, such as plumbing, hood clearance, emissions, etc., and before you make a final decision as to your own plan of attack, you might investigate this booklet (only $1).

AK MILLER ENTERPRISES

Few known hot rodding personalities have been involved in automotive turbocharging as long as the "Pico Rivera Flash". Miller has been interested in performance combined with good fuel economy and low exhaust emissions for many years, and has done a lot of development work with propane fuel and turbochargers together. He and the IMPCO propane carburetion people developed the IMPCO TC-2 boost controller that is used by many kit designers. His company now distributes a wide-coverage line of street turbocharging kits for performance and RV applications, from the little Pintos to the HD 534 Ford truck engines. As major distributors for the AiResearch line of turbochargers, Ak Miller Enterprises offers street and competition kits for the fours found in

Pintos, Capris and the new Ford Courier pickups, Toyota 2000RC engines, Capri and Mustang II V-6's, Ford, Chevrolet and Chrysler six-cylinders, the smallblock and big-block Chevy V-8's, 360-390 Ford trucks, 350 Chevy truck engines, Porsche 914 and 911's, and the Dodge Ramcharger 360 4 x 4's (with new kits constantly under development). Most of the Ak Miller kits can be ordered with IMPCO propane carburetion if you desire, for a truly clean-burning engine with cheap, high-octane fuel.

If you've ever visited the Ak Miller Enterprises shop, yours was probably the only naturally-aspirated vehicle in the parking lot! Everyone who works there has something huffed-and-puffed to drive, from Ak's blown-propane Pinto with high boost and an adapted 5-speed, to Jon Meyers' twin-turbo smallblock Chevy station wagon, and Bill Edwards' turbo'ed Ford pickup (complete with a turbocharged big-displacement motorcycle strapped to the bed). This has been home base for a variety of turbocharged race cars, too, including Ak's twin-blown 351 Cleveland sprint car for Pike's Peak (which Ak has won eight times); Bill Edwards' perennial Bonneville runner, an early Ranchero with twin turbos, two wastegates and Bosch fuel injection on a smallblock Chevy; and the famous Jack Lufkin streamlined sports car (298.26 mph, world's fastest sports car, fastest car (of any type on gasoline) with twin-turbo 454 Chevy.

In addition to the full-fledged kits, Ak Miller Enterprises also sells a complete line of accessories for the do-it-yourselfers. High-flow exhaust components, from 2½-inch tubing bends to the Corvair turbocharged mufflers, water injection kits using Pinto washer

bottles, special cast-iron exhaust manifolds for various engines that allow simple bolt-on installation of an AiResearch turbo, water-heated carburetor adapters for draw-through applications, and cast aluminum inlet manifold adapters (for blow-through) are among the goodies they can supply you with. Technical assistance for the DIY'er by phone or letter is also offered.

ROTO-MASTER TURBOSONIC

If you've been looking for the familiar ACCEL name in this chapter, you won't find it. Accel and Roto-Master are both subsidiaries of the Echlin Manufacturing Corp., and the Turbosonic product line originally advertised by Accel is now handled by the newly-acquired Roto-Master group. Roto-Master has been in the turbocharger rebuilding business for some time, and has recently begun a massive expansion program in the hope of becoming *the* turbo company in the future. Already they are manufacturing complete turbos for a variety of industrial, diesel and gasoline street uses, and are constantly expanding the Turbosonic line of bolt-on turbo kits. Their turbochargers are built to exacting standards on precision, computer-controlled machines, and the rotating parts are balanced down to milligrams.

The current Roto-Master brochure lists kits for Pinto, Colt and Vega four-cylinder engines, and kits for Ford and Chevrolet smallblock V-8's, as well as a "universal" kit for V-8's and V-6's, and a universal inline kit for fours and sixes. Their book lists turbocharger recommendations for various sizes of engines, and the required installation kits are listed separately, due to the

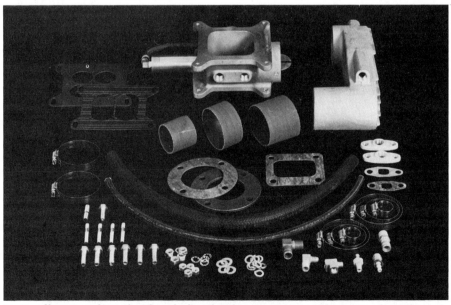

In an effort to reduce the throttle lag that is sometimes evident on a draw-through setup (where the carb is a long way from the manifold) Roto-Master came up with their very effective priority valve assembly. This is their Universal V-8 Module.

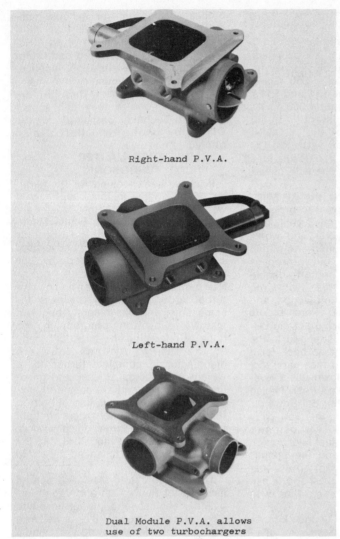

Right-hand P.V.A.

Left-hand P.V.A.

Dual Module P.V.A. allows use of two turbochargers

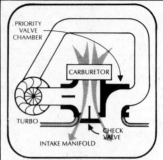

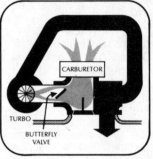

Diagram "A" shows the air/fuel mixture flow under very light engine load conditions. The mixture enters the large Priority Valve Assembly chamber, passes thru the check valves in the bottom of the chamber, and enters the engine's intake manifold. Under these conditions of light load and very high engine vacuum, no boost is occurring. At this point the engine is normally "aspirated".

Diagram "B" shows the transition phase from normally aspirated to boost pressure. As engine load increases to a medium level, the compressor begins to draw a portion of the air/fuel mixture into the compressor inlet. The mixture is compressed and returned to the intake manifold where it joins the mixture still entering thru the check valves.

Diagram "C" shows the engine operating under full load condition at maximum attainable boost. The high engine load is generating a great deal of exhaust output, so the turbine and compressor wheels spin much faster. Now all the air/fuel mixture is being drawn into the compressor, compressed and forced into the intake manifold. The check valve has been forced shut due to the higher pressure in the intake manifold.

Diagram "D" At this point a critical factor called "boost control" comes into play. A boost control butterfly valve located in the passageway leading to the compressor inlet remains open during normal conditions up to the boost limit. As soon as boost pressure reaches the 6-8 lb. range, the butterfly valve begins to close and stabilizes the boost condition in this range, eliminating the possibility of engine destruction.

In normally-aspirated running, A) the air-fuel mixture flows through the carburetor in normal fashion. When boost begins, B) air-fuel enters the engine through both P.V.A. chambers; but as boost increases, C) the check valves in the primary chamber close off and all the mix goes through the turbo. When the preset boost is exceeded, D) an automatic boost limiter throttles down the intake side.

The Roto-Master priority valve assembly is available in a variety of mounting modules. The valve is basically a boost-activated assembly, operated by a piston, which is attached to the large butterfly by a simple rod. As boost rises to the preset level, the piston-and-rod combination closes the butterfly to reduce boost and slow the turbo speed.

wide variation in usage possible for a given engine. Roto-Master recognizes the limitless variations in optional equipment possible on a production car/chassis, but wherever possible they have included information to accommodate the air conditioning systems of most vehicles. Their kits will require you to do the fabricating of the exhaust system leading from the turbine and the usual hookup of carb linkage, fuel lines, etc.

All of the Turbosonic V-8 kits utilize the unique "priority valve" method of induction. This is a dual-chamber aluminum casting on which your four-barrel carburetor sits 4¾ inches higher than the intake manifold. In one chamber, underneath the carburetor, the bottom is closed to the intake manifold except for two holes fitted with studs on which two air valve discs ride. The second chamber is connected to the manifold and to the outlet side of the turbocharger compressor. When

the engine is not under load, the engines breathes a fuel-air mixture directly from the carburetor through these two holes into the manifold. When boost reaches a certain level, the pressure in the intake manifold rises enough to close the two air valves against their seats and force all the fuel-air mixture to go through the turbo before entering the manifold. The idea behind the priority-valve concept is to keep the carburetor as close to the original location on the manifold as possible to reduce emissions, improve throttle response when transitioning from normally-aspirated to boost conditions, and keep the kit plumbing to a minimum. Roto-Master claims the priority valve virtually eliminates "turbo lag" in street applications. In all but their competition kits (for Pinto, Vega and Colt), Roto-Master supplies a boost controller that works on the intake side of the compressor and is connected to the priority-valve module. To

get the benefits of the priority-valve module on most V-8 applications, you may have to build or bolt on a hood scoop to clear the raised carburetor and air cleaner.

The instructions that come with Roto-Master kits are without a doubt the most thorough we've ever seen for any piece of aftermarket equipment. Not that the installations are overly-complicated or only for engineers, but the details and recommendations for the 351 Ford Cleveland engine, for example, comprises 33 pages! Where required, photos and illustrations are provided, as well as listing the tools you'll need, linkage recommendations, start-up checklist, and several pages on fine tuning the system when you're done.

Naturally, as one of the largest turbocharger manufacturers, Roto-Master has a complete line of replacement parts, as well as a variety of accessories such as water injection, priority-valve modules and adapters for dual-turbo setups on V-8's, boost gauges, Ford and GM ignition-retard kits, gaskets, turbo mufflers and IM-PCO boost controllers. Rotomaster's motto is "more power to you", and with their complete line of turbo goodies, they apparently mean what they say!

SPEARCO PERFORMANCE PRODUCTS

If you own one of the popular minicars such as Pinto, Vega, Mustang II or Capri, you're probably already well aware of this company. In addition to their line of dress-up and handling goodies for these cars, Spearco is also a major distributor of Rajay turbochargers and offer a number of street kits and parts. Rajay has been in the business of turbocharging high-performance aircraft since 1961, initially using TRW turbochargers, and they took over the TRW turbo production in 1969, moving the operation to Long Beach, California. George Spears of Spearco first developed the Rajay turbo kit for 1500 and 1600cc Volkswagens and still sells this "double-your-horsepower, double-your-fun" kit, as well as many newer kits. Since 1974, Spearco has handled all of the automotive kit business for Rajay, allowing the company to devote full attention to their growing turbocharger manufacturing facilities.

The Spearco kit for 2000cc Pintos was designed to be as easy to install as possible, and can be used with factory air conditioning and without relocating the battery, as is required on some other Pinto kits. As supplied, the kit will produce 7 psi of boost with 45% improvement in power, and what's more impressive — this kit can be run with 91-octane unleaded fuel! For a bunch more performance on premium fuel, Spearco offers a low-restriction exhaust system and different turbo exhaust housing for 14 psi boost. They recommend you run water injection with this setup and have the cylinder head O-ringed to prevent gasket trouble. The kits for the V-6 Capri and Mustang II (2600 cc and 2800 cc) are equally impressive. Compared to the stock induction, the Spearco turbocharger dropped 0-60 mph times from 10.4 seconds to 8.1 while increasing fuel economy by 5% in city driving and 7% on the highway. The V-6 Mustang II produced 10.2-second 0-60 mph, down from 13.4-seconds in stock trim, and fuel economy improved to the tune of 9% in the city and 12% on the road. Both of these V-6 kits will fit on factory air-conditioned cars and run a maximum of 9-10 psi boost, with water injection and premium fuel recommended. All existing emission hardware is compatible with the Spearco kits.

Newest in the Spearco line is their complete kit for the Chevy smallblock V-8. It will fit under the hood of almost any Chevy-powered vehicle without requiring a hood scoop, although the air conditioning may have to be relocated to the left side (if so equipped).

In addition to the Injectronic water injection kit mentioned previously for normally-aspirated engines (it will also work on turbo setups), Spearco also has a less expensive injector using a washer bottle and pressure-electric switch. Other goodies include cast-iron exhaust manifolds built to accept the Rajay turbo, check valves for boost-pressurized water injection systems, IMPCO boost controllers, various carburetor adapters (including one that drops the carburetor down low for extra hood clearance with large air cleaners), and turbocharger gauges such as an exhaust-gas temperature meter and a combination vacuum-boost gauge. As a major distributor for Rajay, Spearco can also sell individual turbos and they will gladly select the proper unit for your custom application.

BUILDING THE TURBO LONG BLOCK

We told you earlier that unless you were running more-than-average boost on your street machine, a stock engine in excellent mechanical condition needed no modifications to make it suitable for a blower installation. This is true for RV and other installations limited to 6-10 psi, but suppose you're a diehard street freak looking for brain-scrambling performance you can demonstrate at every intersection. If you're going after the 10-psi and above type of installation, then perhaps there are a few considerations you should give to the proper assembly of the shortblock and heads. Sure, there are in-numerable street installations that have gone over 10 psi on stock engines without trouble, but the answer really is in the style of driving. If you're going to be using high boost frequently, then there are some things you should consider to add a little extra durability above and beyond the factory assembly techniques. We'll assume that you don't have a fresh stock engine just waiting for a turbocharger, but that you have collected a few of the basic components to build a motor and you just haven't put it together yet. Perhaps you had planned to build a high-performance naturally-aspirated engine and now you have decided to try a turbocharger. You will want to know how to approach the blueprinting and parts-selection process.

Actually, the techniques for building a high-performance engine are basically the same for any use, at least as far as the attention to details in assembly is concerned. Parts selection for a turbo engine is quite a different matter and you may be surprised to find out how much money you can save on "trick" parts in building a motor for an "air-wheel" installation.

Shortblock assembly procedures follow standard hot-rodding practices. The block should be deburred around the lifter gallery area, and loose casting flash ground off, especially inside the oil return slots. Machine shop work, if any, should consist of the usual align boring of the mains, surfacing of the block for straightness, thorough cleaning of all the oil passages, thread chasing of head-bolt and main-cap bolt holes, and installation of new cam bearings. You can skip the align boring of the main caps if the bearing bores aren't more than 0.001-inch out-of-line with each other (as measured with an accurate straightedge). If you

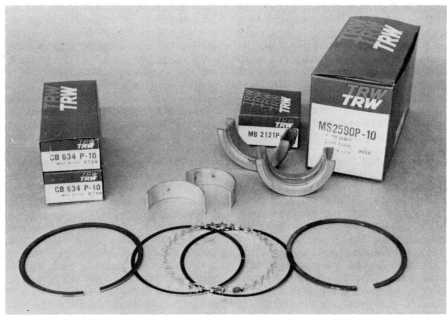

If you're going to be building a turbo engine from scratch, start with good parts.

do have the align boring done, check to make sure that the crank holes haven't moved up in the block or you could wind up with slop in the timing chain, or if your engine has a gear-drive cam (like Ford 240-300 sixes) the gears would bind. After the block is finished, it should be subjected to the most thorough cleaning you can give it, first with the usual steam cleaning and then with hot soapy water and a variety of brushes to reach all the passages where dirt or chips may hide.

The rotating-reciprocating assembly will require some attention. If there are two areas of concern with a turbocharged engine, it is having a strong bottom end and a strong top end (head gasket area). You won't be turning ungodly engine speeds to make power with a turbo, but just the same, it helps to have things "right on" in the lower end. Naturally, if you have a choice for your engine between a steel crank and an iron one, use the forged steel one, but it isn't imperative due to the generally moderate engine rpm. Likewise, for the four-bolt main caps, if you've got 'em, fine, if not, don't worry about them. The crank, especially if it is a new "green" one, should be sent out for magnafluxing (X-ray inspection if available in your area), shot-peening, and polishing of the journals. Chamfering the oil holes in the crank is a wise move to keep the holes from chewing up the inserts and to insure a free flow of oil. During the polishing, some turbo engine builders like to leave the shot-peening finish in the radius areas, rather than polishing the radius smooth.

Select the best set of rods you can. We don't mean that you should spring for a set of racing Carillo rods, but select the best stock rods you can find. They should all pass a magnaflux check and be shot-peened and resized at both ends. You should select a high quality set of bearings and step up one size in rod bolts if that's practical with your engine. At the least, you should use new rod bolts and nuts, and it's a good idea to have them magnafluxed and tested for hardness. Some of the aftermarket "trick" bolts may have a very high Rockwell rating but are so hard as to be brittle. Your rod bolts should test (at a well-equipped machine shop) to a Rockwell "C" rating of 36-40, and the nuts to 28-34. The bolt-nut seating areas on the rod and cap should be made parallel to each other and square to the bolt holes, then polished lightly to reduce the chances of a crack starting on a sharp edge.

What you put on the small end of the rod, the piston, is the most important part of a turbo engine shortblock. Forget cast pistons if you plan to use more than 10 psi boost for any length of time. Some stock pistons will survive, but examine the skirt areas for

Depending on your budget, the block can be treated to the usual align-boring, deck trimming and quality hone job that would be a part of any high-performance engine build.

strength. If there are long slots in the skirt behind the oil rings, they'll be too weak. Those with round holes are better. Forged pistons do make more noise when cold than standard cast pistons, but they'll have the strength when you need it. Most engine builders have had good success with the TRW forgings that are made as direct replacements for stock, low-compression pistons. The shape of the piston head would seem to be of little importance on a low-compression piston, but in wedge engines there should be a distinct quench area. In order to have some quench and still have the low compression, the shape may have a raised area around the circumference of the head with the center depressed to keep the volume up. Some piston manufacturers refer to this as a *reverse deflector* shape. Having a lot of surface-to-volume ratio in the quench area keeps the portion of the mixture cool that would otherwise contribute to early detonation.

Use standard high-performance rings, but resist the temptation to go trick and don't use thin rings, Dykes rings or stainless. The finish and straightness of the bores these rings will ride in is of course equally important. If you have to machine oversize to get straight walls, machine bore then power hone on a Sunnen Cylinder King to size.

We've already mentioned some of the requirements of the oiling system for the turbo engine. You don't need to spend hundreds of dollars here, just install a good performance oil pump, and secure the pickup so that it won't come off the pump. If yours has a pressed-in oil pickup tube, then braze it to the pump body to prevent it from coming

loose, or if yours is a bolt-on pickup as found on some Fords, then drill and safety wire the bolts together. If you have sufficient clearance in your chassis, it wouldn't hurt to add a little extra oil capacity, since you're now supplying extra oil to the turbo for lubrication and cooling. The cheapest way to enlarge your oil pan is to get a similar pan at a wrecking yard. Cut the bottom out of the original sump, cut the full sump (say two inches in depth) off the junk-yard pan and weld this onto the original pan. You now have a stock-like sump that is an extra inch or two deeper. Careful measurements before and after will show you how much to extend the oil pump pickup to correspond to the new pan depth. Cadmium irriditing, like you see on all the trick racing pans, costs about $5, looks neat, and stands up better than paint. Just remember to weld in the new oil drainback fitting for the turbo (above the oil level!) before you send the pan out for cad plating. You may also want to add some kind of windage tray, too. If there is a factory high-performance windage tray available for your engine, it's worth every penny, but you can make one to weld onto the pan yourself. Leave holes at either end for oil return, but restrict the area around the top of the sump to keep the bulk of the oil around the pickup during hard acceleration and braking.

The cylinder heads are an area where going trick can be a waste of money. The little turbocharger will produce more than enough flow, without having to mess with elaborate porting and polishing. You may want to match the ports to your gaskets (both manifold ports and head ports), on the intake and exhaust side, but leave the port

Some builders of turbocharged engines like to leave the shot-peen effect in the crank radius, rather than polish it out all the way. Your whole bottom end should receive a good balancing job.

wall finish as it is to promote mixture turbulence. Likewise, spending extra money for a set of heads with larger cast ports is not worth it. One modification that can be a good investment for a moderate-to-high boost engine would be to have the heads O-ringed. Take them to a good machine shop and have an O-ring groove cut about 0.035-inch deep around each combustion chamber. When you reassemble the engine, you can install some 17-gauge copper wire in these grooves and it will stick out of the groove enough to provide a good, tight seal and prevent head gasket blowout under periods of high boost.

The valve train calls for a little thought, too. A good, concentric valve job is a must, with much wider valve seats than you would run on a hi-po normally-aspirated engine—at least 0.080-inch for the intake seats and 0.100-inch for the exhausts. This is important to give the valves a chance to get rid of the extra heat encountered under high boost conditions. The valves should also be quality pieces, correctly sized for stem clearance, but the expense of special stainless steel valves is unnecessary. In a propane application, the seats should be hardened, since there's no lubricating quality in propane (just as there is none in unleaded gasoline). Use the factory late-model heads that have induction-hardened seats (because of the no-lead requirement) and valve rotators, or have hardened-steel seats installed in your old heads. This is an expensive operation at a good machine shop, but valve recession (where the valves keep going up into the head) will be less of a problem.

Valve springs and retainers are im-portant, to say the least. If there was only one thing you could change about a stock engine to run it with a turbocharger, it should be the valve springs. When the engine is experiencing boost, the valve springs have to work against much higher pressures. The exhaust valves have to fight the extra back pressure that the turbo creates, especially one with a small exhaust housing, and the intake valve spring really has a job pulling the valve closed when boost pressure is trying to keep it open. You can calculate just how much extra pressure is there by figuring the area of the valve head in square inches and multiplying it by the boost pressure. It may surprise you. If you've ever run a racing engine you know how quickly valve springs can lose their strength, so it's necessary to have better-than-stock quality springs in this ultimate turbo motor we're building on paper. Correctly shim the springs to the manufacturer's recommended installed height, but don't shim them such that coil-bind will take place when the valve is fully opened. Lightweight retainers have always been a favorite hot-rodding trick to make the motor rev a little easier, but more important in a turbo application is their strength and durability. Forget about the pretty anodized aluminum jobs, valve springs tend to chew them up. We've repeated over and over that you don't need to run high speeds to gain equivalent horsepower from a turbo engine. This is true, but, to make another case for better-than-stock valve springs, you may be running higher speeds than if you left the engine stock. A stock, late-model smog engine will probably float the valves at 5000 rpm or even less, and you may be running that high with your turbo setup, even if getting that same power by some other hot-rodding methods would mean turning 8,000 rpm. The presence of a turbocharger under the hood is a devilish temptation for your right foot when you feel the rush of the boost coming on, so watch your tachometer!

Also in line with cautions against the high boost pressures, watch your rocker arm wear points carefully. They're under a lot more strain from the higher cylinder pressures and higher valve spring tensions. Screw-in studs are always a good investment for any performance engine, and a set of

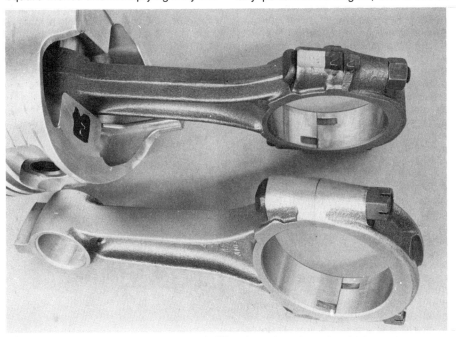

You don't have to go all-out in rod modifications, but they should be resized, shot-peened, flashing ground off, and a good set of new nuts and bolts selected.

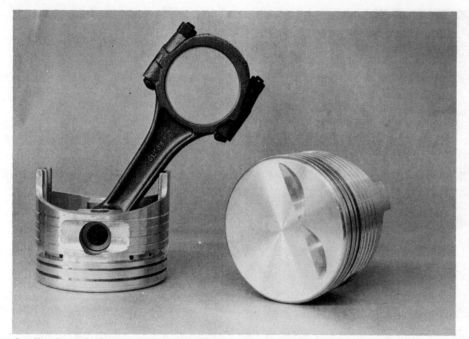

Quality forged pistons are a must if you plan on very much boost. The low static compression required means you'll be using a flat-top or reverse-deflector piston.

grooved rocker balls will keep a supply of oil at the rocker when you need it. Your stock pushrods, if they pass the straightness test (rolling them on a sheet of glass to check for wobble) are perfectly adequate, even with the higher-than-stock spring pressures.

Every performance enthusiast likes to say that he has "a cam" in his engine. Of course, he has to have some kind of cam in there or it wouldn't run, but what he means is that he has a hot rod cam, with a lumpy idle meant to induce fear in the stoplight opposition. To some enthusiasts, how the engine responds to this cam in normal driving isn't nearly as important as creating that visceral impact from the "high-horsepower sound". Such an enthusiast will be disappointed with a turbo installation because the engine will probably make less exhaust noise than it did stock, and the camshaft will provide a normal, smooth idle. For these and other reasons, the turbo is the perfect answer for those who desire a sleeper vehicle, because by the time the other guy hears that whooshing sound he's watching your rear bumper. Almost every street turbo application will operate best with the type of cam that gives the widest possible power band, which is why typical hot rod cams designed for high engine speeds are out. The stock cam presently in your engine does as good a job as any in providing smooth operation, just leave it in there. Yes, there are some specialty cams which are made for turbocharged applications, but unless you're building a "killer" you won't need one.

Iskenderian markets a line of profiles he calls the "Turbo-Cycle" cams, and Crane has quite a few cams listed for turbocharged applications. The Crane-Schwitzer turbo manual lists four categories of boost-performance levels, and makes recommendations for most popular engines as to which of their cams works for each boost level. What you must avoid is a cam with a lot of overlap, so the lobe centers should be far apart, as they are in some of the current "mileage-torque" cams being offered by many cam grinders. Experimenting with cam timing and duration can sometimes show gains in performance, but this may be at the expense of engine and turbocharger longevity. Just a minor increase in intake duration, for example, can feed the engine a great deal more air and fuel, since the turbocharger is forcing it

in whenever the valve gives it a chance, but the exhaust gas temperature may be rising out of sight, too, unless you run a pyrometer to keep track of it. Your best bet is to run a stock cam, complete the engine and turbo setup, then see what kind of performance you get. If it turns out that you're not satiated even then, you may just need to crank in a little more boost pressure by making the exhaust system less restrictive (like using a split-Y coming out of the turbo and running two 2½-inch pipes and two turbo mufflers), changing the exhaust housing of the turbine, or just the "horsepower screw" if your setup is equipped with a waste gate and you're not in danger of detonation. Detonation, in the end, is the only real limitation to your power output on gasoline.

Your lifters may require some close scrutiny. There's almost no reason today to run a mechanical lifter camshaft in a street engine. In a turbocharged application, there will probably be some portion of the plumbing that overhangs one or both of the valve covers, which would make the frequent lash adjustments required by a solid-lifter cam a very unpleasant ritual. Stock hydraulic lifters should be able to handle the engines speeds you'll be running, but if you desire, there are special "anti-pump-up" hydraulic lifters that are good to about 7000 rpm, giving an extra margin for unusual applications.

We've already touched upon some of the considerations of the turbocharged engine ignition system. A stock distributor in good shape with a hot coil or a CD system should provide the necessary hotter spark to fire your dense mixtures, with some good plug wires and heavy-duty plugs to take the heat. Other than the turbo system, that's

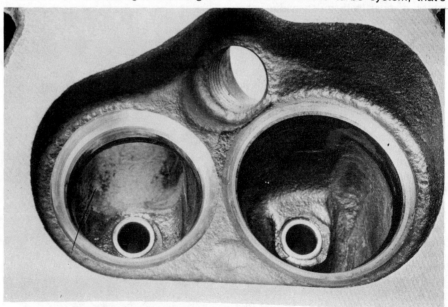

The heads need no trick work other than a good, concentric valve job, but make sure the seats are wide enough to cool the valves.

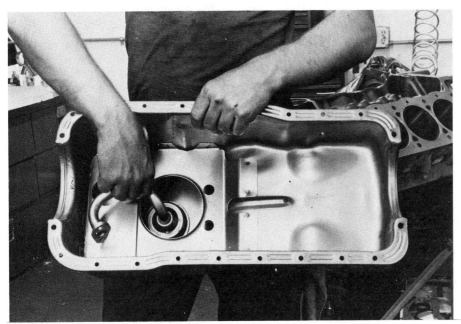

Providing plenty of oil even under hard acceleration will probably mean a special oil pan with windage tray, deeper sump and longer oil pump pickup tube.

all there is to building your engine, except perhaps the intake manifold. Unless you're running an inline engine of small displacement, you'll probably be using a four-barrel carburetor. For any application with a turbocharger, one of the new single-plane performance manifolds is probably the best bet. You could get away with a stock-type dual-plane manifold in a blow-through application, but on a draw-through, the potential mixture distribution problem calls for the best manifold you can get. Some of the single-plane manifolds are developed from racing manifolds in which the open plenum requires high engine speeds to maintain mixture velocity. Even the street derivations of these manifolds can have a touch of this velocity problem, but it's not a problem at all when there's a 100,000 rpm turbine pushing the air-fuel mixture into the plenum.

INTERCOOLERS

If you're running a draw-through installation, you will want some sort of water-heated carburetor adapter ahead of the turbo. This takes care of the carburetor heat, and there's no need to have an exhaust passage through the intake manifold for this purpose, for it would only add to the already hot mixture coming out of the turbocharger. Race cars use sophisticated methods to cool the intake charge, with one or more intercoolers mounted between the compressor and the intake manifold. These heat exchangers may be one or a combination of several types, including air-to-air or air-to-liquid. The mixture from the compressor is routed through the intercooler housing, through which is circulated the air or liquid cooling medium. By dropping the intake charge temperature, more power can be developed, but the space and plumbing of an intercooler makes it somewhat impractical for a street-driven car with a low-profile hood. There are, however, some changes you can make to the intake system to improve the situation in your installation.

Hot oil and crankcase fumes swirling around under your intake manifold (on a V-type engine) can add heat to the intake charge. While this is not such a problem on a normally-aspirated street car, where the extra heat adds to vaporization of the fuel and aids driveability, it's unnecessary heat on a turbocharged engine with a draw-through (remote-mounted) carburetor. You can cut some of this heat transfer from the oil by using one of the sheet-metal plates used by drag racers for this same purpose. These plates fit such that they cover the whole valley under the intake manifold and simply snap in place with two spring-steel clips. Another tract would be to utilize one of the single-plane intake manifolds used by drag and circle-track racers which has a separation between the bottom of the manifold runners and the top of the oil valley. For racing, this air gap provides air circulation through the manifold to aid intake leg cooling. While this type of manifold wouldn't be suitable for a street-driven normally-aspirated car, it may be just the ticket for a turbocharged engine. Another source of intake heat in a standard manifold is the water passages at each end that connect the left and right cylinder heads. Depending on the engine water temperature and intake charge temperature, these water passages could be either increasing intake charge heat or helping to reduce it. If you wanted to take the time and trouble to experiment with it, you could conceivably divorce the water passages from the manifold itself, using external tubing to connect the two passages between the heads. The water passages could be blocked off at the manifold-head juncture and separate water outlets would have to be drilled in the heads. Moroso currently offers a "Y-Block" conversion similar to this for racing engines, but the idea could be adapted to turbocharged street engines.

Typical of marine-type intercoolers, this single-radiator Gale Banks intercooler is used on his "medium-boost" performance kits. It will provide enough mixture cooling to noticeably lower the knock limit, thus allowing more boost to be used in a marine performance engine.

For the "Super Whamo" high-boost Gale Banks kit, this dual-radiator intercooler is provided. By increasing the radiator area with two Harrison cores, this intercooler allows considerably more boost (up to 15 lb) to be used, even in day-to-day ski boats.

It may sound like we're making more out of this intake charge cooling than is necessary for a street engine, but consider that the best reason for doing this is not just to gain a few percent more power, because there are easier ways to do that, but that every drop you can make in the charge temperature means a lessening of tendencies for the combustion chamber to develop hot spots that lead to detonation. In other words, the charge cooling can allow you to reduce the octane requirement or use more boost or more ignition timing without incurring preignition. Here again water injection should be mentioned. If you're running a high static compression ratio (like 9:1) or you're adding boost of over 6 psi on gasoline, water injection provides a form of intake charge cooling. Some engine "experts" call water injection a "crutch". Be that as it may, it's a necessary crutch if you're trying to use an appreciable amount of boost with the lower-octane gasolines available today.

If you want to dabble with intercoolers, there are some excellent units made for marine applications, such as the air-to-liquid units built by the Harrison radiator division of GM. Check with a marine engine builder like Gale Banks for specifics on these. Those of you with ambition and ingenuity could build your own unit to fit your particular setup. You could start by taking a good heater core (actually just a small radiator) and building a sheet-metal box around it through which you could plumb the output of the compressor. Naturally, the box would have to be sturdy enough to withstand the internal pressure of the

boost level you're running, and no leaks would be allowed, since you would lose boost and vent a highly-flammable fuel-air mixture in the engine compartment.

The idea is to circulate a "cooled" liquid through the heater core, over which the intake charge can pass, giving up its heat to the liquid. In some racing situations alcohol or acetone or even freon is used as a medium, but these could be dangerous if improperly controlled. It is more practical to settle for water, an excellent heat exchanger. However, your engine water is already up to 180°F or more, so that's not what we're going after

(even though it might have some slight cooling effect because the intake charge may be considerably hotter than that). How about a system that you could turn on and off at the dash? You could plumb the heater core to a water reservoir tank located elsewhere on the car; it wouldn't necessarily have to be under the hood, you've already got a crowded situation there. You could locate this water tank under the floorboards or even in the trunk, and use an electric pump to circulate the water. For years, drag racers have used the Jabsco marine electric pumps to circulate water through their engines, either to speed up the cool down between runs or to eliminate the power-robbing belt-driven water pump. One of these 12-volt pumps would work fine for your homemade intercooler, with a switch on the dash so you could turn the cooler only when you needed it. Certainly, with a captive water supply like this, you could only run the system for a brief period before the water would be heated to the point that most of the cooling effect would be lost. However, you wouldn't have to use it all the time, and the length of plumbing back to the water tank could help cool off the water after it came out of the intercooler. You could conceivably use an air-conditioning condenser underneath the car instead of a water tank. The condenser would act as a second radiator, using the ambient air to carry off the heat put into the water by the intake charge. If you wanted to get even more elaborate, you could mount the condenser in a sheet-metal shroud and use an electric fan to draw air over the condenser. The electric fan could be controlled by the same dash switch that turns on your auxiliary water pump, or both of them could be

When simplicity and reliability prevent high boost levels, intercooling may not be necessary. In these instances Banks also has a simple plenum without water cooling passages that can be mounted directly to the stock manifold plenum.

controlled by a pressure-switch on your intake manifold, so that the intercooler system was turned on only when you had boost, like your water injection. Anyway, it's something for do-it-yourselfers to ponder about on these long winter nights out in the garage.

INSTRUMENTATION

With everything bolted in place for the last time and the final worm-drive hose clamp tightened around your turbo plumbing, there's one other aspect worthy of your consideration. You'll never know how good a job you've done on your system until you have the proper gauges to indicate the engine operating conditions. A turbocharged street machine should be equipped with all the extra gauges found in any performance car, such as an ammeter, tachometer, oil pressure gauge, and water temperature gauge, plus a few others. Stock idiot lights are just that, for idiots.

The basic gauge used in every turbo installation is a combined vacuum-boost gauge. Most of the specialty gauge companies have these, but you won't find them at the local accessory shop, since they are only useful on a blown car. All of the turbo kit companies can supply you with one, though. This one gauge reads both vacuum and pressure, usually with a range of from 0-30 inches of vacuum on the left side of the scale, and 0-20 psi pressure on the right. The usefulness of the boost side is obvious, you can see just at what rpm (by your tach) your boost is coming in under load,

The heart of most current intercooler systems is this Harrison water-to-air heat exchanger. Though a small and relatively light radiator, this unit proves very effective, especially in marine applications where sufficient cooling liquid is easily obtainable.

how much boost you're actually getting, and whether your boost control is working or not. If you're using a wastegate and it isn't plumbed back into the exhaust outlet but left open, then you'll be able to hear the wastegate when it starts to dump the excess exhaust pressure. It's kind of like a Bronx cheer device on your exhaust system, only a little more expensive than the novelty store type. By watching the boost gauge you can tell if you have the right control spring in your compressor controller or the right amount of turns on your horsepower screw. It'll help you determine at exactly what level of pressure your engine encounters detonation, and then you can take steps to correct it.

The vacuum side of the gauge can be equally useful. If you have driven your car for some time with a vacuum gauge when the car was normally-aspirated, then you know what the vacuum is under various driving conditions. This can be helpful comparison after you've turbocharged it. Reading the vacuum side when the engine isn't running in the boost mode can be helpful in engine tuning and diagnosis. For example, doing your carburetor adjustments by the vacuum gauge can be better than using the tach. Just adjust the idle mixture fo the highest steady vacuum reading rather than the highest idle speed. Fluctuations in the needle movement on the vacuum side can warn you of vacuum leaks, leaky valves, sticky lifters and other engine problems. If you know what the previous vacuum was during freeway cruising, then a comparison with what it reads in that mode with the turbocharger installed tells you what the turbo is doing for your engine. If under the same conditions (and assuming you don't have a rough idle or vacuum leak) you show less cruise vacuum with the turbo than before, it indicates that the turbo is doing some work to help the engine breathe, even though boost isn't showing. If the car in normally-aspirated form was showing 15 inches of vacuum on the highway (which isn't bad) at 55 mph, and with a turbo it only shows 10 inches at the same speed, it means the turbo is turning fast enough to take some of the load off the engine. This is an ideal cruising situation, because when it's taking away from the vacuum side of the gauge, you're getting your best fuel

Water plumbing on a turbocharged marine engine can be a "bag of snakes." Normally water from the hull pickup is directed into the intercooler first to gain maximum cooling effect. From there it is routed into the oil cooler (if an external cooler is used), into the engine block where it picks up heat and, finally, through the carburetor plenum box where the heat is used to prevent fuel fall out. Then, it is dumped back overboard.

This turbocharged 240Z Datsun features a pyrometer lead for each cylinder. This is not as expensive as it seems, since only one gauge is used for all six leads.

economy and emissions, and it also means that the turbo is ready at any instant to deliver boost when you step on the loud pedal. As load conditions change, you'll be able to see how the turbo works and even predict it without looking at the gauge. When you come to a grade, the vacuum side may go down to 5 inches or even zero, and some steep grades will even require some boost. You can "float" over most grades like they weren't there and the engine won't be acting like it's ready to turn in its warranty card and drop to the pavement in an oily mess.

Another highly useful gauge for your turbo car is the exhaust gas temperature gauge, or pyrometer. If you've seen these before, they were probably on a large diesel truck. Basically, these gauges read from about 400°F to 1900°F, using a bimetallic thermocouple probe you install in your exhaust (ahead of the turbine) and wires that run back to the gauge. Reading the exhaust temperature can be a tuning aid in diagnosing carburetion. Exhaust temperature will be hotter under the same load and rpm if the carburetion is lean, and conversely, cooler when the carburetion is rich. There is no way we can tell you exactly what the exhaust gas temperature should read for your particular installation under a certain condition because this depends on a variety of factors, including the engine, camshaft, ignition timing, fuel and turbine housing size. But after you've used one for a while, you'll get as used to it as an aircraft pilot. Pyrometers are frequently used by engine dyno technicians to read each cylinder of an engine, to

check mixture distribution and fuel-air ratios at each port. If you have an eight-cylinder engine this doesn't mean that you have to buy eight pyrometers, just eight probes. Each probe is equipped with a length of insulated cable about four feet long, which you must not cut or splice. From the end of the cable you can use standard wires to the gauge. So on your Camaro or Mustang or whatever, you simply install a probe in each exhaust port (easy if you are using tube headers) and wire

all the leads to an eight-position switch from an electronics shop. The switch is then wired to the gauge. When the engine is running, you can turn the switch to get readings on each of the eight cylinders. This should give you an indication of whether you're getting good cylinder-to-cylinder mixture distribution from your intake manifold on your draw-through installation. If you're consistently running at the top end of the gauge, then something is wrong and you'd better take a look at things before the high heat destroys the turbine.

John Anderson, who distributes the Turbotest line of gauges by Westach, has something that is really neat for the turbo enthusiast. It's a combination gauge with vacuum-and-pressure readings at the top of the gauge and a pyrometer at the bottom. It's a three-inch gauge (about the size of a typical aftermarket tach), and comes with the mounting cup to attach it to the steering column for easy reading. Anderson also has four-inch pyrometers, and two-inch pyrometers (about the size of standard engine gauges). They're very accurate instruments and reasonably priced. You can get them with a white light or a green light for illumination, the latter closely matching the green dash lighting used on many late-model cars. Another four-inch gauge available from John has a dual pyrometer, which can be used when you have two turbos and want to constantly read the exhaust temperature going into each one. This gauge is available with a 4, 5 or 8 station switch for reading engine cylinders selectively.

In this same Z-car, the boost gauge and pyrometer are mounted on the steering column. Below the pyrometer is a six-way switch that allows the driver to read the exhaust gas temperature in each cylinder, so he can tune the engine accordingly and check for proper mixture distribution.

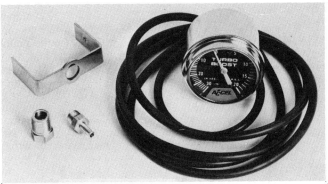

Instruments are important to keep track of any engine, and particuarly a blown one. Most of the major aftermarket gauge companies and turbo kit companies have available gauges that read pressure (boost) and vacuum. This one is in Roto-Master's TurboSonic line.

John Anderson distributes the line of Turbo-Test gauges that include these large and small boost gauges, pyrometers, and the combination boost and pyrometer at right.

TURBOCHARGER MANUFACTURERS

If you are interested in turbocharger flow information or buying a unit, contact one of the following companies for the name of their nearest dealer.

AiResearch Industrial Division
3201 Lomita Blvd.
Torrance, California 90505

Rajay Industries, Inc.
PO Box 207
Long Beach, California 90801

Roto-Master, Inc.
7101 Fair Avenue
North Hollywood, California 91605

Schwitzer Division, Wallace-Murray Corp.
1125 Brookside Avenue
Indianapolis, Indiana 46206

TURBO KIT MANUFACTURERS

With new companies coming into the turbo kit field every day, it would be impossible for us to list every one. This list covers only the major kit makers and installers we have discussed in the chapter.

Ak Miller Enterprises
9238 Bermudez St.
Pico Rivera, California 90660

John Anderson Turbocharging
3748 Ilium Court
Napa, California 94558

BAE Division of Turdyne Corp.
3032 Kashiwa St.,
Torrance, California 90505

Gale Banks Racing Engines
929 S. San Gabriel Blvd.
San Gabriel, California 91776

Crane Cams, Inc.
PO Box 160
Hallandale, Florida 33009

Crown Manufacturing Co.
858 Production Place
Newport Beach, California 92660

Ak Miller Enterprises
9238 Bermudez
Pico Rivera, California 90660

Roto-Master, Inc.
7101 Fair Avenue
North Hollywood, California 91605

Spearco Performance Products
2054 Broadway
Santa Monica, California 90404

OTHER MANUFACTURERS

IMPCO Carburetion Co.
16916 S. Gridley Rd.
Cerritos, California 90701

(propane carburetion equipment)

Filtron (distributed by)
Hooker Headers
1032 W. Brooks
Ontario, California 91762

(air filters)

Edelbrock Equipment Co.
411 Coral Circle
El Segundo, California 90245

(intake manifolds)

Offenhauser Sales Corp.
5230 Alhambra
Los Angeles, California 90032

(intake manifolds)

Accel Performance Products
PO Box 142
Branford, Connecticut 06405

(ignition systems)

NITROUS OXIDE INJECTION

INTRODUCTION

Twenty-five years ago, before freeways crisscrossed the Los Angeles basin, there was an old trolley car planted by the side of the highway leading into Riverside, California. It was much like the diners of the depression era, except that this particular concessionaire advertised "laughing gas" instead of hamburgers. For twenty-five cents you could stop in and get the giggles.

Today, the serving of nitrous oxide, or laughing gas, to human beings is strictly regulated. In fact, its use as an anesthetic requires a prescription and a licensed administrator. However, in the last couple of years, thousands of doses of nitrous oxide have been administered to internal combustion engines by competent mechanics, and the results have been anything but anesthetizing. Laughing gas puts people to sleep, but it has exactly the opposite effect on race car, boat, and airplane engines. Automotive engineers have gathered very little concrete data about the effects this amazing gas produces when injected into the fuel-air stream of an engine, but racers all over the country are proving beyond a doubt that nitrous definitely does produce lots and lots of horsepower.

Nitrous oxide was first obtained by Joseph Priestly (the discoverer of oxygen) in 1772. It is a colorless gas, heavier than air, with a faint pleasantly-sweetish odor and taste. In 1800, Sir Humphry Davy conducted a careful study of nitrous, determining its composition as N_2O, and discovering both its stimulating and anesthetic physiological properties.[1] That is, he found that it was respirable and produced anesthesia, preceded in some cases (when mixed with air or oxygen) by pleasurable symptoms and laughter. Hence, its common nickname of laughing gas. Nitrous Oxide was the first anesthetic discovered for medical use, and it is still employed today by some dentists for this purpose. However, should you ever get the urge to experiment with this gas yourself, you should be forewarned that the type of nitrous available for automotive use is an industrial grade, which is not fit for inhalation; and you should be even more strongly warned that *prolonged inhalation of nitrous oxide causes death.* Once you try it in your car, you will get all the kicks you need just by stomping the accelerator to the floor.

More to the point of our discussion, it was also discovered quite early that pure N_2O would rekindle glowing chips, and would support the combustion of car-

[1] H. Davies, "Researches, Chiefly Concerning Nitrous Oxide", 1800.

A Pontiac Trans-Am is a healthy machine in today's factory market, but the owner of any modified street racer has little fear of a car like this at a street light.

bon, sulphur, phosphorous, and iron wire when these substances were burning vigorously enough to start the decomposition of the gas. Chemists found that nitrous oxide could be obtained in the laboratory by heating ammonium nitrate (NH_4NO_3), which produces nitrous oxide and water, but they also noted that if too high a temperature were maintained in the system, an explosion would occur. They also discovered that mixtures of nitrous oxide and ammonia are explosive. It seems reasonable, then, that somebody would eventually try using nitrous oxide as a motor fuel additive.

Just who that first someone was remains unclear, but the first general use of nitrous oxide as a motor fuel "stimulant" occurred during World War II. The fact that nitrous was being used on aircraft engines throughout the war by the Germans and the British and being tested by the Americans was kept a well-guarded secret until late 1945. During '45-'46 a few detailed articles which described nitrous oxide "supercharging" or "power augmentation" systems and studies appeared in some of the aircraft publications. Unfortunately (for us), however, by the end of the war almost the entire attention of the aircraft industry had focused on a much more promising power source—jet propulsion—and the discussion of nitrous oxide was already being treated more as history than as development. Since much of it pertains directly to today's applications of nitrous oxide, some of the details of the German, British, and American wartime nitrous testing will be outlined in a later section.

Aircraft engineers of the second world war developed this power boosting system for a slightly different reason than simply to make airplanes fly faster. Piston engines rely on the oxygen content of air to make power. But the higher an airplane flies, the "rarer" becomes the air; that is, the less oxygen it contains. Consequently, any naturally-aspirated airplane has a limit to the altitude it can attain (its *ceiling*), and this limit is greatly dependent on the amount of oxygen available at that altitude. By the same token, the maximum speed of an airplane drops off drastically the higher it flies, because the engines cannot maintain full power. So you can see that it would be advantageous, especially in time of war, to devise means for increasing the oxygen intake of airplane engines, even for short periods, when flying at high altitudes. Two methods for achieving this goal are well-known—supercharging and turbo-supercharging—but these methods rely simply on pushing a greater quantity of air into the cylinders so that a greater amount of oxygen can be extracted from it. Such a technique is limited in extremely rarified atmosphere.

So it was logical that various types of oxygen-releasing compounds, as well as straight oxygen, should be tested to see if they could be injected into the engines when a greater boost was needed in the oxygen-deficient air. Several compounds were evaluated and tested, including hydrogen peroxide, nitrogen peroxide, carbon monoxide, nitrous oxide, liquid oxygen, and others.

At the same time, a cure to a second problem plaguing supercharged high-altitude aircraft—detonation or "knocking"—was also being sought. If the engine were supercharged to the point of knocking, no further power gains could be extracted from it. But experiments dating to before 1900 had shown that cooling the intake charge with water or another suitable substance could reduce knocking and therefore allow the engine to develop greater power. During the war, various types of internal coolants were tried, including water-alcohol (the alcohol being added primarily to keep the water from freezing at high altitude), gasoline injection upstream of the supercharger, methanol injection, and mixture enrichment. Both the internal cooling devices and the oxygen-injectors were commonly grouped together under the classification of power boosting or power augmentation systems. There were decided advantages and disadvantages to each particular system—and it is not too surprising that the three national powers disagreed on which was the best—but the power boosting systems most often used were straight water-alcohol injection, liquid oxygen injection with water-alcohol, and nitrous oxide injection in either liquid or gaseous forms.

The Germans were probably the first to use nitrous oxide, having fitted their Me 109F Messerschmitt fighter with a pressurized N^2O system surprisingly similar to that being used in cars today. This system was designed primarily for increasing the low-altitude speed of fighters operating on the Russian front; but when they found that these superior planes didn't really need the extra boost, they shifted their development of nitrous to reconnaissance aircraft (such as the Ju 88 and 188) which needed utmost speed at high altitude while flying over England. This second system used liquid nitrous oxide at atmospheric pressure and very low temperature (thus eliminating the need for heavy high-pressure tanks to contain the N^2O).

The British also used a pressurized nitrous system similar to current ones, but due to the weight of the system (about 600 pounds, full), they used it only in larger aircraft such as their Mosquito bomber. The Mosquito was a twin-engined light bomber, large enough not to be severely affected by the weight of the nitrous tanks, but highly dependent on its extra boost. It was officially described as "an unarmed bomber that would depend for its defense on sheer performance." Obviously the power created by nitrous oxide was well-respected by the British . . . and they put substantial trust in it!

The Americans, as far as can be ascertained from available documents, never actually used nitrous oxide equipment in combat during the war, presumably because our airplanes were quite highly developed and could rely on other means for necessary power and altitude. However, the National Advisory Committee for Aeronautics (NACA) did perform tests with both liquid oxygen and nitrous oxide, and in their annual report for 1946 briefly discussed the rela-

A casual glance under the hood reveals little more than a stock Pontiac 400.

tive merits of each as follows:

An emergency means of increasing the engine power for short intervals of time at high altitudes is the introduction of additional oxygen either from high-pressure storage tanks or some suitable chemical compound. The use of oxygen resulted in increases in engine power for a given manifold pressure. The addition of oxygen, however, led to high combustion temperatures with consequent overheating and a tendency toward preignition and knock. This tendency could be overcome by drastic increases in fuel-oxygen ratio. This response to this enrichment was limited and some means had to be used to increase the internal cooling. Results of investigations of various internal coolants indicated that large flow rates would be required to prevent knock and overheating.

The use of nitrous oxide instead of oxygen was proposed because it has been found that nitrous oxide did not appreciably lower the knock limit and did not result in as high a degree of overheating as had been experienced with oxygen. An investigation conducted with nitrous oxide showed that, when the knock was not a limitation, the overheating caused by the addition of nitrous oxide could be con-

trolled to best advantage by the use of mixture enrichment. When knock is a limitation, the use of internal coolants is necessary.

We should point out that the nitrous oxide tests to which the NACA annual report refers were conducted with gaseous N^2O and that (as we shall see later in a discussion of the test results) the benefits found for liquid nitrous were even more pronounced, especially with respect to cooling the cylinder and producing extra power. The major conclusion from this test and the practical use of nitrous oxide by the British and the Germans, is that the nitrous—especially if injected as a liquid—combines the benefits of both the added oxygen and the internal coolant to produce a two-fold gain in usable power.

In all of the above examples it should be noted that extra fuel (enrichment) was also added along with the nitrous oxide, though it was done more to control the burning of the charge rather than to increase power. The extra oxygen was needed just to burn the fuel already being inducted during operation in oxygen-deficient atmosphere. In current applications for ground-level use, one of the major reasons for introducing an oxygen-releasing compound into the cylinder is specifically to burn *more* fuel

But that sleepy smog motor comes alive to the tune of 150 extra horsepower when the nitrous oxide injector is turned on! Visible components of the system include: 1) the N^2O and fuel enrichment solenoids with braided hoses leading to two nozzles tapped into the stock manifold, just below the carb; 2) the throttle-actuated triggering switch; and 3) the enrichment fuel line splice.

than is possible even with oxygen-rich air. One of the major lessons to be learned from these early developments of nitrous oxide is that systems quite similar to current ones were actually employed, under the most demanding and critical circumstances, on several occasions—and they worked very successfully.

After the end of the war the main reason that nitrous oxide was pursued no further for use as a motor fuel, despite its tremendous power potential, was that it is a very impractical day-to-day propellant for airplanes, autos, trucks, boats, or any other combustion-engined vehicles. Even when compressed to a more compact liquid form, far too much nitrous must be carried on board for even a few minutes of extra horsepower. To gain an extra fifteen-minute burst of speed, the Mosquito bomber had to carry almost six hundred extra pounds of payload (including the liquid N^2O, its pressure bottles, extra petrol, and apparatus). Nitrous oxide is far from "economical" fuel; it takes lots of nitrous to make more horsepower (in addition to the extra gasoline or fuel needed). This is not to mention the fact that the metal tanks used to contain liquid nitrous at pressure are themselves far from light.

It wasn't until much later that a new

application for a high-potency, short-duration motor fuel appeared on the scene—drag racing. This relatively recent short-sprint automotive competition is perfectly designed for a fuel like nitrous oxide. However, by the time drag racers reached the point that they were searching for and experimenting with fuels more potent than gasoline, the few secretive sorties of N^2O-charged RAF bombers and Messerschmitts had all but been forgotten. Drag racers instead turned to more common and better understood high-powered racing fuels such as methanol and nitromethane.

Supposedly, one or two early drag racers did remember something about the wonders of laughing gas, and tried it in their dragsters; but the attempts were crude at best (straight N^2O dumped directly into the carb or injector throats), and the results weren't worth repeated tries. Besides, the big blown engines of the early sixties were already pumping out many more horses than the chassis or the tires of the time could put to use on the drag strip.

By 1962 a fellow named Ron Hammel, who worked for the Wilcap Company in Torrance, California, began some serious testing of gasoline-powered engines spiked with doses of nitrous oxide and extra gasoline. He had been reading the works of the British engine-de-

sign genius, Sir Harry Ricardo, and he had been intrigued by Ricardo's brief description of the effects of N^2O when it was injected into the air-fuel stream of an internal combustion engine. Hammel conducted his tests primarily on Wilcap's engine dyno, and the process apparently took considerable study because he did not install a nitrous unit on a competition car until 1969.

By this time nitro-burning fuelers were still creating just about as much horsepower as they could handle, and they weren't really looking for alternatives. On the other hand, competition in the gasoline-only classes, both in drag racing and in other fields such as stock cars and drag boats, had developed to the point where any extra edge could make a big difference. Also, the methods for detecting cheating, both in terms of engine modifications and fuel additives, had become equally sophisticated. So once again there was a very practical—albeit clandestine—application for nitrous oxide injection. Other additives to pump gasoline could easily be detected by a fuel sample either from the gas tank or from the carburetor bowl; but since nitrous oxide is contained in a separate tank and injected apart from the gasoline into the intake manifold, it could not be detected by the usual fuel sampling methods. And since the nitrous pressure tank looks almost exactly like a normal fire extinguisher, the nitrous system was very easy to disguise from the unsuspecting tech inspector's eye.

The applicability of such a concealed nitrous system on a stock class drag car should be obvious. A five-pound bottle of N^2O would provide enough fuel for several twelve-to fourteen-second blasts down the drag strip; it would not add appreciably to the car weight; and the extra boost in horsepower would give a decided superiority to one "stocker" over another.

A hidden nitrous system in a circle-track stock car was equally attractive, but for a different reason. A Grand National stocker could not carry enough nitrous for an entire five-hundred mile race; but a short shot of N^2O when it was really needed—like when one car was in position to get around another—was just the thing that many car builders had been searching for. Additionally, a nitrous hook-up for a fast qualifying lap could take quite a bit of pressure off back markers who weren't quite sure if they could make the field or front runners who needed good starting positions in the pack—not to mention the appeal of sizable "top qualifier" purses.

It was stock car racing, in fact, that actually brought nitrous oxide to the attention of other racers and the general racing audience. After a couple of the well-known drivers were caught with illegal laughing gas systems on board, the se-

51

The nitrous oxide system can be engaged or disengaged by a flick of this toggle. When switched on, N2O and extra fuel will be injected into the manifold at full throttle.

cret was out and tech inspectors began looking very carefully for nitrous systems on all of the fastest cars. Since it was so unknown in the early days, it is very difficult to say just how many cars were using nitrous assist. Few of the big names in Nascar are willing to admit they have raced with nitrous assist, but Ron Hammel says that he supplied a few units to drivers on the Grand National circuit in 1969, and, without mentioning names, he stated simply that they were on "some of the faster cars." Ron also claims that the fastest qualifying record at Talledega in 1970 was set with assistance from one of his nitrous units.

Undoubtedly one of the first stock car builders to fool around with nitrous oxide was Smokey Yunick. The way Smokey tells it, he was visiting his dentist one day back in the mid-fifties and they got to talking about the anesthetic, nitrous oxide. Smokey was curious about the stuff and the dentist told him that it was primarily an oxygen-releasing compound. "Hey, that's just what I need to get more power from my engines," was Smokey's immediate reply. The dentist put him in contact with a supplier of nitrous oxide in Daytona Beach and Smokey rigged a system for injecting it into the engines of his famous Hudson Hornet stock cars.

At this time the NASCAR rules stated simply that a car "must be run on gasoline" to be legal, and Smokey interpreted this ruling to include his setup, since the car was, in fact, running on gasoline. The system itself was anything but sophisticated, consisting of a nitrous pressure bottle mounted under the driver's seat, with a screw valve and a pressure regulator attached to the bottle, and a length of rubber fuel hose running to the mouth of the carburetor. The nitrous was "injected" directly out of the end of the hose above the carb's air horn, and it was drawn into the engine, in a

gaseous state, along with the inducted air.

The stock cars of this period were severely hampered by the limited air-flow capacity of their small carburetors, and Smokey's reasoning for using the nitrous oxide was to provide more oxygen in the cylinders so that larger jets could be used in the carbs. Consequently, a greater quantity of fuel could be combusted in the cylinders. By experimenting with this simple rig he determined the amount of nitrous that could be injected into the engine, with an over-rich carb, before the exhaust temperature rose to over 1500° (at which point the engine would be in danger of burning pistons or valves from an overly-lean mixture). When he got the system worked out, his formula was four turns on the nitrous bottle valve. It wasn't too sophisticated—but it worked. Smokey would use the setup for qualifying, when the car would be fitted with the rich carburetor, and he would simply instruct his driver to give the bottle four cranks on the valve when he was coming out of turn four—and to hold on!

It took quite a long time, but eventually other drivers figured out that Smokey had something they didn't, and within a few years the NASCAR rules were changed to read that a car must be run on "gasoline *only*" as fuel. This precluded the use of nitrous oxide, and Smokey says he gave up using it at that time (about 1958).

During the next decade the subject of nitrous oxide injection remained almost dormant around the circle tracks. Just before 1970 (about the time Ron Hammel says he began building some units for stock cars), NASCAR began a program of awarding sizable cash prizes

to the number one qualifiers at major races. A $10,000 incentive to turn one fast lap suddenly reminded many of the car builders about the significant boost available with nitrous oxide, and within a short time several units were being hidden in Grand National racers. The problem was that the technology for using nitrous properly was not very advanced at this time, and most of the nitrous experimenters found that spare engines were also a necessary part of the system. They were going for large horsepower boost from the nitrous, and if they didn't get enough extra fuel metered properly into the engine at the same time, a severe lean-burn situation developed, which didn't do much for the life of the pistons, rings, and valves. Smokey recollects "One year, when the big teams were just starting to use nitrous, they must have blown fifteen or twenty engines, shooting for the pole" but many of the big-money teams figured that an engine or two was worth one large top-qualifying purse.

At this time the secret of nitrous oxide was known to little more than the ones using it (the builders had used great ingenuity to camouflage their handiwork); but some of the less well-sponsored teams became tired of shelling out for new engines in attempts to keep up with the pack. Supposedly one or two of them decided to even the competition by "snitching" on the guys who could afford the price of going fast on laughing gas. Darrel Waltrip, one of the two top qualifiers sent to the back of the field at the '76 Daytona 500 for using a nitrous system, reasoned the situation this way: "If you don't cheat, you look like an idiot. If you do it and don't get caught, you look like a hero. If you do it and get

The standard, and safest, location for the N2O bottle is in the trunk.

caught, you look like a dope. Put me in the category where I belong." Who's to say just how much nitrous oxide is being used on stock car tracks these days? Those who are or who have used it will not discuss the subject.

The NASCAR rule book covering Grand National cars was changed again a couple of years ago to read "no pressure systems allowed" under the section on fuel and fuel cells. In 1976 it was further and more specifically amended to: "No pressure systems allowed. Any concealed pressure type containers, feed lines or actuating mechanism are illegal even if inoperable." That means any nitrous oxide is illegal.

Today the fraternity of nitrous users includes an almost unbelievable assortment of racers. Units have been built for everything from pylon-racing airplanes and unlimited hydroplanes to go karts and model airplanes. We even know of one unit adapted by 303 Enterprises for a motorized skateboard! Alcohol-burning dirt trackers are using nitrous, drag bikes are using it, and match racers are using it. Several units have been built for snowmobiles in the northern U.S. and Canada, and even motorhome owners are installing nitrous units so that they can more easily pass slower traffic and make it up steep hills. Whether it has been tried at Indianapolis or on the Grand Prix circuit yet, no one will admit, but no doubt someone has considered it.

Naturally, as more and more racing associations become aware of nitrous oxide and its uses, they will institute new regulations and checking procedures in order to keep their competition equal. Logically, any class permitting open fuel should allow the use of nitrous oxide, since it is nothing more than a fuel itself. However, some associations have already ruled it illegal, supposedly on the premise that if one or two cars run it, all will have to install nitrous to remain competitive. Nitrous is legal in Top Fuel drag racing (though very few fuelers are using it at this point), and it is, of course, legal in bracket racing (where its advantage is somewhat dubious).

The largest group of nitrous users, by far, are the street racers and street rodders. A hidden nitrous injector under a tame-looking four-barrel manifold is the perfect decoy for late-night, money-down drag racing. In fact, it was primarily on the streets of Los Angeles and Orange County that the typical nitrous system was developed, both by Ron Hammel and by street racer Marvin Miller. Today, young cruisers of Van Nuys and Whittier Boulevards are proud to boast that their Boss Mustang or V-8 Vega is "on the bottle." That is, unless they are dickering with another machine that they suspect is not as well equipped.

Actually, it is surprising that nitrous

Nitrous oxide will also add a significant power boost to modified engines, such as the big-block Chevy in this ski boat. This exposed 10,000 RPM unit uses mechanical valves rather than electric solenoids.

oxide injection has been able to maintain its "underground" status because it is a logical and practical way to increase the performance of an automobile engine. It is perhaps the most practical—and economical—piece of speed equipment yet devised for street-driven or "dual-purpose" cars. Consider, for a moment, the amount of modification necessary to increase the output of a typical V-8 engine by 100 to 150 horsepower. Next, consider the cost in both dollars and in man-hours for such modification. Finally, think how such a modified engine drives through traffic and how seldom you actually call upon all those horses you built into the machine. A street-driven car with a drag race engine is a poor compromise at best. If you are serious about drag racing (either on the strip on weekends or on the street at night), you must sacrifice almost all your driveability if you want to be competitive. On the other hand, if you tame down the engine enough to make it

behave in traffic, you're not going to win many "confrontations" with it.

A nitrous oxide injection system, however, can actually give you both—a situation you supposedly can't achieve in the real world. Because of the very peculiar burning properties of N^2O, you can add it to the air-fuel mixture of a completely stock engine and gain 50 to 150 or more extra instantaneous horsepower *when you want it*. Unlike most other speed equipment, you need add no other components to make the nitrous do its job properly. So when you are not blowing somebody's doors off, you can motor around town quietly and comfortably and you can even burn cheap gas. On the other hand, if you feel that a hot rod just isn't right without a couple of carburetors and a rough idle, the addition of N^2O will still give a proportional increase over the horsepower you have built into the engine. As Ron Hammel puts it, "Nitrous doesn't know how modified the engine

One great advantage of nitrous systems is that they can easily be hidden. On this ski boat installation the only visible clue is the nitrous storage tank.

Nitrous oxide injection can be combined with Roots-type superchargers or turbochargers for real eyeball-flattening performance. On this Gale Banks turbocharged engine the nitrous injector is hidden in the carb plenum.

is." In other words, nitrous oxide increases power differently than most other hop-up techniques, adding its contribution to total engine output irrespective of other engine modifications.

Therefore, nitrous oxide is not really going to replace common speed parts and modification techniques as we have known them. But it is certain that more and more nitrous systems will be used both in conjunction with these components and in place of them by rodders who drive their machines on the street. Rather than tearing his engine down and installing a bigger cam, higher compression pistons, stronger rods, and reworked heads, the typical rodder in search of a lot more go when he steps on the gas can simply add nitrous oxide to the normal list of bolt-on accessories. The more serious street racer may still want to raise his compression ratio (though not too much), port the heads, or add a more efficient intake; but with a nitrous system he can choose a milder cam and use less ignition advance, so that driving around town between throttle stabs will be easier, both on the passengers and on the engine. Of course, expertly concealed nitrous systems will always be sneaking into the highly competitive fields of motor racing of all types—though in the future they will be harder and harder to conceal successfully.

HOW NITROUS WORKS

It was mentioned earlier that nitrous oxide was a fuel but this statement is not entirely correct. An engine could not run on nitrous oxide alone since N_2O does not burn. Nitrous is, rather, an oxidizing agent. That is, when heated (to approximately 572°F) it separates into

oxygen and nitrogen, and the free oxygen supports (or in this case greatly enhances) the burning of some other flammable substance (i.e., the fuel). It was primarily for this reason that nitrous oxide was first injected into a piston engine, as pointed out earlier when discussing the use of N_2O in high-altitude airplanes. They could not, at that time, foresee a practical use for such a system on any other type of piston-engined vehicle, due to the fact that nitrous boost could be employed for only a short burst of extra power. As far as the aircraft industry was concerned, the future would be given to jet propulsion.

They were, of course, correct, but at least one developer of internal combustion engine theory was not yet ready to concede that the piston engine had reached its ultimate perfection. Sir Harry Ricardo had been writing books on internal combustion engine theory and had been designing his own engines since the twenties. His last work, *The High Speed Internal Combustion Engine*,[1] published in 1953, has been read and admired by many of the best engine builders—both in and out of hot rodding—throughout the past twenty years. Besides his enlightening theories about sleeve-valve engine design, cylinder turbulence, quench area, and other topics, he also made a brief mention in his last book of the phenomenon produced by nitrous oxide when introduced into the air-fuel charge. His discussion is short, but it was the only mention of nitrous made in book form and it does give a good idea of how nitrous works in the engine:

[1]Sir Harry Ricardo, LL.D., F.R.S. *The High Speed Internal Combustion Engine,* 4th Edition (London: Blackie and Son, Ltd., 1953).

"Later, nitrous oxide was used in preference to liquid oxygen, for this could be stored and carried as a liquid, in light cylinders, at normal temperatures and under quite moderate pressure (compared to other gases such as oxygen). Nitrous oxide was found to have very great advantages, not the least of which was that, to the surprise of everyone, it proved to be a very effective anti-knock or, to be more exact, it permitted of a large increase in power, at least 40 per cent, without any increase in detonation, and so could be used safely even below the rated altitude. By the use of nitrous oxide at high altitudes, it was found possible to augment the power by as much as 40 to 50 per cent at a consumption of slightly under 5 lb of nitrous oxide per additional 100 H.P. per minute. Since the time during which such power augmentation was required was generally only a matter of seconds, i.e. in order to close with, or break away from, the enemy, this relatively high consumption was not a serious objection.

The large power augmentation obtained by the use of nitrous oxide was due to:

(1) The liberation of free oxygen.
(2) The liberation of a large amount of heat by its dissociation into oxygen and nitrogen.
(3) The high latent heat of the liquid, the whole of which was evaporated within the supercharger, thus lowering the temperature and increasing the density of the normal supercharge and adding thereby to the supply of atmospheric oxygen."

Many of the early experimenters of nitrous oxide injection in race cars or boats listed Ricardo's book as their initial source of information on the subject, and stated that the "five pounds of nitrous oxide per additional 100 horsepower per minute" mentioned by him was their beginning point in developing rates of nitrous injection to be used in automotive engines. It should be remembered, however, that Ricardo was talking about aircraft engines of approximately 1500 cubic inches operating at high altitudes; that no mention is made of adding enrichment motor fuel; and that he calls the five pounds per minute "relatively high consumption."

In 1953 Ricardo was at a loss to explain the reason why nitrous inhibited detonation, stating: "Much more difficult to explain is the action of nitrous oxide, a high endothermic oxygen carrier, which, by all the rules, should intensify greatly the tendency to detonate but which, in fact, has precisely the opposite effect." The fact that it would provide additional free oxygen was well understood—this is the reason it was used in the first place. The liberation of extra heat (which of course translates to work—or power—in an internal combustion engine) upon its separation into nitrogen and oxygen when heated by combustion in the cylinder was also an easily predictable effect. The third benefit of nitrous oxide mentioned by Ricardo—its high latent heat of evaporation—bears some further discussion, however, since this property of nitrous oxide contributed almost as much as the oxygen content to increasing power in engines.

To change a substance from a liquid to a gas (evaporation or "vaporization") requires an input of energy, usually in the form of heat. The boiling of water is a common example; or perhaps more apt is the cooling effect of water when applied to a hot substance—the water evaporates, and thus "removes" heat from the substance. The latent heat of evaporation (or vaporization) of a liquid

is the amount of heat required to change its state from liquid to gas at its boiling point; or, put another way, it is the amount of heat absorbed by the substance as it changes from a liquid to a gas, or evaporates. This figure can be expressed in various units of heat energy (BTU's, calories, CHU's, joules, etc.) per weight of substance (pounds, grams, moles, etc.). The unit BTU/lb for latent heat seems the most common terminology these days; so a substance's latent heat of vaporization in BTU's per pound would be the number of BTU's (British Thermal Units) required to change the state of the substance from a liquid to a gas at its boiling point (the temperature remains constant while the change is occurring) and at atmospheric pressure. Some substances require much more heat for this change than others do, and nitrous oxide's latent heat of vaporization is relatively high. Perhaps even more important, the boiling point of nitrous oxide is extremely low (-129° F), and the N_2O will maintain this temperature as it is allowed to change from a liquid to a gas once it is released from pressure.

Therefore, when liquid N_2O is injected into the air stream above the carburetor, or into the air-fuel stream in the intake manifold, it must absorb a great quantity of heat from that air stream as it turns to a vapor. Additionally, it will absorb even more heat as it rises from its very low vaporizing temperature to try to equalize with the much higher temperatures in the intake manifold and the combustion chamber. The result is that the temperature of the air charge entering the cylinder is significantly reduced, which in turn means that it is greatly condensed. If you have studied the basic thermodynamics of an internal combustion engine, you should realize that the denser the air charge, the more air-fuel will be packed into the cylinder before compression, and the greater will be

the resulting power. In other words, the significant cooling effect of the vaporizing N_2O as it enters the air stream produces the same result as supercharging does, only perhaps even more efficiently (since a supercharger actually heats the air as it compresses it). Furthermore, since the nitrous condenses the air charge in a different manner than a supercharger does, the two can be used in conjunction with each other to "double" the boost.

To show how effective this condensing action of evaporating N_2O is, you might compare it to other fuels. Methyl alcohol (methanol), for instance, actually contains less internal energy (heat value) per pound than either gasoline or benzol does, but it has a very high latent heat of vaporization (463 BTU/lb at its boiling point of 148.4° F). According to Ricardo, its temperature can drop as much as 250° F upon evaporation (to approximately -100° F). In another instance he notes: "It is true that more power is obtained from ethyl alcohol than from, say, petrol or benzol, but this is due rather to the fact that, owing to its higher latent heat of evaporation, the final temperature of the mixture at the end of the suction stroke is lower, and the density of the charge is correspondingly greater." It takes much more methanol than gasoline to run an engine (its best stoichiometric air-to-fuel ratio is approximately 7:1 compared to 14½:1 for gasoline), but its cooling effect can pack much more air into the cylinder. Consequently it has much more oxygen to support combustion. As we well know, race cars run much faster on methanol than they do on gasoline.

The above comparison might lead you to ask whether there would be any point in using nitrous oxide rather than a more common high performance fuel or, since they both appear to create power in the same way, would it be feasible to combine nitrous and alcohol. Although the latent heat of nitrous oxide is not as great

Nitrous injection can be used in engines of all sizes and types. This nitrous injected Kawasaki KZ-900 looks stock but has half-again as much power as a stocker.

Street stockers or all-out racing engines can benefit from a dose of "the bottle." This Weber-carbureted and nitrous-injected smallblock Chevy is a real handful, even on a race course.

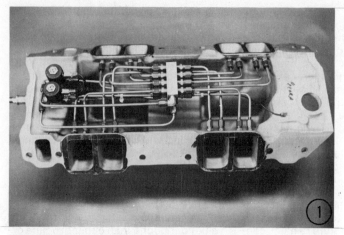

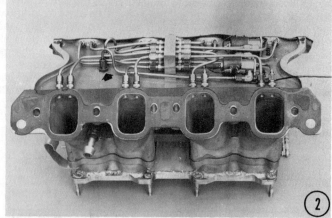

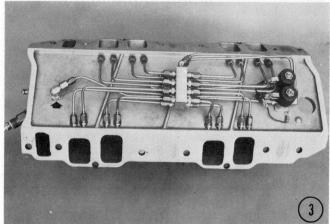

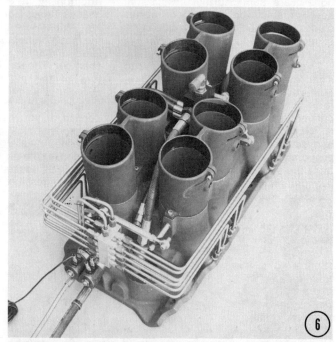

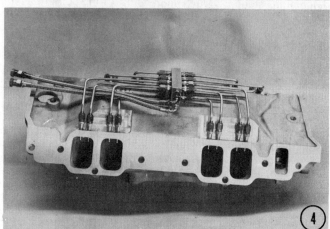

As simple as nitrous injection is, some guys go to great pains to hide their efforts. Here is an array of intake manifolds that have been modified to accept nitrous injection nozzles along with extra nozzles for the fuel enrichment circuit: 1) a system hidden beneath a smallblock Chevy tunnel ram manifold along with electrical solenoid valves, 2) a similar system installed under a Ford tunnel ram manifold; note where fuel and nitrous lines feed through the manifold valley cover to the solenoids, 3) another example on a single four-barrel mani- fold, note the nitrous feed through the water outlet (on top of manifold) and through the floor of the valley cover to the nitrous system, 4) another single four-barrel installation with the injection nozzles plumbed to external control valves, 5) this is an example of an exposed nitrous system on a fuel in- jection manifold (there are also several hidden systems around on fuel-injected cars); the most difficult work is obviously the routing of the fuel and nitrous lines, 6) another neat plumbing job on a fuel injection manifold; note here that the solenoid valves are mounted directly on the manifold.

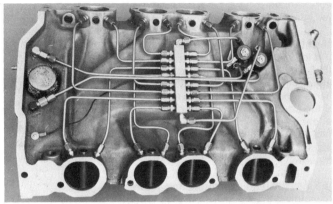

Those who would rather keep their nitrous injector a secret can have all the plumbing and the solenoids hidden underneath the intake manifold, like Marvin Miller did for this

427 Ford. N²0 and gasoline hoses attach to two fittings at the back of the manifold.

as that of methanol, its boiling point is considerably lower. Besides the heat absorbed by nitrous oxide to change its state from liquid to gas, it absorbs another large amount of heat *after* it becomes a gas (at approximately -130°F) and then begins to rise in temperature in the engine. The nitrous oxide actually cools the charge in two ways—by absorbing a large quantity of heat while it vaporizes, and then by absorbing more heat as it warms from its very low boiling point. Even though the latent heat of vaporization of methanol is exceptionally high, it also has a relatively high boiling point (+148.4°F), as do most other liquid motor fuels.

Secondly, remember that the condensing of the air charge is only part of the benefit of nitrous oxide. Put very simply by Ricardo, "The power output of an engine is determined by the amount of oxygen it can combine." In common terms, combining with oxygen means burning, and the more fuel an engine can combine (burn) in the cylinder, the more power it can make from that fuel. Under ideal conditions, it takes approximately thirteen to fourteen parts of air to completely burn one part of gasoline. Add more gasoline to the mixture than that and you are just wasting fuel and fouling your spark plugs. The hot rodder's trick in the past has been to add more carburetors or a supercharger in order to get *air* into the engine, so that it can in turn burn more fuel. With the addition of nitrous oxide, *besides increasing the volumetric efficiency of the engine, you also provide more available oxygen so that a greater quantity of fuel can be completely burned in the cylinder* (thus increasing the thermal efficiency of the engine). For this reason, as we shall see later, current N²O injection systems are designed to inject both nitrous oxide and an extra quantity of fuel into the air stream at the same time.

This oxygen-liberating quality of nitrous oxide is so significant that, even when added to the air stream as a gas (and thereby losing the cooling benefit of its latent heat of evaporation), it can

still add greatly to the power output of an engine. Remember, under normal conditions much of the gasoline in the cylinder is left unburnt even when the air-fuel ratio is properly maintained. In one test case, some gaseous N²O was directed towards the air horn of the air cleaner, from a distance of about a foot, under the hood of a Grand National stock car, and an increase of forty horsepower was recorded at the rear wheels.

In respect to its oxygen-releasing quality, nitrous oxide is much like nitromethane. Nitro creates large quantities of power because it not only is a fuel of high heat value, but because it also contains a large quantity of its own oxygen to enhance combustion (in addition to the oxygen in the inducted air). Because nitromethane adds so much oxygen to the air-fuel charge, detonation is a severe problem—so adding greater quantities of oxygen via nitrous oxide would probably only aggravate the problem. However, if a smaller per-

centage of nitro were mixed with methanol and nitrous oxide were added to that, the possibility of creating a more potent racing fuel might exist (see the discussion of this point in the nitrous-with-superchargers section). The nitrous oxide could provide the needed extra oxygen, but in a form that would not promote detonation like nitro does; the N²O and alcohol combined would produce a very dense charge; and the nitrous oxide would very likely enhance the burning characteristics of the slow-burning and difficult-to-ignite nitromethane—allowing less advance to be used in the ignition. Even with plain old gasoline, the addition of nitrous oxide will yield two of the major benefits of both alcohol (charge cooling) and nitromethane (extra oxygen), without most of their drawbacks, in one simple to use, safe form that can be turned on and off at the touch of a button.

However, the possibility of over-leaning an engine is one of the biggest problems when setting up a nitrous oxide

CHARACTERISTICS OF N₂O (DINITROGEN MONOXIDE)

Molecular Weight	44.02	
Oxygen Content	36.35%	by weight
Boiling Point	−129.1°F	at 1 atmosphere
Freezing Point	−151.6°F	
Latent Heat of Vaporization	124.9 BTU/lb	at boiling point
Heat of Formation	691 BTU/lb	of gas at 64.4°F and 1 atmosphere
Temp at which dissociation begins	572°F	at atmospheric pressure
Critical Temperature	102.2°F	
Critical Pressure	1278.03 psi	
Liquid Pressure in Container	800 psi	at room temp (70°F) in form of gas over liquid in pressure cylinder
Density of Liquid	81.2 lb/cu ft 39.1 lb/cu ft	at −130°F at 86°F
Volume of Gas	8.7 cu ft/lb	at 77°F and 1 atmosphere

COMPARATIVE PROPERTIES OF FUELS AND N₂O

	Boiling Point Degrees F	Latent Heat of Vaporization BTU per lb	Heat Value BTU per lb
Gasoline	110°	140	19,000
Benzene	176.2°	169	17,300
Methanol	148°	473	8,600
Nitromethane	214.2°	243	4,998
Nitrous Oxide	−129°	125	—

system, and it is one reason why many of the early experimenters with nitrous oxide ran into difficulties. Remember that nitrous oxide is an oxidizer; it is injected into the engine so that more fuel can be burned in the combustion chamber. If no extra fuel is added at the same time that the nitrous is injected, or if too small a proportion of extra fuel is added, the temperature inside the chamber will climb dramatically, producing the same results as a severely lean mixture.

If the nitrous oxide is injected as a liquid into the intake manifold and allowed to vaporize there, it will dramatically cool the incoming charge and thereby reduce cylinder head temperatures, allowing a slightly leaner charge to be burned without damage to the piston, rings, or valves. However, this cooling effect also increases the amount of air that is effectively taken in by the engine, thereby increasing the air-to-fuel ratio and again causing a leaner situation. If the nitrous oxide is injected as a gas or if it is allowed to vaporize before it reaches the intake manifold, the possibility of damaging the engine becomes much more critical, largely because an increased burning temperature will result in the combustion chamber at the same time that the extra quantities of oxygen are added. *The situation can be controlled only by carefully matching the correct proportion of extra fuel that must be added to the nitrous as it is injected into the engine.* The current manufacturers of commercial nitrous oxide systems have determined these proportions through several years of assiduous testing, but their work springs from earlier studies.

EARLY OXYGEN-AGENT INJECTION SYSTEMS

As mentioned earlier, the Germans, the British, and the Americans carried out studies of oxygen-agent injection during the war, and that results of these studies were published in 1946, along with findings from actual use of nitrous oxide and liquid oxygen injection systems in aircraft, in at least two lengthy articles. These articles are very difficult to locate these days but—even though these data relate primarily to large displacement, supercharged, reciprocating-piston engines used in high-altitude aircraft—much of the information set forth in them still pertains to the understanding of how oxygen agents increase horsepower in the types of engines we are running today.

The first public detailed summary of nitrous oxide (and liquid oxygen) injection studies and flight tests appeared in an article by E. P. Hawthorne in the October, 1946, issue of the British magazine *Aircraft Engineering* (pp. 330-335). In it the author describes the use of

NITROUS OXIDE AND OXYGEN INJECTION SYSTEMS ON WW II AIRCRAFT

Aircraft	Oxygen (liquid) Spitfire	N₂O (press) Mosquito	N₂O (unpressurized) Me 109	Ju 88	Ju 188
Number of engines	1	2	1	2	2
Designed total power increase, HP	300	600	330	660	1,000
Quantity of oxygen-agent carried, lb	80	180	310	355	2,120
Duration of injection period, min	9.0	6.3	23.5	27	53
Total weight of system (full), lb	118	475	410	956	2,500
Specific weight of system, lb/100 hp increase/min	4.37	12.5	5.3	5.36	4.71

SPECIFIC CONSUMPTION RATES (German Tests)

	Induction Temp. deg C	Specific Consumption lb/min/100 hp increase x=0	x=100
Nitrous Oxide liquid, pressurized	−20	4.4	3.81
	0	4.36	3.94
	+20	4.3	4.22
liquid, unpressurized	−88.5	4.5	3.41

(x=percentage of N₂O evaporated in air intake before supercharger)

CALCULATED SPECIFIC CONSUMPTION RATES (British)

	Liquid Temp. deg C	Specific Consumption lb/min/100 hp increase
Nitrous Oxide liquid, unpressurized	−88.7	3.42
Nitrous Oxide liquid, pressurized	0	4.55

ACTUAL TEST RESULTS WITH PRESSURIZED N₂O (British)

N₂O Consumption lb/min	BHP w/o N₂O	B.H.P. increase	N₂O Specific Consumption lb/min/100 hp observed	calculated
6.5	796	144	4.52	4.64
10	773	230	4.35	4.83
12	773	257	4.67	4.82

NACA NITROUS OXIDE INJECTION TEST RESULTS
N₂O INJECTION AT CONSTANT MANIFOLD PRESSURE

N₂O-Air Ratio	N₂O Injected as Gas at 210°F IMEP	Per Cent Increase	N₂O Injected as Liquid at −128°F (calculated) IMEP	Per Cent Increase
0.00	237	—	237	—
.05	255	8	275	16
.10	271	14	311	31
.15	285	20	338	43
.20	297	25	369	56
.25	307	30	406	71

KNOCK-LIMITED PERFORMANCE
(with 33R fuel; fuel-oxygen ratio 0.410)

N₂O-Air Ratio	N₂O Injected as Gas at 210°F knock-limited manifold pressure (Hg in abs)	knock-limited IMEP lb/sq in	% increase	N₂O Injected as Liquid at −128°F (calculated) knock-limited manifold pressure	knock-limited IMEP	% increase
0.00	80.5	385	—	80.5	385	—
.05	79.6	405	5	75.0	404	5
.10	78.8	420	9	69.1	415	8
.15	78.0	436	13	64.5*	422*	10
.20	77.0*	452*	17	—	—	

*Extrapolated values

nitrous both by the British and by the Germans (as far as data was available), and for his British information he acknowledges the assistance of "J.M.F. White, formerly of the Royal Aircraft Establishment, who carried through the initial development of the British systems."

Hawthorne's article begins by contrasting various possible oxygen-carrying agents: oxygen, hydrogen peroxide, nitrous oxide, nitrogen peroxide, and carbon monoxide, stating that the choice of a suitable agent should be based on:

a) the degree of charge cooling resulting from the injection of the agent into the air intake. It should be possible, therefore, to inject the agent as a liquid, so that its latent heat of vaporization can be fully utilized.

b) the oxygen content of the resulting charge.

c) the increase in internal cylinder temperatures due to the combustion of the oxygen. This determines the detonation limit and cylinder cooling requirements and therefore fixes the maximum quantity of oxygen-carrier which can be injected.

d) the corrosive effect on metal and the effect on the lubricating oil.

e) the supply and maintenance problems.

None of the potential agents satisfied all of the desired properties. Hydrogen peroxide has a very high latent heat (almost seven times greater than N_2O), but it wouldn't vaporize in the air intake, due to its high boiling point. Nitrogen peroxide was too unstable, formed acids in the engine, and caused detonation. Carbon monoxide is highly exothermic upon formation and therefore would absorb heat during its dissociation in the cylinder, thus detracting from engine power. Nitrous oxide was deemed to have "average heat values and a low oxygen content" in comparison to the others, but is easily stored as a liquid under pressure, and was chosen primarily for this reason—coupled with the fact that it had none of the other major drawbacks. The Germans also decided upon nitrous oxide as the best possible oxygen agent, though they ultimately preferred to use it in a cooled, unpressurized, liquid state (for high-altitude use).

The article then gives three equations—one for the temperature of the oxygen-agent/intake air mixture; one for the relationship between power, air consumption, and air intake temperature; and one for the increase in manifold boost pressure created by the lower inlet air temperature due to the oxygen agent. The author states that "by a process of trial and error" they can be used together to give "values of the charge, air

temperature drop and percentage of power increase in terms of the injected agent consumption and initial air consumption before injection." In other words, by figuring the amount of extra oxygen available in a given quantity of an agent like nitrous oxide, calculating the amount of extra air that would be inducted due to the cooling of the N_2O, and then determining the amount of fuel that could effectively be burned by this combined amount of oxygen—they could theoretically calculate the

CHART A

N_2O Consumption lb./min.	B.H.P. w/o N_2O	B.H.P. Increase	N_2O Specific Consumption lb./min./100 h.p. increase	
			observed	calculated
6.5	796	144	4.52	4.64
10	773	230	4.35	4.83
12	773	257	4.67	4.82

horsepower gains that should result from the injection of a given quantity of the agent.

As shown in the accompanying tables and graphs, a number of interesting and helpful statistics resulted from these theoretical calculations. Figures are given for liquid oxygen, liquid nitrous oxide at atmospheric pressure (refrigerated), and pressurized nitrous oxide. Obviously, the pressurized N_2O figures are the ones that will relate to nitrous systems like the ones being used today. The figures used in the Hawthorne article were calculated for a theoretical engine producing 1,930 brake horsepower at 28 pounds of supercharger boost under static sea level conditions. Probably the most interesting result of these calculations was that they found a direct relationship existed between the amount of oxygen-carrier injected and the resulting power increase. That is, the amount of extra horsepower produced is directly proportional to the amount of nitrous oxide injected (by weight), and this relationship can be plotted as a straight line on a graph. Consequently, they could calculate a *specific consumption rate* for each oxygen agent, which would remain constant, and which they expressed in pounds-of-agent-injected-per-minute-per-100-horsepower-increase. Thus, if the specific consumption of the oxygen carrier is known, the horsepower increase can be adjusted accordingly. For instance, if the specific consumption rate for N_2O were (to use a round figure) 5 lb/minute/100 horsepower increase—injecting 2½ pounds per minute would give a 50 horsepower increase; injecting 10 pounds per minute would give a 200 horsepower increase, and so on. These calculations should prove correct for any size of engine.

The theoretical specific consumption rate arrived at by the British for optimum

utilization of N_2O injected as a pressurized liquid was 4.55 lb/min/100 hp increase. However, in actual testing in aircraft and on bench test engines (testing which they admitted gave "scanty and slightly inconclusive" results due to lack of testing time available) varying figures were obtained. The discrepancies were attributed to the fact that in the real engines the full advantage of the extra oxygen was not being gained. Tests with pressurized nitrous oxide gave the results shown in Chart A.

Although he does not say exactly why, Hawthorne then concludes that, "From these and other results a practical figure of 4.75 lb/min /100 hp increase for the nitrous oxide specific consumption was eventually decided upon." The Germans, using unpressurized liquid nitrous oxide, employed a rate of 4.0 lb/min/100 hp in their aircraft.

The foregoing discussion might lead one to assume that there is no limit to the horsepower that can be created by adding an oxygen agent such as nitrous oxide to the engine. This is, of course, not true. The two major limiting factors (as we shall hear reiterated in the section on nitrous injection with superchargers) are the physical strength of the engine components themselves, and the point at which the engine begins to knock or to detonate. Concerning engine physical limitations Hawthorne cites tests made on Mosquito bombers prepared for low-altitude attacks in July of 1945. These planes were fitted with high-powered engines "which were already operating at their maximum permissible power at about 3,000-ft altitude." That is, their compression ratio and supercharger boost were set to the maximum for the "weight" of air at that altitude. At higher altitudes their power fell off rapidly, so it was decided to try nitrous oxide injection to help boost power when needed. A rate of 12 pounds-per-minute was used, which gave an increase in speed of 20 mph at 5,000 feet. However, "There was considerable risk of bursting the engines if the nitrous supply was not switched off when approaching 3,000 ft." Hot rodders might not put it quite that way, but they will experience the same results if they attempt to create more horsepower with nitrous oxide than the engine can handle.

Concerning the limits due to detonation (Hawthorne uses the terms *detonation* and *knock* interchangeably), he

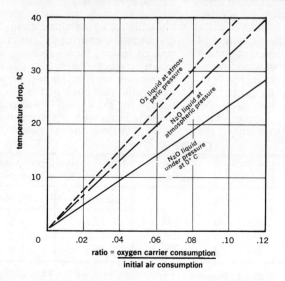

ESTIMATED TEMPERATURE DROP OF CHARGE AIR CAUSED BY INJECTION OF OXYGEN OR NITROUS OXIDE INTO AIR INTAKE BEFORE SUPERCHARGERS

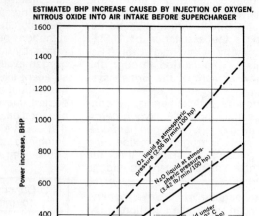

ESTIMATED BHP INCREASE CAUSED BY INJECTION OF OXYGEN, NITROUS OXIDE INTO AIR INTAKE BEFORE SUPERCHARGER

states that severe detonation problems were encountered with the use of straight injected oxygen. However, though actual data had not been collected, it was expected that the knock limit with nitrous oxide would be considerably higher for two reasons: "Nitrogen is an inhibitor to detonation, and it is probable that the nitrogen liberated from the nitrous oxide serves to offset the pro-knock effect of the added oxygen"; and, "The higher latent heat of nitrous oxide gives a greater degree of charge cooling than is possible with the same quantity of oxygen. Thus . . . nitrous oxide will give appreciably greater power increases. . . ."

The remainder of the Hawthorne article describes the specifics of the N^2O and O^2 injection systems as used on the Mosquito bomber, the Ju 88 and 188, and on single-engined fighters. Those interested in further study of these systems might be able to locate a copy of the magazine at a well-stocked college or technical library specializing in aircraft or aviation history.

The second major early study of nitrous oxide was outlined in a post-war NACA report. In the early part of 1945 the U.S. National Advisory Committee for Aeronautics (or NACA; the name has since been changed to NASA) was asked by the Air Force to conduct tests and research on nitrous oxide as a possible temporary power augmentation device for piston-engined aircraft. The results of the study were published as Memorandum Report #E5F26, "Nitrous Oxide Supercharging of an Aircraft-Engine Cylinder," by Max J. Tauschek, Nester C. Corrington, and Merle C. Huppert. The paper was not released until later, and it is currently cataloged as NACA Wartime Report #199, or WR E-199; though it is not found in any of the NACA indexes.

The actual research for this study was conducted only with gaseous nitrous oxide, on a single-cylinder test engine of 1710 cubic inches, but a set of *extrapolated* figures were also calculated for injection of nitrous oxide as a liquid at its vaporization point.

It is unfortunate that actual tests were not carried out with liquid nitrous, but the researchers do present several data or theories in the study that should be of specific interest to current builders of pressurized liquid nitrous oxide systems.

It is also unfortunate, though typical of this sort of project, that the American researchers did not consult nor collaborate with the British scientists who were working on the same subject. It is probably even more unfortunate for us that the Americans used a completely different set of measurement units than the British did; so without going through awkward conversions, comparing the results of these tests with the prior ones is going to be like comparing apples and oranges.

Most of the modern nitrous oxide developers measure the proportions of injected N^2O in terms of pounds-of-N^2O-per-minute - per-100 horsepower-increase (the British system). Weighing the nitrous bottle as the liquid is being discharged seems to be the most practical means for measuring the quantity flowing to engine, and it appears that *pounds-per-minute* will be the standard measurement these days.

In the NACA test, however, the researchers decided to express the flow rate of the N^2O as a function of the air flow, determining a *nitrous oxide-air ratio*. This is the ratio of the mass flow of N^2O to the mass flow of intake air, and it is expressed as a decimal. For instance, they found that the nitrous oxide (gaseous) increased the power of the engine 14% when added at a nitrous oxide-air ratio of 0.1 (that is, one part of N^2O per

ten parts air), and by 25% when the ratio was increased to 0.2 (or one part N^2O to five parts air). This figure would compare to the British actual N^2O consumption figure in pounds-per-minute, rather than their specific consumption figure (expressed as lb/min/100 hp).

Then, to describe the fuel mixture strength when nitrous oxide was added, they devised a *fuel-oxygen ratio* which would take into account the oxygen in the air plus the extra oxygen available for combustion in the nitrous oxide. Unfortunately, this ratio is the reciprocal of the standard air-fuel ratio, so we have listed below four fuel-oxygen ratios tested in the experiment, below which are equivalent fuel-air ratios (discounting the nitrous oxide), and the equivalent air-fuel ratios as commonly expressed today.

Fuel-Oxygen Ratio

0.410
.453
.495
.539

Fuel-Air Ratio

0.095
.105
.115
.125

Air-Fuel Ratio

10½ to 1
9½ to 1
8.7 to 1
8 to 1

The 0.410 fuel-oxygen figure is the basic "correct" fuel-to-oxygen ratio for any engine. What the NACA researchers did was to compute the percentage of increase in total oxygen content of the intake charge with N^2O added, and then increase the fuel flow to maintain this basic 0.410 fuel-oxygen ratio (thus increasing, or enriching, the fuel-air ratio). After the various ratios above were tested on the engine, they judged the 0.410 figure optimum.

It must be remembered that these tests were all conducted with gaseous nitrous oxide at room temperature and atmospheric pressure. The nitrous was completely vaporized in an evaporator, and it was then thoroughly mixed with the intake air in a surge tank. The nitrous oxide and air charge was then mixed with the correct proportion of fuel and completely vaporized in a second evaporator. These are typical idealized laboratory procedures, necessary to the accurate collecting of data—but far removed from conditions in the real world.

Since gaseous nitrous was being used, they encountered significantly increased cylinder head temperatures, leading to preignition. This was countered by installing colder spark plugs, however, it didn't lower the head temperatures, which the authors listed as "the main problem associated with the use of nitrous oxide." To overcome this problem with the gaseous nitrous they tried both water-alcohol injection for internal cooling, as well as adding large quantities of enrichment fuel (beyond the extra amount already added for complete combustion with the N_2O). Of course, the use of liquid nitrous would considerably reduce this problem.

Of greater interest to current users of nitrous oxide is the fact that even the gaseous nitrous used in the NACA test greatly increased the knock limit of the engine (that is, with a given fuel the power output of the engine could be increased beyond the point at which detonation would previously occur). Using fuels of two different octane ratings (28-R and 33-R), the knock limit was increased in both cases; with an N_2O-air ratio of 0.1 the indicated mean effective pressure increased 9% while the manifold pressure decreased 2%. With a 0.2 N_2O-air ratio these figures were 17% and 4%, respectively. In all their data, the NACA researchers used indicated-mean-effective-pressure (IMEP) rather than horsepower to reflect power increases, but they did find, like the British, that, "the power output increased almost linearly with the nitrous oxide-air ratio."

Other useful data collected from the gaseous nitrous induction tests showed that optimum spark timing was retarded and that fuel consumption was reduced appreciably. The results noted that "in all cases the optimum spark timing was retarded as the percentage of nitrous oxide in the charge was increased; this effect became more pronounced as the mixture was enriched. . . . Increasing the oxygen concentration in the charge by the addition of nitrous oxide increases the flame speed and permits optimum operation at a much more retarded spark timing." Even though a greater quantity of fuel is fed to the engine with the N_2O, it is interesting to note that the actual consumption-rate-per-work-produced is lowered (that is, fuel economy is increased). "This increase is probably caused by two effects: 1) nitrous oxide has a positive heat of formation and therefore liberates energy as it dissociates in the combustion chamber, and 2) the increased concentration of oxygen in the charge causes high equilibrium flame temperature, which increases the engine efficiency."

Although the NACA research was conducted exclusively with gaseous nitrous oxide, the report does give estimated results of the use of N_2O in liquid form, injected at its normal boiling (vaporizing) point. Equations for calculating these results are given in the paper, and these estimations were derived for a theoretical engine maintaining a constant manifold pressure (which is not the usual case in practice). The report posits that "in a multicylinder engine the nitrous oxide would probably be injected into the induction system as a liquid rather than as a gas because of the comparative similicity of the liquid system and because of the charge cooling obtained by the evaporation of the liquid." Their estimated conclusions were that liquid nitrous would yield about double the power increase of gaseous N_2O at all values of nitrous oxide-air ratio. It is very interesting to note that they also theorized that, owing to data showing that the knock-limit of gaseous-nitrous dropped as mixture temperature was lowered, "The lowered inlet-mixture temperatures brought about by injection of the nitrous oxide as a liquid would be of doubtful value where the knock limit is concerned." They estimated that knock-limited power would increase only about half as much with liquid N_2O injection as with gaseous

Ron Hammel of 10,000 RPM Speed Equipment has been developing and testing nitrous oxide injection devices on his dynamometer for over fifteen years.

Hammel recently tested a 350-hp 327 Chevy with one of his bolt-on nitrous oxide injectors. Other than a Weiand manifold and a Holley carburetor, the engine was completely stock, and a gain of 150 horsepower was recorded with the nitrous.

N²O. However, these estimates are based on their *optimum* fuel-air ratio of 0.410, and they note that at richer fuel-oxygen ratios the knock-limited power increased as the mixture temperature was lowered.

Another very interesting theory presented in the paper concerning liquid injection of N²O— and one which is still being debated by the current manufacturers of nitrous systems—is the problem of mixture distribution and the optimum location of the nitrous injection nozzles. According to NACA, "The nitrous oxide, however, lowers the inlet-mixture temperature so much when injected in this manner that little of the fuel would be vaporized at the time of induction into the cylinder, which would probably lead to mixture-distribution difficulties with the multi-cylinder engine . . . . The best solution for these difficulties would be to inject the nitrous oxide into the intake manifold as near as possible to the individual cylinder ports. The desirable feature of higher charge-air density (due to lower mixture temperature) would be partly lost because of lack of time for complete vaporization and mixing before induction into the cylinder; this loss would be compensated for in some measure, however, by the high density of the liquid nitrous oxide entering the cylinder."

These two papers might be a little confusing to the average user of a nitrous oxide injection system or to the enthusiast looking to buy an "over the counter" bolt-on system. But to the stu-dent of nitrous oxide as a power source for internal combustion engines they give considerable insight into the development of such systems. It is unfortunate that the two articles use such widely differing systems of measurements and methods of nitrous injection. At least they do give some actual figures for amounts of nitrous oxide and enrichment fuel used. Individually, they give documented scales for measuring power gains available from N²O injection, but together they put forth theoretical statements and questions which have proven to be points of contention even as the state of the art exists today.

CURRENT THEORETICAL STUDIES

Obviously the art of injecting nitrous oxide into automotive engines has seen some changes and developments beyond Ricardo's observations and the testing during World War II. Much of the latter day testing has been conducted behind closed doors and the results remain secret, but there are at least two major spokesmen for commercial nitrous injection systems, Ron Hammel of 10,000 RPM Speed Equipment and John Callies of 303 Enterprises.

Ron Hammel, as mentioned earlier, pioneered nitrous oxide injection in the field of hot rodding and auto racing. He has been testing nitrous on automotive engines almost continuously for over fifteen years. According to Ron, approximately fifty per cent of the power increase netted with N²O is due to the cooling of the intake charge, and the other fifty per cent is due to the release of extra oxygen and the burning of more fuel. Ron estimates that the nitrous in his systems emits from the injector nozzle (usually located under the base of the carburetor) at -20° F, cooling the fuel-air charge from approximately 120° F down to 60° F. He has found that the cooling effect of the injected nitrous can increase vacuum in the manifold by more than sixty per cent (from a normal of 1½ inches to 2½ inches of mercury). In other words, a lot more air is rushing into the cylinders as it becomes much denser. These figures can vary with changes in ambient air temperature, altitude, humidity, and under-hood temperatures.

As for exactly how much extra gasoline can be injected (and burned) along with the nitrous oxide, Ron was reluctant to say since this would be giving away trade secrets that he has worked long and hard to develop, but he would admit that he has seen *double the amount of gasoline* efficiently combusted. He tailors his units to give set horsepower increases depending on the application and on how long the customer would like his bottle of nitrous to last. But he uses a ½ hp-per-cubic-inch increase as a "rule of thumb" for a standard unit. He claims to build a 10%-15% safety margin into his units, so that a lean-burning situation will not develop. Ron also pointed out that a nitrous oxide injector is much like a carburetor in terms of getting it set just right. "You can't just turn it on and have it work," he says, meaning the fine tuning and matching of the unit to a given engine is important to optimum nitrous performance, just as it is with carburetion.

We must not forget the third significant benefit of nitrous oxide, the one that so surprised earlier users—its ability to reduce detonation. Harry Ricardo and other initial experimenters were almost dumbfounded—though obviously overjoyed—at this phenomenon. Today the nitrous experts are still theorizing about what actually takes place in the combustion chamber when N²O is present. Ron Hammel explains the action this way: N²O dissociates into nitrogen (N²) and oxygen (O) at temperatures above 575° F in the combustion chamber. At this point free oxygen is released for the burning of more gasoline, but at the same time a quantity of free nitrogen is also released in the combustion chamber. While the oxygen works to increase combustion, the nitrogen has almost the opposite effect. Rather than simply quenching the flame, according to Ron, it instead gradually retards the propagation of the flame front, producing a very even-burning pattern in the cylinder. Thus, rather than having the fuel explode violently at extremely high temperatures, or detonate, the flame is allowed to burn at a more reasonable

John Callies, owner of 303 Enterprises, distributes Marvin Miller nitrous injectors and uses a very exposed N²O system with four Weber carburetors in his street-driven '37 Simca coupe.

temperature completely across the face of the piston and down into the cylinder as the piston descends on the power stroke. Thus nitrous oxide not only produces more power in the cylinder, but it distributes the pressure of the expanding gases more evenly. For this reason it can be used to develop great quantities of horsepower in engines with stock pistons, rods, crank and bearings. There are no hot spots to burn holes in pistons, and the cylinder walls sustain less wear (especially near the top) since pressure on the rings is more even throughout the cycle. Ron has also noted that the temperature of exhaust valves remains lower when an engine is run on nitrous oxide, thereby greatly extending their life. This also points out that much more work is being extracted from the fuel in the cylinder (that is, the thermal efficiency of the engine is being increased).

Philip H. Smith, in his book *Tuning for Speed and Tuning for Economy*, states that there are four major ways to increase the thermal efficiency of an internal combustion engine: 1) reduce heat losses to exhaust and cooling system, 2) achieve ideal air-fuel ratio for complete combustion under operating conditions, 3) increase the compression ratio, and 4) achieve the ideal burn rate of the charge. Our discussion thus far indicates strongly that nitrous oxide injection satisfies requisites 1, 2, and 4; and, by increasing the volumetric efficiency of the engine, it compensates for a lower compression ratio.

John Callies, whose 303 Enterprises is

Nitrous injection will give a showroom stocker a 2 second, 12 mph boost in the quarter mile. But to see what the gains might be on a finely-tuned, record-holding AHRA formula stock drag race car, C.J. Baker of Hot Rod Magazine added a 303 Enterprises unit to his 396 Chevelle and gained 2 mph while lopping a quarter second from his elapsed time.

one of the major distributors for Marvin Miller's N²O injection units (the only other commercial manufacturer of automotive nitrous systems at this time), is a full-time engineer with the title of Senior Projects Engineer for the Pontiac Division of General Motors. His explanation of how nitrous works in the engine closely parallels Ron Hammel's, and he similarly emphasizes that, "We don't know exactly why N²O retards detonation in the combustion chamber. It is strictly a theory." The theory is deduced largely from inspection of engines that have been disassembled after many miles of running on nitrous oxide. "We can't look inside the engine to see what is happening, but when we tear down an engine we don't find hammered bearings or distressed rods." John likes to call the nitrous oxide in the chamber a *catalyst* since it changes the burning rate (it isn't strictly a catalyst in the combustion process, but the effect on the burning rate can be likened to that of such an agent). He also states that the even burning it promotes "acts like a shock absorber on the piston and rod." Further, John theorizes that nitrous in the cylinder reduces the quench area in the combustion chamber, noting that spark plugs burn almost completely clean (showing no deposits) when running on nitrous—an indication of very complete combustion of fuel in the cylinder.

The fact that nitrous oxide-injected engines produce sizable increases in horsepower and live longer than engines making equal amounts of horsepower by more conventional means can, in part, be explained by the fact that nitrous produces horsepower gains at lower engine speeds. Most traditional methods of increasing engine horsepower rely on increasing the rpm potential of the engine (the horsepower curve increases directly with engine speed until the point where volumetric and mechanical efficiency losses overcome the power gains). However, nitrous oxide increases the thermal efficiency of the engine—which means that more work is being extracted from the fuel in the cylinder on each stroke—*thereby increasing the Mean Effective Pressure within the engine.* In other words, the nitrous oxide allows the burning air-fuel charge to expand with more force per revolution, thereby "pushing" harder and longer on the piston each time the cylinder fires. Consequently, the engine can work harder (that is, produce more power) even at lower engine speeds. And, the high stress on reciprocating engine parts

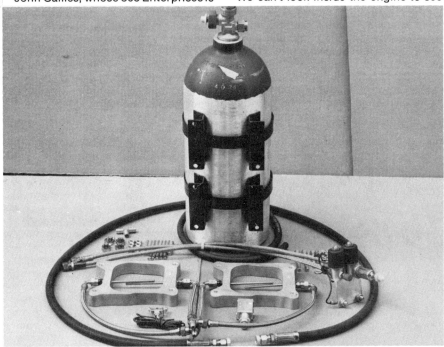

A typical carb-plate nitrous oxide injector, this one for dual four-barrels, would arrive from Miller Manufacturing like this. Included is a filled 10-pound nitrous oxide bottle with mounting hardware, carb plates with nozzles and connecting lines, two solenoids with braided steel hoses, a bottle-to-solenoid covered braided hose, electrical switches, and all necessary hoses, clamps, and fittings.

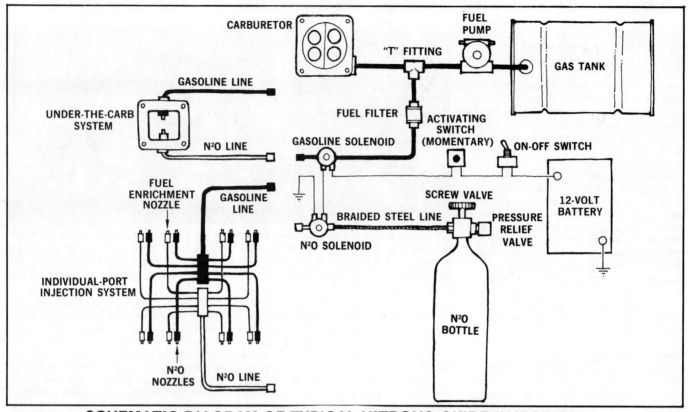

SCHEMATIC DIAGRAM OF TYPICAL NITROUS-OXIDE INJECTION

(pistons, wrist pins, rods, bearings, crank) directly related to engine speed can be reduced, at a given horsepower output, when the engine is running on nitrous oxide. It is for this reason that nitrous oxide is such an attractive proposition for engines that are relatively stock internally.

Concerning the cooling effect of the vaporizing N_2O in the intake manifold, Callies states that his units drop the temperature of the incoming charge approximately 150°, which results in an increase in volume of the fuel-air charge in the cylinder of up to 230°. By maintaining full pressure (approximately 800 psi) from the nitrous bottle, through the lines, to the valve (which is kept as close to the nozzles as possible), Miller systems can, under ideal conditions, inject liquid nitrous oxide directly into the manifold where it vaporizes at -128° F. Under these conditions the full effect of the latent heat of vaporization can be put to work to condense the incoming charge. The resulting decrease in temperature actually lowers the temperature of the cylinder considerably (thus reducing energy loss to the cooling system). Callies has also recorded temperature drops at the exhaust valve of 75° F.

CURRENT NITROUS OXIDE INJECTION SYSTEMS

Since there are, and have been for the past couple of years, only two major commercial manufacturers of nitrous oxide injection systems—10,000 RPM Speed Equipment and Marvin Miller Manufacturing— it is fairly simply to categorize the different types of systems in current use. In all cases, the setup is basically the same. It consists of a pressurized bottle of liquid nitrous oxide, with a screw valve, and a length of high-pressure braided-steel hose leading to an actuating valve near the intake manifold. A second actuating valve is fed by a length of low-pressure hose spliced into the regular fuel (i.e., gasoline) line with a tee fitting between the fuel pump and the carburetor inlet.

The two actuating valves are, in most cases, electric solenoids which are jointly triggered by a push button located either under the accelerator pedal or at some point in contact with the throttle linkage. This button is adjusted so that the solenoids are triggered only at full throttle. A second switch, an on-off toggle, is located ahead of the push button so the entire system can be activated only when the user wishes. A second type of system, less common these days, employs mechanical actuating valves (instead of solenoids), which are attached to the carburetor throttle linkage by an adjusting rod, much like a

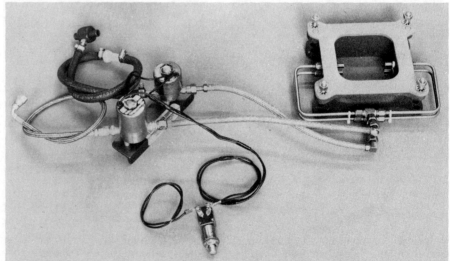

A 10,000 RPM carb-plate injector differs slightly from Miller's in nozzle design and layout, but is equally as simple. Except for the N_2O bottle and an off-on switch, this unit is ready to bolt on and run.

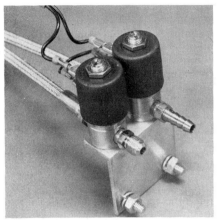

12-volt electric solenoids trigger the flow of nitrous oxide and enrichment fuel simultaneously. Miller uses 3,000 psi solenoids for both.

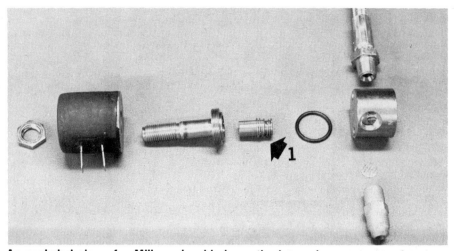

An exploded view of a Miller solenoid shows the internal components. A unique teflon tip on the plunger (1) insures positive sealing when the switch is off.

progressive multiple-carburetion linkage. In special systems on some types of competition machines, the actuating valves are triggered by hand, rather than by the throttle linkage.

Current nitrous oxide systems are also divided into two other categories: hidden and exposed. A simple exposed unit locates the N²O and extra gasoline nozzles in a base plate or spacer between the carburetor(s) and the manifolds. In the case of a single carburetor, two nozzles are fastened into the base plate (one for nitrous and one for extra fuel), and each is attached to the respective valve by a short length of hose. The entire N²O line, from pressure tank to injector nozzle, must be of high-pressure hose (normally 3,000 psi braided steel aircraft line); the gasoline line (including the valve) can be of low-pressure materials.

A hidden system is much more complicated. To conceal the nitrous and extra gasoline lines and nozzles, these components are placed underneath the intake manifold, with two nozzles (again, one for N²O and one for extra gasoline) tapped directly into the bottom side of

each manifold runner, near the port. These nozzles are then connected by a maze of -3 AN stainless steel tubing to a pair of fuel blocks, also mounted under the manifold. Each block is then connected by similar tubing, or by braided stainless line, to the respective actuating valve. The mechanical or solenoid valves can be hidden behind the firewall, inside the bellhousing, or—in the most recent Miller units—under the manifold along with everything else. This latter type of concealed system requires solenoids that are impervious to oil and to temperatures encountered in the valley chamber of an engine; and in any hidden nitrous system great care must be taken to prevent any leaks, especially of gasoline into the oil system.

An under-the-carb (exposed) nitrous injector has several advantages. Since it is less complicated, it is therefore both easier to install and easier to service (should servicing be necessary—though this is rare). Perhaps more important to the typical street rodder, vanner, or motorhome owner, this simplicity of construction means that such a system is considerably less expensive to pur-

chase. Since it is self-contained, it can also be removed from the engine in a matter of minutes and transferred to another if the owner wishes. If the new application calls for a different type of carburetor, or if the user wishes to switch to a different type of manifold—even to multiple carburetion—he can usually order a new base plate(s) to fit his needs without having to purchase a whole new setup. Thus the exposed nitrous system is more versatile than a concealed unit.

The total power potential available from any nitrous injector depends greatly on the temperature and pressure that can be maintained in the N²O lines. Placement of the injector nozzles to optimize the density of the charge the vaporizing N²O produces is also important. Under normal ambient temperatures, unpressurized nitrous oxide is a gas. If it is injected into the air stream in the gaseous state at the ambient temperature it will have a minimal cooling (condensing) effect on the charge. Pressurizing the nitrous oxide to approximately 800 psi, at room temperature changes it to a liquid state. If this

Ron Hammel uses a higher pressure solenoid for the N²0 than for the gasoline.

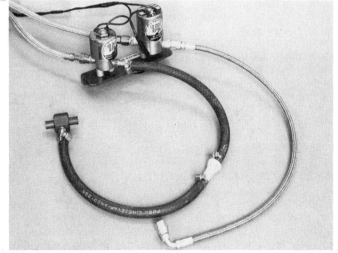

Rubber hose is fine for fuel, but high-test braided line must be used for the nitrous.

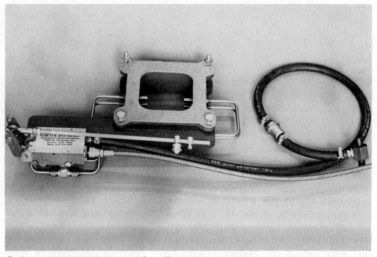

Mechanical valves can also be used to actuate the nitrous and gasoline flow, and these are normally tied into the carburetor linkage with a slip rod so that they can engage at full throttle.

Only 10,000 RPM currently offers this mechanical valve system.

pressure is maintained by the nitrous tank, the high-pressure nitrous line, and the high-pressure solenoid control valve, this nitrous will not vaporize and the cooling action will not begin until this pressure is released (such as when the solenoid valve is opened to allow the N_2O to flow to the injector nozzles). When the distance between the solenoid and the nozzle is great and the ambient temperature surrounding the high-pressure line between these two points is high (the line is usually located in the relatively hot engine compartment), the compressed nitrous has a greater opportunity to begin vaporizing *before* it enters the intake manifold—where it is supposed to be doing its cooling. *Therefore, it is essential to maintain full pressure from the bottle to the solenoid, and it is very beneficial to place the solenoid as close to the injection nozzles as possible.*

In the case of most exposed systems, the N_2O valve can be placed very close to the base of the carb, requiring only a short length of hose to connect it to the nozzle. Therefore the heat gain will be minimal. In some concealed units, where the gasoline and N_2O solenoids must be hidden behind the firewall, under the dash, or in some place removed from the engine, the hoses carrying the unpressurized nitrous to the intake manifold must be quite long and, even worse, it is often routed through the engine itself, or through the hot water hoses of the cooling system. In such cases the N_2O may vaporize completely in the hose, before it reaches the nozzles. Though it will still be colder than the ambient temperature and the temperature in the carburetor venturi, it will nevertheless have lost much of the potential cooling power.

The second problem arising from a long line between the N_2O solenoid and nozzle is that the system might have a noticeable "lag" between the time the button is pushed and the time the low-pressure line fills and cools with nitrous oxide. Concealed systems of the latest type, which place the solenoids right under the intake manifold, only a few inches from the nozzles themselves, obviously overcome this heating problem.

There is dissention between Callies and Hammel, as well as others, over the optimum location for nitrous injection nozzles. Hammel claims to have found, through his dynamometer testing, that units using individual N_2O nozzles placed near the intake ports yield less temperature drop at the intake valve than do units with the nozzles located closer to the carburetor. He claims that he has experienced as much as a 30% increase in intake temperature with a direct-port injector as compared to an under-the-carb type of system, and he believes that this difference is due to the fact that an injector located close to the intake port doesn't have enough time to effectively cool the incoming air-fuel charge before it enters the combustion chamber. For this reason, when he builds a concealed system for a customer, or when he adds nitrous to a direct-port induction system such as fuel injection, he prefers to locate the N_2O and extra fuel nozzles at some point on the manifold runners or velocity stacks farther away from the ports. He also noted that the

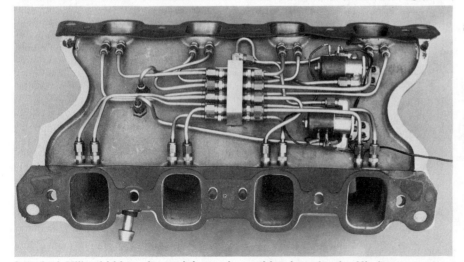

A typical Miller hidden nitrous injector is anything but simple. His latest versions tuck everything, including the solenoids, under the intake manifold where they will be hidden in the valley chamber of the engine.

Miller uses a variety of nitrous oxide and fuel enrichment nozzles, made by his shop to fit the application.

Hammel often uses regular fuel injection nozzle blanks, but drills them to his own specifications. The nozzle on the left is an experimental aerated type.

This top-of-the-tunnel-ram installation reflects Ron Hammel's theory that nitrous injection nozzles work best further away from the intake ports.

majority of his sales are of under-the-carb type systems (of which he markets about 20% more than concealed units).

John Callies, on the other hand, is a firm believer in the direct-port nitrous system. He states that the current Miller concealed units (with the solenoid valves located under the manifold) can create approximately double the horsepower of the carb-plate types. He theorizes that the cooling effect produced by the vaporizing nitrous oxide at the base of the carburetor can be partially lost through convection to the hot intake manifold and heads, thus allowing the condensed charge to re-expand somewhat before it gets into the cylinder. Such reheating of the intake charge might be more pronounced in tall tunnel-ram manifolds, or in aluminum manifolds that are splashed on the underside by hot valley-chamber oil. Even more advantageous, according to John, is the fact that an N_2O nozzle located near the intake port will be able to direct its cooling spray towards the intake valve. By cooling the valve surface with nitrous oxide, as well as cooling the intake port and the combustion chamber itself, John feels that the optimum cooling benefit of the nitrous can be gained. However, John also states that one of the major reasons for greater horsepower gains with the concealed unit is the fact that the eight N_2O and fuel nozzles can inject greater quantities into the engine than single nozzles can.

Unfortunately, few conclusions can actually be drawn from the above "controversy" since Callies and Hammel are working with slightly different types of nitrous systems and they have conducted all of their testing independently of each other. Hammel does his testing almost exclusively on his engine dynamometer, while Callies prefers to test systems on operating vehicles. There are even differences of opinion among experts as to which is the better test bed for engine equipment: "The dyno doesn't lie," says one group, while the

other retorts, "But you can't drive a dyno." Remember that the use of nitrous injection in high-speed internal combustion engines is still in the infancy of development compared to most other types of engine modification procedures—and the experts argue vehemently over the fine points of many other systems (take valve timing and cam profiles as but one example) that

have been around a lot longer than nitrous oxide. In the years to come, as nitrous injection inevitably gains in popular use, further comparative and scientific studies will be conducted—and many more miles on practical nitrous applications will have been run—allowing a more accurate analysis of the variables in the systems.

Disregarding the exact location of the

Quarters are admittedly cramped on this supercharged, nitrous-injected, Crosley-powered slalom racer. However, the distance between the solenoids (1) and the point of injection (2) is greater than optimal. Placing the solenoids next to the carburetor rather than near the bottle would maintain the N_2O in a pressurized, liquid state until injected.

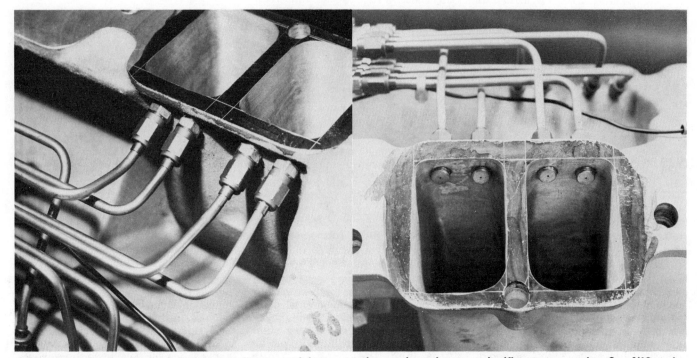

Callies and Miller, however, both feel that direct port injector nozzles produce the most significant power gains. One N²O and one extra fuel jet is located at the base of each manifold runner.

nitrous and extra fuel nozzles, however, it might be helpful to compare under-the-carb and individual-port setups in terms of other direct-port induction systems. The comparison might not hold up on some counts, but the difference between a carb-plate nitrous unit and a unit employing individual nozzles for each cylinder of the engine (be it a concealed system or one that is mounted on the outside of the manifold) could be likened to the difference between a normal carburetor-and-manifold induction and a direct-port fuel injector. In a study conducted by Arthur W. Judge and reported on in his book, *Carburetors and Fuel Injection Systems,* the author lists seven benefits found for injection over carburetion:

1) Higher charger or volumetric efficiency because of the increased capacity of the injectors over a carburetor venturi, and because restrictive passages in the carburetor (such as the choke) and the manifold are eliminated
2) Better distribution to the cylinders
3) Uniform mixture strength in each cylinder
4) Better fuel economy (because of 2 and 3)
5) No necessity to heat inlet air for vaporization
6) Better acceleration response, since the increase of fuel is sprayed directly into the ports
7) Better cooling of the inlet valves, due to the latent heat of the fuel

At first sight, it would seem that numbers 2, 3, 6, and especially 7 would apply directly to a nitrous injection system which locates both the N²O and extra fuel nozzles near the individual ports. In fact, other than not being able to compensate for the limitations of a carburetor listed in point #1, the addition of an individual-nozzle nitrous system to a carburetor and manifold would seem to give all the benefits of a fuel injection system once the nitrous is turned

Locating concealed nozzles under some manifolds can be tricky, though. In this instance a portion of the manifold was milled away and long-reach nozzles were used.

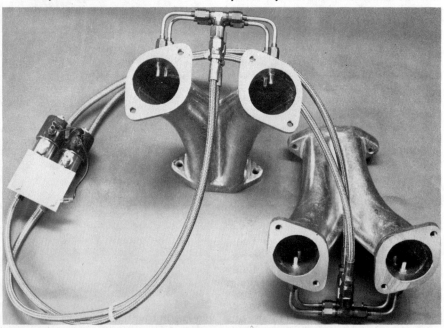

This Miller-Autohaus setup for a Weber-carbureted Volkswagen illustrates a good compromise in the nozzle-location debate: injectors placed at the top of a short, smoothly-flowing manifold, a few inches above the intake ports.

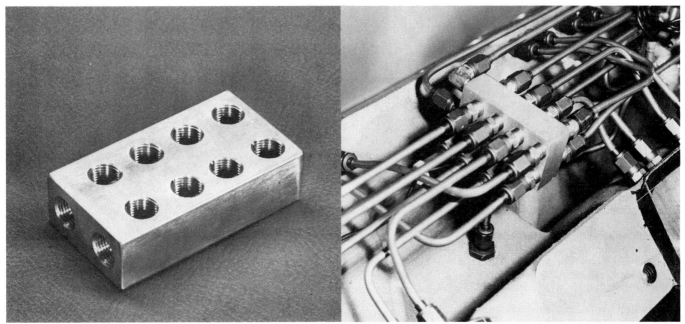

For individual port injectors, a compound block is used to divide the flow from the two solenoids. One passage of the block feeds nitrous oxide to eight cylinders while the other carries extra fuel. Double-flared AN fittings and -3 stainless AN line connect the distribution block to the nozzles.

on. At that time, it would be injecting the majority of the fuel, as well as the nitrous, individually into each port. Of course, the maximum benefits of *both* a fuel injector and a nitrous injector could be gained by simply combining the two since, as pointed out earlier, nitrous oxide can add its horsepower increases to those already built into an engine. However, it is not practical to drive a Hilborn-injected machine around in city traffic. But, by adding a direct-port nitrous injector to a regular carburetor and manifold, it is possible to gain most of the benefits of each systems—a simple and tame carburetor for driving around town and, at the touch of a button, a direct-port fuel (gasoline) and N_2O injector.

Once again, dissention exists on this subject. Certain users of nitrous oxide feel—like those who espouse the "plenum chamber" design of intake manifolds—that better distribution of the nitrous and extra fuel can be gained by injecting both at the top of the manifold and letting it disperse throughout the chambers or runners evenly. The condensing effect of the cold nitrous will increase mixture velocity within the manifold (resulting in a quicker throttle response), and the relatively high pressure of the nitrous stream, plus the fact that it is vaporizing very rapidly, could provide for quick dispersion in the manifold.

Others, such as the NACA researchers, believe that the severe cooling of the N_2O would inhibit proper vaporization of the primary fuel, both from the carburetor and from the enrichment nozzles. The low temperatures created by the N_2O in the manifold

might even cause the atomized fuel to recondense into droplets, which could in turn impinge on the walls of the manifold or the ports because of the increased velocity of the air charge, creating substantial distribution problems. The NACA researchers felt that locating individual N_2O injection nozzles very near the ports—though allowing less time for optimum charge cooling—might be the best compromise.

On the other hand, an individual-nozzle nitrous system must rely on very accurate metering and constant, equal

flow of both N_2O and extra fuel to each jet in order to function properly. If for some reason one of the individual nitrous or gasoline lines delivers more or less than it should (such as might happen if it becomes clogged with a dirt particle), an uneven distribution situation would result. If one or more cylinders receives too large a dose of N_2O or too little extra fuel, an over-lean condition could result—leading to damage in the cylinder. In short, an individual-nozzle nitrous injector is more complicated than an under-the-carb type, and there-

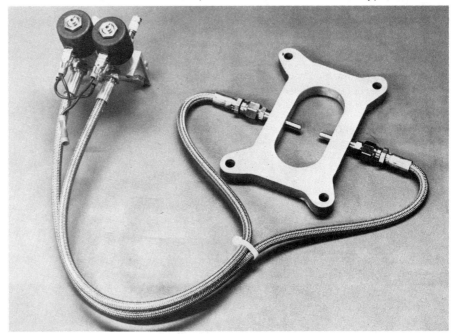

The simplest way to add nitrous oxide to your engine is with a carb-plate adapter. Such a system is exposed, but it can be installed or removed in minutes and can be transferred to another vehicle.

fore has more possibilities for malfunction. However, either system, if properly designed, installed, and maintained, should deliver the horsepower increases it is supposed to, without undue problem.

One might wonder, at this point, which type of nitrous oxide system is best. It is best to discuss each specific of your application with the individual manufacturer and listen to their suggestions. Decide whether a concealed system or an exposed system is necessary for the intended purposes. Consider whether you might want to transfer the nitrous unit to another vehicle at a later date (if so, an under-the-carb unit is your wisest choice in most cases). Finally, consider how much extra horsepower the engine can stand, as well as how much nitrous apparatus your pocketbook can afford.

INSTALLATION

Once you have decided that a nitrous oxide injection system is a practical and potent hop-up device for your car, boat, motorhome or snowmobile (which shouldn't take much arm-twisting at this point), and have decided on the type of system that best suits your needs, it is time to get to the business of installing the components. Most of the distributors of either 10,000 RPM or Miller units can bolt them on your engine for you; but the actual installation of a prefabricated nitrous oxide injector takes

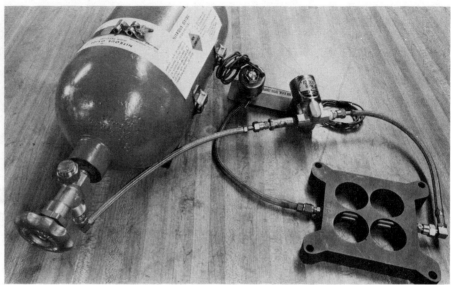

This complete carb-plate bolt-on system is surprisingly simple and can deliver up to 150 extra horsepower to a stock V-8. If you don't need a concealed injector and aren't building an exotic race car, it's the best bet for the money.

very little time or special skill. A few important pointers will, however, insure the accurate and unfailing performance of the total package.

First, decide where to mount the N²O bottle. This decision must be predicated by: 1) the size of the bottle itself, and 2) whether your system will be open or concealed. If you plan to use nitrous illegally in a closely-supervised racing situation, both the size of the bottle and its possible locations will be severely limited. In the well-publicized "capture" at the '76 Daytona 500, Darrell Waltrip finally surrendered his nitrous bottle to the tech inspectors when they threatened to tear his car apart looking for it. It was in his pocket! It was a very small 10 oz -bottle, with a special quick-connect fitting, that he could carry undetected in his fire suit and hook up once he was in the car. Such a small con-

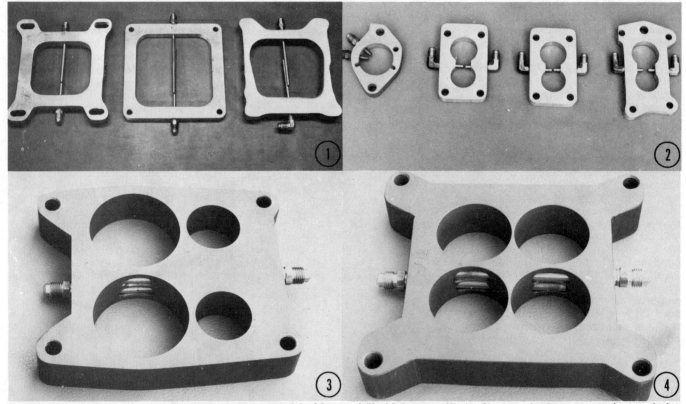

Carburetor adapters are available for every conceivable application. This makes a system extremely versatile if carb or manifold changes are anticipated: 1) typical 303 Enterprises four-barrel plates with centrally-located tube with drilled injector orifices, 2) several adapters are also made for two-barrel carbs, 3) 10,000 RPM plates include a sample for a Quadra-Jet carb (note the nitrous is sprayed only into the secondary bores), 4) and a plate for the Holley four-barrel.

Nitrous oxide bottles are available in a variety of sizes to fit any application: 1) rated by the weight of N²O they hold, this lineup from 10,000 RPM ranges from 25 lb to 2 lb , 2) Miller units use aluminum bottles which are more expensive but are reputed to control corrosion. Each bottle has a siphon tube inside running to the bottom and turning in the direction of the valve outlet.

tainer would be of little benefit except in the most critical qualifying situation. And, carrying a filled N²O bottle on one's person is about as safe as completely replacing the fire system with nitrous oxide (which has also been tried). Nitrous is relatively harmless under most conditions, but if it should for some accidental reason begin to escape, the vaporizing liquid N²O would have the same tremendous cooling effect it has in the engine and can cause severe cold burns if it comes in direct contact with your skin. For this reason, only federally-approved and tested pressure bottles should ever be used to store nitrous oxide (the 10,000 RPM and Miller bottles are U.S. approved to 1800 psi). Only high-pressure test lines and valves should be used for the N²O systems, and all connections should be tight, sealed, and double checked. The manufacturers of nitrous oxide units use only the highest quality components—do not substitute anything of inferior quality. If installed properly, they claim that nitrous oxide should be completely harmless.

The painstakingly-concealed nitrous system is the exception rather than the rule. The most common application on street-driven or part-time race cars is rather the "casually-concealed" setup. The engine will appear to be normally-aspirated when the owner lifts the hood, but it will not have to stand up to any detailed tech inspections or tear-downs by experts. Therefore, the most common choice for a nitrous bottle is a five- or ten-pound tank and the most logical place for it is inside the trunk. Some users might want to select a smaller bottle and tuck it up under the dash—which makes it slightly more difficult to detect and which requires much shorter lines—but remember that a bottle full of nitrous (especially a small one) doesn't last very long, and the better you hide it the harder it will be to remove and replace every time you have to fill it.

It is advantageous to mount the nitrous bottle in a relatively cool location. If the nitrous tank or the braided hose that connects it to the actuating valve becomes heated, the liquid N²O inside will try to expand, increasing the pressure in the system. The nitrous bottle should have a safety pressure-relief valve built into its screw valve, and most are set to release at 1800 psi. Every high-pressure gas system should have a safety valve at some point. There is a slight chance, if the bottle becomes excessively heated, that it might "pop off" through its relief valve. Such an occurrence would be very rare, but John Callies did discover that it can happen. He was carrying some full bottles of N²O in the back of a station wagon, and failed to realize until too late that the hot sun beating through the window glass directly onto one of the bottles could heat

A fine example of a "casually concealed" nitrous oxide injector has been installed on this 302 Ford-powered Pinto street racer.

An early Miller direct port model, it has the solenoids mounted externally. Also visable in this photo is the fuel line tee fitting, located just after the fuel filter.

it considerably. The safety valve did release, but luckily no one was near the tank at the time. Of course, the pressure valve is a safety device and activating one will cause no harm other than loss of the nitrous oxide—unless the bottle were placed in close proximity to passengers in the vehicle. The wisest safety precaution is to keep the N²O bottle and line away from excessive heat, and to be sure that the bottle is never overfilled.

Of more practical importance to the installer of a nitrous system is the position of the bottle in the vehicle. Unlike large industrial tanks, smaller N²O pressure bottles for on-board use have a siphon tube built inside. This tube runs the length of the bottle and turns at the bottom to face the same direction as the outlet of the valve at the top. The pressurized nitrous is a liquid, so the bottle must be positioned so that the liquid can be drained until the bottle is empty. Otherwise, you'll be refilling the N²O more often than necessary or you will run out of N²O before you have utilized the bottle's capacity. Since the liquid will also be affected by the motion of the vehicle, the siphon tube should be positioned so that it will pick up the nitrous when the vehicle is accelerating. If the bottle is mounted vertically, the valve should be at the top with the outlet facing the rear of the vehicle. If it is mounted horizontally, it can either be placed with the valve end to the front of the vehicle and the outlet pointing down, or it can be placed laterally in the chassis with the outlet pointing down and slightly towards the rear of the vehicle. If the car or boat is to be used in left-turn oval competition, a laterally-mounted bottle should, of course, have the valve on the left side of the vehicle (so the siphon tube is to the right). In any type of horizontal bottle mounting it is a good idea to place the valve end slightly higher than the siphon end.

By far the most important consideration when installing a nitrous injector on a vehicle is cleanliness. The nitrous system is an amazingly simple mechanical apparatus. It has only two moving

All of the plumbing and the sixteen nozzles are hidden under the manifold, fed by two braided lines which attach at the rear.

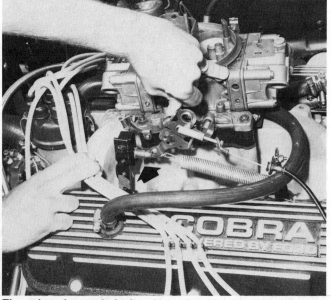

The triggering switch for the solenoids is mounted on a bracket so that it engages with the carb linkage at full throttle.

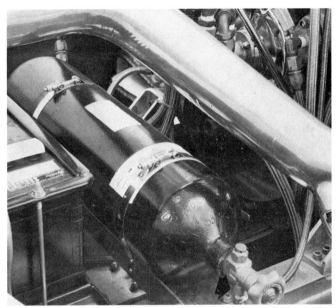

The ten-pound nitrous bottle mounts at the rear of the Pinto's luggage compartment, but it is neatly camouflaged as a fire extinguisher with red paint, an appropriate lable, and a dummy hose.

A laterally-mounted bottle, such as in this ski boat, should have the valve pointing down as shown. If used in left-turn oval racing, the nozzle should be to the left so that the siphon tube will be to the right.

parts—the actuating valves—and a unit as supplied from the manufacturer needs little or no adjusting or further calibrating. It is much simpler than even the least-complicated carburetor. However, like the carburetor, dirt or foreign particles of any sort are the worst enemies, and the orifices in a nitrous injector are much smaller than those in most carburetors. It is imperative that a good fuel filter be placed in the gasoline line, preferably near the gasoline valve itself. Likewise, a filter should also be incorporated in the N_2O line. Miller units use a special stainless steel strainer in the nitrous solenoid and 10,000 RPM units have a similar strainer in a small brass fitting which screws into the inlet

side of the nitrous valves or solenoid. The only maintenance necessary to keep a good nitrous oxide injector functioning properly is to keep these filters clean and to keep dirt particles out of the lines. If this is not done, three possible problems could result. A dirt particle clogging an N_2O nozzle will simply cut off nitrous to one cylinder or to the whole engine (in an under-carb unit) Not only will the effect of the nitrous be lost, but the extra gasoline being injected will richen the mixture, causing the engine to run worse. A dirt particle clogging a gasoline nozzle could be more dangerous. It would allow too much nitrous to be injected into the engine or into one cylinder in proportion to

the gasoline, and would result in a lean situation in the cylinder (which can lead to burned valves or pistons). A dirt particle caught in one of the actuating valves will cause the valve to jam open, or not to shut off completely, thereby injecting a steady stream of either nitrous or gasoline into the engine.

This last example has been the unfortunate experience of a few users who found out too late the necessity of keeping their system clean. In one case, a Late Model Sportsman racer was using a clandestine nitrous injector for a race at the Riverside Raceway. When he pulled into the pits, those present heard a strange hissing sound coming from the engine compartment. He had just run a

Placing the bottle in the engine compartment reduces the length of the connecting hose, but increases the temperature of the N_2O. This bottle should also be turned around for proper delivery of the liquid nitrous oxide under acceleration.

A neat installation of a 10,000 RPM exposed injector makes an extremely potent package of this Ford-powered Sunbeam Tiger. Note that inline filters have been added to the inlet sides of both the gasoline (1) and the nitrous oxide (2) solenoids.

Dirt or rust particles in either the fuel or the N²O are the system's worst enemies and are the most common reason for failure. An inline fuel filter has been attached directly to the gasoline solenoid in this case.

The latest Miller solenoids incorporate small, fine-mesh, stainless steel strainers in the inlet passage. These should be removed and cleaned periodically.

Hammel's N²O solenoids have similar strainers in screw-in brass cartridges. Such filters are available at aircraft supply houses.

very fine qualifying lap, but, unfortunately, his nitrous solenoid would not seat properly because it had a dirt particle trapped in it. The N²O continued to release even after he had shut the car off, and the cause of the hissing sound was quickly determined by officials. In another less fortunate case, the owner of a nitrous-equipped street machine had just made a couple of strong runs, shut off his engine, and then went to restart it a few minutes later. He didn't notice that a small quantity of N²O was leaking through the solenoid while the car was sitting. When he tried to start the engine it coughed once through the carburetor—and the nitrous-filled manifold exploded, literally blowing the top off. It should be emphasized, however, that these examples are given only to underscore the necessity for keeping the system clean. They are the result of an avoidable circumstance. A professionally-manufactured and properly-maintained nitrous injector system should not experience such calamities.

Hooking up the plumbing of a typical nitrous system is straightforward. Since most units are made with the same size fittings for both the N²O and gasoline lines, you must, of course, attach them to the proper valves. In all Marvin Miller systems the N²O fittings are marked with red Dy-chem; in the 10,000 RPM systems the N²O injector nozzles are placed above the gasoline nozzles, and the lines should be hooked up accordingly. The nozzle orifices may look the same to the naked eye, but the secret to the proper functioning of a nitrous system is the perfect metering of a specified amount of N²O with a specified amount of extra fuel. These amounts are not the same, and the unit will not work properly if the lines get switched. Also be sure, if your setup uses high-pressure lines and solenoid for the nitrous and low-pressure components for the gasoline (as in 10,000 RPM electric systems), that you do not use the low-pressure components with the nitrous oxide. The N²O lines and valves should be rated at no less than 1275 psi.

Wiring a solenoid-operated system is also quite simple. The solenoids operate on 12 volts DC current, and should already be pre-wired in parallel so that they will both open at the same time when current is applied to the single lead. This lead can be attached to any type of actuating switch with the opposite terminal of the switch attached to any hot wire or terminal on the vehicle.

The most common wiring setup utilizes one momentary actuating button connected in series to an off-on toggle switch, which is then connected to the 12-volt source. The momentary switch or button can then be placed either under the accelerator or at some other point where it will contact with the linkage in the wide-open throttle position. The off-on toggle can be placed in

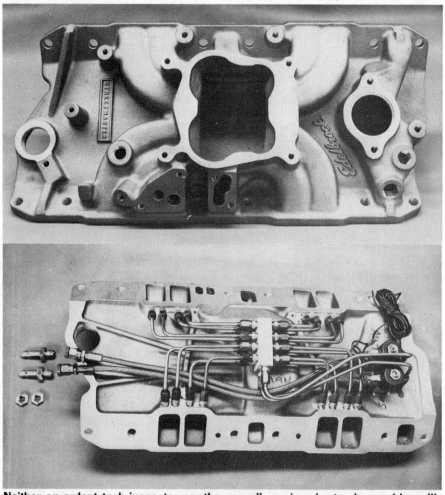

Neither an ardent tech inspector nor the casually-curious bystander would readily guess that this manifold is completely plumbed for nitrous oxide injection, but turn it over and the fact is obvious. The two fittings at far left mount in holes drilled through the back of the engine block, and the solenoids are attached to them with the flexible hoses. The N²O and fuel feed lines are attached to the fittings from inside the bellhousing.

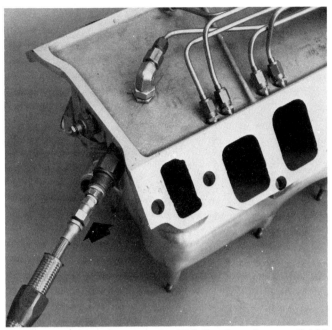

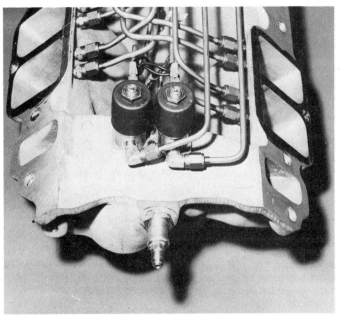

Another sneaky way to run the N²O line into the manifold is through a dummy water hose. A braided hose shows no bulges and it is difficult to detect the inner lines.

The nitrous line can also be installed in a regular rubber water hose fitting. Some users have hidden nitrous lines inside operative radiator hoses, but the heat transferred to the N²O might cause it to vaporize prematurely.

the dash or some other place within easy reach of the driver. When the toggle is switched on, the system will be "ready," but the nitrous will not be injected until the accelerator is tromped to the floor. When the toggle is off, the car can be driven normally, even at full throttle, without using any of the nitrous supply. If the system will be turned off for any length of time, it is also highly recommended that the safety valve on the bottle should be closed, just as a precaution.

A new two-stage nitrous system is currently being tested. Since the horsepower created by nitrous oxide is so tremendous, some drag racers are experiencing traction problems coming off the line under full throttle and full nitrous boost. Rather than cutting back on the power of the nitrous or having to switch on the system part way down the strip, the new system employs two pairs of solenoids—one pair will give a limited initial dose of nitrous and another will add more as the car gets under way. Such a system has been tested on a drag car by Marvin Miller, and was found to be quite effective.

No internal modification of an engine is necessary before fitting it with a moderate nitrous oxide system. If the engine has been modified, the N²O will just add more power to that already built into the engine. However, there is no need for most of the traditional "beefing" that is required when engines are built for high-rpm horsepower gains. Similarly, since the engine will be producing horsepower increases at lower rpm ranges, there is no need to increase clearances or extensively alter the oiling system, unless the rest of the engine has been modified in the traditional manner. When beginning with a highly-

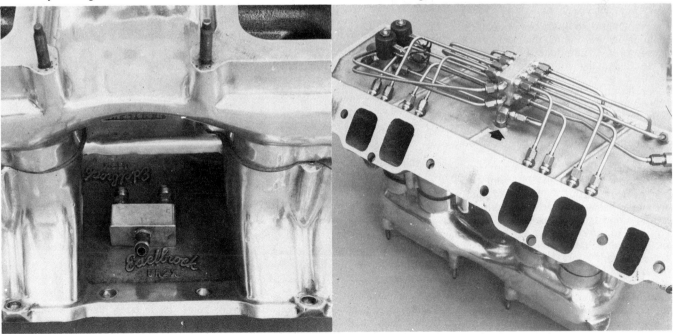

An easy way to conceal the extra fuel line to the injector is to mount a fuel block to the manifold and then tap into it from the underside.

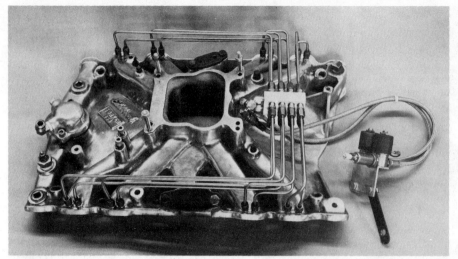

A direct-port nitrous injector doesn't have to be concealed. This 455 Olds boat manifold has been tapped on the outside because the owner liked the looks. Such a system would be easier to install, easier to maintain, and should run cooler (thus more efficiently) than hidden types.

more extra horsepower than all of these other modifications combined and since half of that increase is due to improved intake efficiency, there probably won't be too great an improvement in performance by adding just one or two of the above items in addition to an N_2O injector. The nitrous will take care of most of the work of getting the air-fuel charge into the cylinders. Of course, if your engine suffers from restrictions at any point along the intake path—carb capacity, intake manifold efficiency, port size, valve size, cam duration or lift—it could be fighting the job the N_2O is doing. Of course, camming and headwork will help exhaust as well as intake; but if you are going to use nitrous oxide to increase your engine's performance, you don't really need to spend more money on the intake side as long as things are adequate—Ron Hammel recommends about a 700-cfm four-barrel on a 350 cubic inch engine. If you want to spend

modified engine or when planning such traditional modifications, do not think that the addition of a nitrous oxide injector will negate the need for certain engine building procedures. If you plan to run the engine or turn high engine speeds only when the nitrous is turned on, you might be able to get away with slightly less bullet-proof pistons, rods, crank, and your rings will probably last longer. If you are using a high compression ratio, long cam duration, solid lifters, etc., then you had better go all the way. Especially important in a high-modified engine are oiling, clearance, tough rod bolts, and all other considerations that relate primarily to high engine speeds rather than to combustion forces. The nitrous, when it is being employed, should help to make pistons, rings and rods live longer in any type of engine. Of course, the closer an engine is built to the limit, the less extra horsepower it can take from nitrous oxide. Especially critical are very high compression ratios or large boost from supercharging (see the section on nitrous and supercharging).

Secondly, there are certain modifications which would produce more significant improvements with nitrous oxide than others would. For instance, the nitrous helps to pack more volume into the cylinder, but it doesn't do anything to help get exhaust out. A good set of headers would help, as would low restriction mufflers and large diameter tailpipes if you plan to run corked-up on the street. Most engine performance modifications currently practiced today—and those which generally produce the most significant power increases—concentrate on getting the intake in: cam timing and lift, head porting and polishing, enlarging of valves, intake manifolding, and the first consideration of almost any hot rodder—carburetion. Since nitrous injection can produce

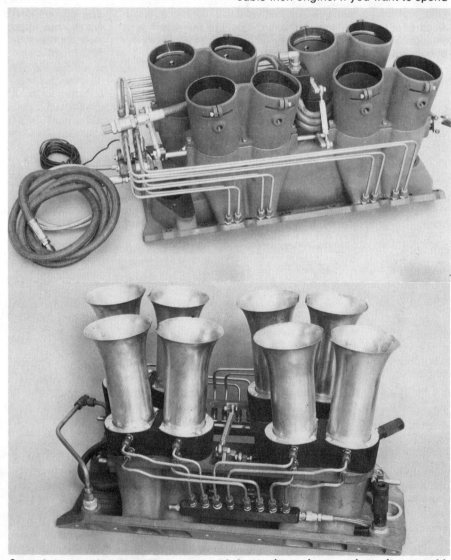

Several types of competition cars and boats have been using nitrous oxide successfully, and the system appears fully compatible with fuel injectors. Marvin Miller recently modified a factory prototype for Crower (above) while Hammel added N_2O to the Hilborn unit (below). The two manufacturers' differing theories on nozzle location are apparent in these installations.

Hammel did point out one benefit to elevated nozzle placement worth considering by racers—if the solenoids should ever stick open, the driver can still close the throttle butterflies, thus shutting off fuel from the engine.

more money on speed goodies, start with areas that aren't directly affected by the nitrous, such as improving ignition and streamlining exhausts.

If you are starting with an engine that is already stock, as long as it is in good mechanical condition, you can get an extra 150 horsepower out of it with nitrous after only a slight amount of modification. First, *you must have a good ignition system* which will insure firing of the plugs on each cycle even with the increased charge in the combustion chambers caused by the nitrous oxide. Manufacturers of nitrous systems agree that a *good* stock ignition system is adequate if top quality wire core spark plug wires are installed (at least eighteen strand; no carbon-core). However, a capacitive discharge electronic ignition would probably be a wise addition to any nitrous-equipped engine. John Callies has also found that the denser charge in the cylinder requires that spark plugs be gapped down to about 0.028-inch. The increased combustion temperatures usually require plugs one step colder than normal in range.

Secondly, besides the addition of an inline gasoline filter, you must also provide an adequate supply of fuel for the extra dose that is added with the nitrous oxide. In all cases a high-value fuel pump is recommended (either mechanical or electric), and *fuel pressure of 4-5½ pounds must be maintained,* even at peak consumption. Consequently, it is advisable to add a fuel pressure gauge to the instrument panel to monitor delivery under all driving and racing conditions. The 10,000 RPM installation instructions stipulate a maximum fuel pressure of 6 psi., which could be controlled, if necessary, by the addition of a variable pressure regulator (such as manufactured by Holley or Filt-O-Reg) on the outlet side of the fuel pump.

While discussing the subject of various types of nitrous injectors, how to install them, and how to make them work properly, it is necessary to broach the subject of burning down the engine. If you talk to very many people about nitrous oxide injection, you undoubtedly encounter several ex-nitrous users who swear at it rather than by it. They will tell you about blown engines, wiped-out rings, melted pistons, and other castastrophies, usually followed by, "But, Lordy, that engine would run like a scalded dog when it was working right." There are several reasons for these scare stories about nitrous oxide. Let's look at one example. More than five years ago a drag boat pilot was running an injected Hemi Chrysler

hydro and his crew was experimenting with nitrous. They had learned about N²O from the V-12 airplane engine-powered unlimited hydroplanes, and had done quite a bit of testing with the stuff themselves. This was still the early days of nitrous use in "small displacement" racing engines. Their system was pretty sophisticated for the time, having eight nitrous nozzles injecting into the upper portions of the injector stacks and eight extra fuel nozzles located next to the regular fuel injection nozzles. They had the standard difficulties, getting an even distribution of nitrous and fuel to the individual cylinders and keeping the N²O from condensing the gasoline as it came out of the injectors. But the real problem was keeping the engine together. As the crew chief later recounted, "We could never get more than four runs out of an engine. After that we'd tear it down and it would be junk. The ring lands would be turned inside out! The exhaust valves would be completely gone." *This destruction was not so much a result of the fact that they were using nitrous oxide, as it was of the* **way** *in which they were using it.* As the crew chief put it, "We were using the nitrous the lazy way. That boat would only run about 130 mph without the nitrous oxide. It really wasn't set up that well. With the nitrous we were getting about 400 extra horsepower."

That, obviously, is not the proper way to use a nitrous oxide injection system. But it is quite easy to get lazy when using nitrous—to rely on it to make all your horsepower for you—because it certainly will add gobs of power to any kind of engine. Likewise, it is also very easy to become greedy. In both respects many of the past users of nitrous

Because nitrous injection increases the density in the combustion chamber, a good ignition system is paramount. A stock distributor, with plugs gapped to 0.028-inch and with high-grade secondary cable, is adequate for stock engines. Better is a CD electronic ignition such as the Speedatron system installed by Hammel on this Mopar wedge.

Here's what happens when the nitrous oxide user gets greedy. Radical cylinder pressure has broken the compression rings and the top of the piston.

oxide have been like those who relied on huge doses of nitromethane to make the power in their engines. The results are much the same in both cases. First of all, both the "shock abosorber effect" and the cooling of the cylinder produced by nitrous oxide work on a scale of diminishing returns. If you are going to dump lots of N²O and lots of extra fuel into your engine, you are going to be burning a lot more fuel in the cylinder on each stroke and that has to result in a considerable amount of extra heat and pressure. Since it doesn't cost much more to make 400 extra horsepower with nitrous than it does to make 100-150 hp, many purchasers of nitrous units figure they might as well get as much as they

can for their investment. When you start making this kind of power in your engine, the nitrous system, and everything else in the engine, has to be exactly right. As in any high-powered engine, a slight malfunction or a weak part is going to make a magnified effect on total results. When you are playing with 400-plus extra horsepower, you can't afford to get lazy.

Secondly, many of the past attempts by racers to use nitrous oxide have ended in failure because of a slightly different type of greed. If an engine is already modified to pump out several hundred horsepower, the addition of a sizable nitrous oxide injector could easily be the straw that breaks it. Some controversy exists on this subject, but most of the racers running big blown-fuel engines—consistently on the ragged edge—seem to be of the opinion, "I can destroy engines with the power I've got built into them already, why do I need nitrous oxide?" Some of these have formed their opinions from experience. The manufacturers of nitrous oxide systems would argue, on the contrary, that a well-designed and properly set up nitrous injector could *replace* some of that destructive power with an equal amount of power in a more reliable form. *The fact remains that the power of nitrous oxide added on top of an already explosive engine package is likely to result in a fragmentary bomb.*

Third, as mentioned earlier, many of the scare stories about nitrous oxide accrue from the early experiments of hot rodders who tried this substance before

much was known about the proportions of extra fuel that must be added when the nitrous is injected into the engine. It was common knowledge that the more nitrous you dumped into the engine, the more horsepower it would make; but getting just the right amount of extra gasoline metered in with it to make it run properly—and not lean out drastically—was a little more tricky. As one such experimenter put it, "The problem was that we lost an awful lot of engines trying to get the system worked out. The effect of the nitrous oxide was so rapid, when it was injected, that you didn't have time to adjust things while the engine was running. If it wasn't right, the engine would scatter before you knew it." For this reason, it seems wise to start with a developed and tested commercial nitrous oxide unit (unless you've got plenty of extra engines in your garage). Such systems have a built-in "safety margin" of 15%-25%, meaning that they are actually set slightly rich in terms of added fuel per dose of N²O. Yet they still deliver plenty of horsepower.

When you are considering a nitrous oxide system for your car or boat, don't be greedy. Unless you are involved in a highly-competitive racing situation and you intend to devote the time and attention all engine tuners in similar situations must spend keeping all systems of their engine in perfect working order—you would probably profit more in the long run from a slightly less potent nitrous setup. Using Ron Hammel's ½-hp per cubic inch "rule of thumb" might be excessive in many cases. In fact, both

The nitrous bottle filling apparatus at 10,000 RPM is elaborate. N²O from the sixty-pound bottle at right is pumped through a refrigerating condenser (the large white cylinder) by a compressor (bottom left), and then into the small bottle (on scales). The condenser cools the N²O to approximately 40°F so that it will remain liquid at a much lower pressure.

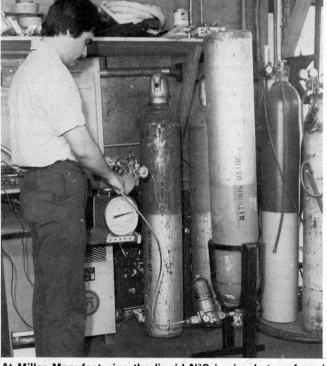

At Miller Manufacturing the liquid N²O is simply transferred by gravity flow from the inverted cylinder to the small bottle (on scales). Note the large filter in connecting line.

Hammel and Miller recommend systems of closer to 150 hp for their average customer (average being a relatively-stock 350 cubic inch V-8). With such a setup, not only will the margin of error be greatly reduced, but the owner will also find that his bottle of nitrous oxide will last considerably longer as well. If you are using a nitrous injector primarily for fun on the street, on your ski boat, or on your motorhome; you should find that 100-150 extra horses is well worth the initial investment, and that making your nitrous last longer between refills is not only more convenient, but more economical as well.

WHERE TO GET NITROUS OXIDE

If you purchase a complete nitrous oxide injection system from 10,000 RPM or Marvin Miller, or from one of their distributors, you will receive with it a full bottle of nitrous oxide. Once you have installed all the components in the car you will hopefully find that the system does everything it is claimed to do and you will be very happy that you purchased it. But after several full-throttle runs you will suddenly find that your nitrous injector has run out of steam. Your nitrous bottle is empty. Then what are you going to do?

Obviously, if you are contemplating the purchase of a nitrous system, you should first determine where liquid nitrous oxide is available in your area. If you live near a nitrous oxide distributor, you can usually get your bottle refilled at the same place where you purchased the system. Both Marvin Miller and Ron Hammel refill nitrous bottles at their shops, as does John Callies at 303 Enterprises, as do some of their distributors around the country. But where do you go to get a N²O bottle refilled if you live in West Virginia or in North Dakota and you bought your nitrous equipment through the mail? You wouldn't want to be stuck in the foolish position of having the only nitrous oxide injected car in town—but having no nitrous oxide to put in it.

The distributors of nitrous equipment leave the problem of procuring N²O strictly to the customer. John Callies of 303 Enterprises, on the other hand, has established an agreement with a national supplier of nitrous oxide to fill his customers' bottles, and John can usually give the customer a name and address of a supplier nearby. Of course, the customer should contact the potential supplier before he buys the nitrous equipment, to make sure that he can get the bottle filled afterwards. If you are planning to buy nitrous equipment from another dealer, you should check with him for possible sources of N²O in your area. He can probably help with suggestions.

Readers might wonder why cylinders of nitrous oxide are not always readily available from industrial gas suppliers, like oxygen and acetylene are. First, there is much less call for nitrous oxide, especially as an industrial gas (although you might be surprised to learn that it is necessary to the manufacturing of whipped cream!). Dentists still use nitrous as an anesthetic, and dentists are located in just about every town in the country. However, most dentists buy their N²O through medical supply houses, and these companies usually will not sell their products to the general public. A problem arises from the fact that nitrous oxide is an anesthetic. Consequently, manufacturers of the gas want to be sure that it does not fall into the wrong hands to be used for non-medical or non-industrial purposes. Unfortunately, "fooling around" with nitrous oxide can be lethal. Anyone attempting to inhale the stuff directly from the bottle will very likely freeze his lungs, and large doses of even gaseous nitrous are deadly. For these reasons a manufacturer or distributor of N²O is not likely to fill a bottle unless he can be sure that it is not going to be used in a harmful way.

It might be helpful to establish some sort of rapport with a dealer of nitrous oxide. If the prospective buyer lives in or near a large urban center, he can usually find a gas supplier who handles nitrous oxide listed in the Yellow Pages under "Gas—Industrial & Medical" or a similar heading. If he lives in a rural area, he should contact the nearest welding supply dealer (preferably one with which he already does business), and ask if the dealer can obtain bottled N²O from his supplier of oxygen and acetylene. He probably can have it delivered along with his regular shipments. If either of these two sources fails, the buyer can try medical supply houses (again, look in the Yellow Pages or ask the family dentist for the name of a supply company), but he will probably find them reluctant to cooperate.

Secondly, he will probably find that an industrial or medical gas supplier won't be too crazy about filling the five or ten-pound nitrous bottle. To begin with, most gas suppliers have an agreement to fill only their own tanks and bottles because of the problem of large rental bottles (such as for welding uses) being stolen and also because any pressure bottles must be periodically inspected and certified for safety. If you buy a nitrous system from either 10,000 RPM or from Marvin Miller, the package includes an N²O bottle (of whatever size) that has been hydrostatically tested and given an I.C.C. pressure rating of 1800 psi. The date of testing must be stamped into the bot-

tle, and this certification is good for five years. No industrial gas supplier will fill any pressure bottle that is not tested and "in date," and neither should you. Nitrous bottles, especially steel ones, are prone to internal corrosion, which can eventually lead to thin spots in the cylinder walls and possible rupture of the bottle. If you have a bottle that is not currently certified and you want to use it for nitrous oxide, you can have it tested and stamped at almost any fire extinguisher or welding supply dealer's. The nominal cost is well worth the insurance (not to mention required by law).

Filling your own bottle is actually the most practical, expedient, and usually the most economical way to maintain the nitrous system. A ten-pound bottle of N²O will provide about 200 seconds of operation on an average V-8. That's plenty of ten-second bursts, but if you run your vehicle a lot, you will have to refill the bottle at least every 2 or 3 weeks. That can be a hassle if you have to take it back to a dealer to have it refilled each time (it can be a hassle for the dealer, too, and he's likely to charge for his inconvenience). You could put a larger bottle in your vehicle, but space might be a limitation, and there is really no reason to carry around thirty or so pounds of extra weight in the car. The practical solution is to rent (usual cost is about $20 per year) a large cylinder for liquid N²O (such as a sixty-pound, or "G" size bottle), and to keep it in your garage to refill your own smaller bottle whenever it needs it. You will find that most industrial gas suppliers will be more eager to sell you nitrous if you buy it in larger quantities and rent the tank from them (if you buy sixty pounds of N²O you've obviously got serious intentions). And, despite the extra cost of renting the tank, you may find, in the long run, that your nitrous will be less expensive if you buy it in bulk. The cost of N²O varies, just as the price of gasoline does, but the average charge for filling a sixty-pound tank is about $50-$60. On the other hand, having a smaller bottle filled with nitrous at a dealer can cost from about $1.25 per pound (Callies' current price) to $2.25 per pound (Hammel's price for filling bottles other than his own).

FILLING THE BOTTLE

If you have opted to create a nitrous oxide refilling station in your own garage, you may need some tips on how to transfer the liquid properly and efficiently from the large tank to the small one. One problem arises from the fact that you want to transfer the nitrous in a liquid state from one tank to the other, and that the small one has a siphon tube inside but the larger one doesn't. A partially-filled nitrous tank

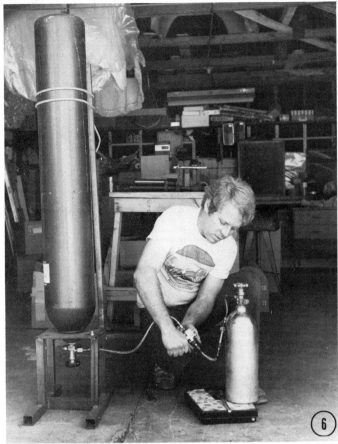

HOW TO FILL A NITROUS OXIDE STORAGE BOTTLE

The simplest and most economical way to keep your nitrous bottle filled is to purchase (or rent) a large sixty-pound cylinder and keep it in your garage. 1) John Callies demonstrates the apparatus needed for a home refilling unit—a stand to invert the large cylinder, a connecting hose with an inline filter (John's also has an off-on valve), and a bathroom scale. 2) A good filter (arrow) is an absolute necessity in the refill line since most cylinders of N^2O contain some dirt or rust particles. These filters can be purchased from most suppliers of aircraft hoses and fittings. Callies also recommends capping the open end of the line when not in use. 3) Empty the smaller nitrous bottle before filling and then weigh it. If a ten-pound bottle, like this one, weighs fifteen pounds empty, it should weigh twenty-five pounds full. 4) Before connecting the coupling hose open the valve on the large cylinder momentarily to purge the line of any possible dirt particles. 5) Connect the hose loosely to the smaller bottle (with its valve closed), open the valve on the larger cylinder, and then tighten the coupling when white spray appears. This fills the line with liquid N^2O, so that no air will enter the bottle. 6) Allow the liquid nitrous oxide to flow from the cylinder to the bottle while reading the scale. If it attains the proper weight, close both valves and you are through. 7) If the bottle does not fill completely, try inverting it a couple of times with the hose still attached and reweigh. If still not filled to capacity, disconnect the bottle, invert as shown so that the siphon tube is elevated, and open the valve to let a slight amount of vapor escape. Then reattach and refill. 8) If you do not have a fixture for inverting the large cylinder, you can lay it on the floor during the filling process, with its bottom end slightly elevated.

contains liquid N^2O with gaseous N^2O above it. If you were to open the valve of the large tank when it is upright, you would get only N^2O vapor out of it (and the nitrous would keep vaporizing as the liquid level dropped). Conversely, an "empty" small bottle will contain some gaseous nitrous which must be removed to make way for the liquid to completely fill it — this gas will, of course, turn to liquid if the N^2O is pumped in under high pressure, but when transferring nitrous from one bottle to another, the pressure in the large bottle isn't sufficient to liquify all the vapor in the smaller one.

So, you must "pour" the liquid N^2O from the large tank, and the easiest way to do this is to build a stand on which to invert it, with the valve accessible at the bottom. Otherwise, you must elevate the bottom of the large tank with something like blocks of wood while it is lying on the floor. The smaller tank can be filled in any position that is convenient, but it might have to be inverted and "purged" of gas, as we shall see in a minute.

Another precaution that must be seriously considered when transferring nitrous oxide at any stage is that of straining out any dirt or rust particles. Nitrous oxide is available in two grades—medical and industrial—the difference being that the medical grade is cleaner and slightly purer. Even tanks of medical grade N^2O can contain tiny rust particles, and filtering is a *must* at the time of filling your own bottle. Inexpensive inline liquid filters are available from 303 Enterprises, and they can also be purchased from most aircraft surplus stores or suppliers of aircraft-type braided hoses and fittings. Be sure to use one in the line between the large N^2O tank and the smaller one when filling, and also use filters in the system on your vehicle if they are not incorporated in the valves. Remember to clean these filters from time to time.

It is easiest to refill your N^2O bottle when it is empty or nearly so. If there is a slight amount of nitrous in the bottle, open the valve to release the N^2O present, and, at the same time, to cool down the bottle. This cooling will help to liquify some of the remaining N^2O, and will lower the pressure inside the bottle. If you have the time, a neat trick discovered by John Callies for easy filling of empty bottles is to store them in your refrigerator for about 45 minutes before filling. This will reduce the pressure inside the bottle and allow the higher pressure in the large N^2O cylinder to quickly fill it. If the smaller bottle is partially filled, you can usually cool it quickly by allowing some of the N^2O to escape.

The first step in filling the bottle is to weigh it. Your bathroom scale will do

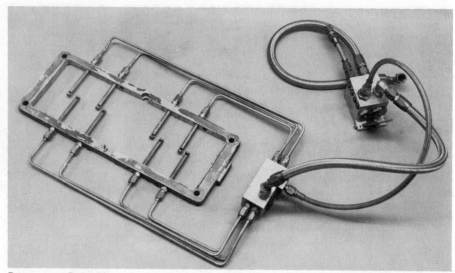

Drag racer Dale Armstrong has been toying with nitrous oxide for several years. He found this setup quite successful on his Donovan-powered Funny Car running on 25% nitro. The nozzle plate fits between the blower and injector; four nozzles inject N^2O while the other four add extra fuel.

fine. A five-pound nitrous bottle is designed to hold five pounds of nitrous oxide. Never fill a bottle with more than its specified weight; this can lead to extremely high pressures, especially if the bottle becomes heated, and might cause the safety valve to release or, if the safety valve should not work, an extremely rare possibility, the bottle may burst. Actually, you will probably find it difficult to get more N^2O into the bottle than it is supposed to carry. The weight of the nitrous oxide is, of course, the difference between the weight of the bottle when empty and its weight when full. If your five-pound bottle weighs ten pounds empty, you will want to fill it with nitrous until it weighs fifteen pounds on the scale.

Once you have recorded the empty bottle weight, attach the line from the large bottle (with filter attached) to the small bottle, but do not tighten it down on the small bottle. Open the valve on the large tank and as soon as white vapor begins to appear around the loose fitting, tighten it. This allows any air in the line to escape, making certain the coupling hose will be full of liquid N^2O. Then open the valve on the small bottle and watch the scale as it fills. If it reaches the specified weight, turn off the valve. If not, invert the bottle a few times and reweigh. If this doesn't help, you may have to turn off both valves, disconnect the line from the small bottle, invert it so that the siphon tube is pointing up and the bottle is resting on the scale, and then crack open the valve until about one pound escapes. This way you will be purging gaseous N^2O from the tank, above the liq-

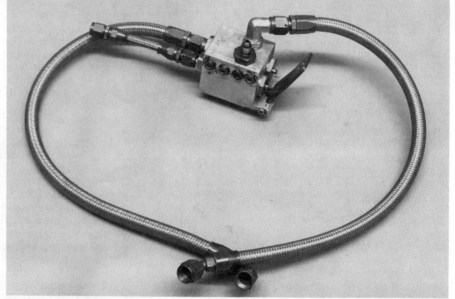

Dale machined his own mechanical actuating valve from an aluminum block. It uses valves from a fire extinguisher and the lever is triggered by a cable from the cockpit.

To insure adequate and precise delivery of enrichment fuel, Dale had a special gear drive made for the front of the engine to mount a separate fuel pump for the enrichment system.

uid—but don't let too much out, because the liquid nitrous will also turn to vapor as the pressure is released. Finally, hook the line back up to the bottle as before and refill it to the correct poundage.

NITROUS WITH SUPERCHARGERS

The name Dale Armstrong should be very familiar to anyone who follows the Funny Car or Pro Comp drag racing circuit. Dale's AA/Blown Alcohol Dragster is currently one of the fastest in the nation and one of the constant winners of national Pro Comp competition. Dale is also very knowledgeable about nitrous oxide.

Armstrong began fooling around with nitrous over fifteen years ago when he was drag racing a 409 Z-11 Chevy in his hometown of Vancouver, British Columbia. He had taken a couple of trips down to the state of Washington to race, and there heard about a guy who was using "laughing gas" in his race car. When he got back home, he contacted a local supplier of medical gases, obtained a dentist's bottle of nitrous oxide, and tried a couple of experiments on an old six-cylinder Chevy pickup. The experiments consisted of removing the truck's air cleaner and, while sitting on the front fender, squirting some of the nitrous directly from the bottle into the throat of the carburetor. Dale says the initial results not only surprised him—but left him a little shook up as well! Concluding that the stuff really worked, he immediately rigged up a home-brew apparatus for injecting the gas into his 409. By today's standards his first system was very crude, but for the time it was actually fairly sophisticated. It was a hidden setup, utilizing a network of 1/8-inch copper tubes fitted to holes drilled

into the underside of the intake manifold. The tubes were connected to a hose that ran to the back seat of the car, where a pair of nitrous bottles were stashed—along with a hiding accomplice to turn the valves on the bottles when Dale gave the signal (how's that for a concealed system?). With 4.88 gears in the car, Dale said he would run through the traps at about 6200 rpm when the car was normally-aspirated. But the first time he tried the nitrous he had to shut down about a thousand feet down the strip because the car was already red-lined and out of gear. To say the least, Dale was convinced that there was a future for nitrous oxide injection in drag racing.

Within a few years Dale moved to Southern California and opened a shop

in Torrance—which coincidentally happened to be next door (at that time) to Ron Hammel's 10,000 RPM Engineering. Ron had, of course, already been experimenting with nitrous for a couple of years, and one day when Dale happened to see a large bright blue pressure bottle next to the engine dyno he remarked, "Oh, I see you're playing around with nitrous oxide." Both were rather surprised.

In the years to follow Dale and Ron worked together on several nitrous experimental projects—some of which made history at the old Lions Drag Strip in Dale's "Canuck" topless Chevy II altered-wheelbase "Funny Car," which ran a 354 ci blown smallblock Chevy and got into the mid-8's back in '65-'66 using nitrous assist. Dale ran this car for over a year, often on nitrous, and never blew the engine.

Armstrong's thinking on nitrous these days still focuses on the benefits as an engine saver. "Adding nitrous oxide to a blown fuel engine running over 50% nitro is useless," says Dale; likewise, "You can't add nitrous to the typical blown alcohol engine running 11:1 compression," (meaning an engine creating approximately 30 pounds of blower boost on top of a static 11:1 compression ratio). Adding the greatly-increased cylinder pressures produced by nitrous oxide to such "built to the hilt" racing engines would mean sure disaster.

When asked about the detonation-inhibiting properties of nitrous oxide, Dale responded, "There are two things which cause detonation—heat and compression." The cooling effect of the vaporizing N_2O might be able to retard detonation slightly in a highly-compressed engine, but the benefit would be minimal compared to the effect of

Ron Hammel offers a bolt-on nitrous and extra fuel injection plate (center) for superchargers, which can be attached to either solenoid or mechanical actuating valves.

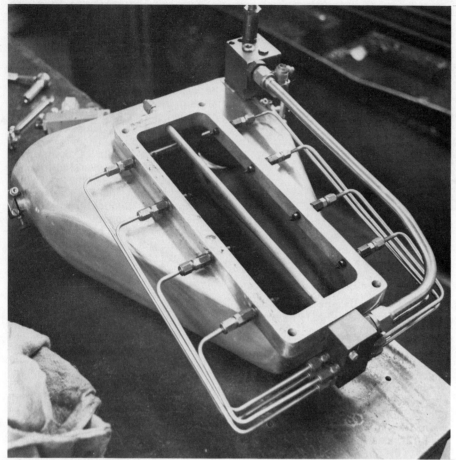

In this blower application a nitrous oxide delivery tube has been added to the center of a standard fuel injector. Enrichment fuel is added via modification to the injector's metering system.

engine package that is much more livable on the strip.

The trick is to reduce the static compression of the engine to approximately 8:1 (which is closer to what the nitro engines use), and to run about 20% nitromethane, plus nitrous oxide injection. This way the engine will be producing about the same horsepower as it would on straight blown alcohol when it comes off the line, so the car could hook up and get underway quicker with a lower gear. At the same time the engine, which is actually a "detuned" version of a 2000+ hp fueler, would be operating at a wider margin from the destruction limit and would consequently have less of a tendency to explode, lift the blower, burn pistons, throw rods, and other antics typical of blown fuelers. Then, once the car is underway, the nitrous can be turned on and the horsepower can immediately be brought up to the 2000+ mark for a full-power blast through the traps.

In other words, the nitrous oxide can be used like a horsepower "valve." Instead of building an engine to the limit with a fixed compression ratio or blower overdrive ratio, or by dumping in heavy continual doses of nitromethane, it would be possible to feed the extra horsepower to the engine in short bursts of nitrous oxide and extra fuel—saving the engine somewhat in the meantime. Of course, as pointed out so many times previously in this discussion, the nitrous itself will offer advantages toward making higher horsepower with less detriment to the engine. The advantages will be considerably less significant than they would be in a much tamer gasoline engine, but there would be some benefit from the cooling capacity of the vaporizing N²O.

The cooling effects may be less pronounced because the alcohol itself (which will be the other 80% of the fuel) has a very high latent heat of vaporization and has a very high knock rating. Nitro, on the other hand, is very prone to detonation—but it is also very slow burning. One of the major benefits of running nitro (besides the fact that it is an oxygen-releaser, like N²O), is that it will continue burning down into the cylinder, yielding a longer power-effective cycle than other types of fuel. You will remember that this is also one of the calculated benefits of nitrous oxide. By combining all three fuels—alcohol, nitro, and N²O—Armstrong feels he can gain most of the major benefits of each, all at once (or in succession, which is preferable). The combination will have a very high knock rating (that is, it will not detonate easily), but it will ignite easily and rapidly, unlike nitro (Dale notes that slightly less total ignition advance can be run in the igni-

the extra power (i.e., heat and pressure) being produced. As Dale added, any engine, running on any type of fuel, has a "mechanical limitation" dictated by detonation. Different fuels have different limits, and alcohol has a much higher detonation limit than either gasoline or nitro does. Any all-out blown racing engine is built (via compression ratio and blower boost) to the fuel detonation limit. Running anything less would mean wasting some of the potential power available from a given engine in a given class, and consequently running slower than the competition.

Given this situation you might think—like most top fuel engine builders today apparently do—that there is little use for nitrous oxide in blown fuel racing. Armstrong disagrees. In fact he feels that the future of nitrous with blown fuel "looks really promising." He reasons, and has found to be true from experience, that the power generated from nitrous oxide can be used to *replace* some of the power built into the engine. The engine will, therefore, still be working to its "mechanical limit," but the power can be handled in a slightly more controllable form.

For example, Dale's blown alcohol

dragster, which creates approximately 1500 horsepower, can use a three-speed Lenco transmission, and can therefore leave the line quite a bit quicker than a Top Fuel dragster. The fuelers, which are making in excess of 2000 hp, use a two-speed or direct drive, and must leave the line more slowly—otherwise they would simply spin their tires and go up in smoke. Of course, the fuelers can put their extra power to work as soon as they get underway, and end up quicker and faster at the traps than an alcohol car. But consider, what if a car were to use alcohol to come off the line, and then were injected with a dose of nitrous and extra fuel as soon as it was hooked up in second or third gear? Theoretically it could get off the line quicker than the fuel car, on less horsepower, but still be able to match the fueler's power and speed on the top end. Sound good?

The one problem is that the typical blown alcohol engine, running 11:1 compression, would not be able to withstand the extra pressures created by the injected nitrous. The solution which Dale has found to be effective on his Funny Car, is one that not only produces power and times equal to most of the nitro burners, but also gives an

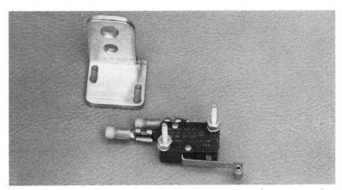

Miller's solenoid-operated bike units are actuated by a small micro-switch mounted to contact the carburetor linkage at full throttle.

A typical nitrous oxide injector for a motorcycle differs from a car or boat system only in the proportions of the components and the addition of a small electric fuel pump for positive extra fuel delivery.

Modern four-cylinder bikes require a machined aluminum adapter which mounts between the ports and the carburetors. N_2O and extra fuel are injected through small holes drilled in the long brass tubes, which are inserted in the adapter.

tion), and yet it will burn longer and more completely, yielding the longer, stronger power stroke. The end result, put simply, is that you can get all the benefits of running large doses of nitromethane—without most of the drawbacks. Of course, putting them all together isn't quite as easy as it sounds (the real key is knowing how much N_2O and what proportion of extra enrichment fuel to meter into the engine). If Dale's testing proves fruitful, the future of nitrous oxide in blown fuel drag classes looks very promising.

NITROUS ON MOTORCYCLES

Dave Zeuschel, who builds 1500+ cubic inch Rolls Royce twelve-cylinder engines, remarked that it is far easier to make nitrous oxide work productively on a big engine than it is on a small engine. The smaller the engine, the smaller the margin for error when calculating the amounts of N_2O and extra fuel that can be added—and the greater the risk that the power generated can become destructive rather than productive.

Nitrous oxide has been, and is being, used effectively on all sorts of small engines, both of the two-cycle and the four-cycle variety. Snowmobiles, go-karts, quarter-midgets, even a few model airplanes have been fitted with nitrous injectors; but probably the largest category of small-engined machines to which N_2O is applicable is the motorcycle.

Adding a nitrous system to a four-stroke motorcycle is very similar to adding the same equipment to a car or boat, except that most of the components are proportionally scaled down to match the displacement of the engine (including the size of the N_2O and extra fuel metering nozzles). One man who has had experience with mo-

torcycle systems is Gary Brunelle of San Bernardino, California. Gary has just installed a Miller nitrous injector on his new Kawasaki KZ-900 LTD, a four-cylinder, four-stroke road bike. Gary is a motorcycle mechanic at Midway Honda in Fontana, California, and in-

You would have to look very closely to detect that Gary Brunelle's street-trim KZ-900 is nitrous oxide equipped.

When Gary cranks the throttle, it's obvious this bike is something more than stock. With nitrous oxide, this "stock" Kawasaki turns the quarter mile in 11.33 seconds at 121.43 mph.

A two-pound N^2O bottle tucks neatly under the seat, and holds plenty of nitrous to feed the bike's small appetite.

stalls nitrous systems on bikes as a sideline. His Kawasaki is his second nitrous-equipped motorcycle, and he has had very successful results with all of his installations.

Since most motorcycles use individual carburetors to feed fuel and air directly to each cylinder with little or no intake manifold to speak of, the simplest and most common method for adding the nitrous and extra fuel nozzles is in an aluminum plate fitted between the carburetors and the in-

take ports. If someone were expressly looking for such a nitrous setup on a bike he could probably find it, but as you can see from the photos of Gary's Kawasaki, it is not immediately noticeable. A small N^2O bottle, such as the two-pound container on Gary's bike, can easily be concealed under the seat. The electric solenoids, which are the same as used on all Miller systems, could be mounted in several places, but Gary found that they fit nicely behind a plastic cover on the right side

of the bike. A small micro-switch was mounted between the carburetors to trigger the system. It rides on the accelerator eccentric and is adjusted to inject the N^2O and extra fuel only at full throttle. For an on-off switch for the system, he converted the stock headlight dimmer switch mounted on the handlebar.

The only major difference between a motorcycle system of this type and an automotive system is the fact that most motorcycles do not have fuel pumps,

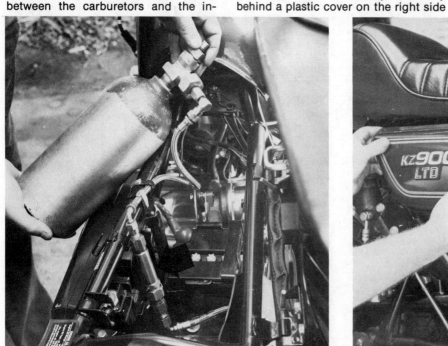

The bottle can be easily removed for refilling, and you will note the large filter (arrow) Gary has added in the nitrous line—good insurance for any N^2O installation.

A dust cover on the right side of the bike conveniently conceals the two solenoids.

Major components of the system include: 1) the N_2O and gasoline solenoids, 2) a small rotary electric fuel pump, and 3) the nozzle adapter plate between the carbs and the head.

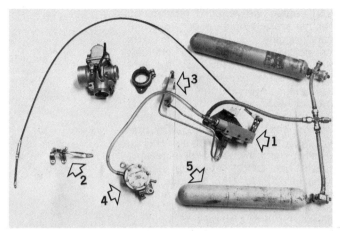

Two-stroke engines respond very well to nitrous injection. This system was developed by 10,000 RPM for a 250-cc flat-tracker and consists of: 1) a pair of mechanical valves, with 2) a handle bar mounted control lever, 3) a carb adapter plate with N_2O and fuel nozzles, 4) a fuel pump, and 5) a pair of small ten-ounce nitrous oxide bottles. Since a two-stroke usually has no auxiliary electrical system, all components must be mechanical.

and to guarantee that a sufficient and constant flow of extra gasoline will be delivered to the nozzles, one must be added. Most Miller bike setups come with a 12-volt electric pump, of a pulsing type. However, Gary experienced some problems with this particular pump and substituted a Carter (P4594) rotary electric pump which is compact and delivers a constant seven pounds of fuel pressure. Another noteworthy substitution on Miller bike units compared to those for larger vehicles is the special small diameter (⅛-inch or 3/16-inch), flexible, high-pressure hose manufactured by Imperial-Eastman, and called *Nyloseal*. It can withstand pressure up to 2500 psi, so it can be used for both the N_2O and the gasoline lines, but it is much smaller (and much more unobtrusive) than the typical braided stainless steel aircraft-type high-pressure hose normally used.

When Gary first installed the nitrous system on his Kawasaki, the bike was completely stock. The only mechanical problem he encountered (and one which seems to be typical of this bike) was valve float at high rpm, and the subsequent tendency to "spit" valve shims. To remedy this problem he installed R.C. Engineering cam followers and high tension S&W valve springs. Of course the bike was given a precise tune-up, but everything else, including the carbs and the ignition, was left factory stock.

After drag testing the Kawasaki both stock and with the nitrous unit as delivered from Miller, Gary felt that more power could safely be gained from the N_2O. He enlarged the N_2O and the extra gasoline jets 0.003-in each. After drag testing the bike once again, he decided to try another 0.003-in on all the nozzles. The dramatic results are given below:

stock	12.46	109.62
with N_2O	11.75	115.83
0.003-in larger jets	11.50	120.64
0.006-in larger jets	11.33	121.45

A Mikuni snowmobile fuel pump, operated by crankcase pressure and delivering 4½ psi, is perfect for a two-stroke nitrous application.

As tested on his motorcycle mini-dyno, Hammel's two-stroke N_2O injector produced an impressive 20 ft-lb torque.

Of course, we wouldn't recommend that the average buyer of a nitrous unit start hogging out the N²O and extra fuel nozzles, especially on a small engine like this, but Gary has had substantial prior experience with the equipment. You will note that the increases were small and gradual. He also tore down the engine after each testing session to make sure that everything inside was living properly—and he stopped increasing nozzle size *before* anything showed signs of distress. Gary is quite happy with an increase of over one full second and almost twelve mph from his 900-cc, full-dress, street-trim motorcycle (and you will notice that his stock times aren't bad, either, which means that the bike was tuned almost to the maximum before the nitrous was added). He has subsequently made several more runs with this bike, and has experienced no problems.

Two-stroke motorcycles—and two-stroke engines in general—are a slightly different case. To see just what goes into such a system, a good example is a 250-cc flat-track racing bike that had been outfitted with one of Ron Hammel's nitrous systems. Of course, as in all nitrous setups, the basic design was the same: a pair of actuating valves feed the N²O and extra fuel to a pair of metering nozzles; and since this is a single-cylinder bike, the nozzles are located in a small spacer between the carb, a 34mm Mikuni, and the intake port. For this particular setup, a pair of small one-pound nitrous cylinders are mounted on the aluminum plate attached to the frame and are coupled together by use of a tee-fitting to feed into a single braided line.

The first difference between this bike system and the previous one discussed (or any street bike) is that the racing bike has no electrical system, other than a magneto to fire the plug. Consequently, mechanical actuating valves have to be used rather than electric solenoids. These valves are controlled by a single cable running to a small lever mounted on the handlebar. Secondly, a fuel pump of some sort is needed to deliver the enrichment fuel, but an electric pump cannot be used. Instead, a small Mikuni "impulse" pump, such as made for snowmobiles, is employed. It functions by using crankcase pressure and delivers 4½ psi, which is just about the perfect pressure for Hammel's mechanical actuating valves.

Installed on the bike and mounted to Ron's special dyno, he found a 20 foot-pound increase in torque all through the rpm range with the nitrous and extra fuel turned on—which isn't bad, even for a high-powered, specially designed racing engine of only 250 cc's (15¼ cubic inches). Ron explained that

The 1650-cid V-12 Rolls Royce Merlin engine was nitrous oxide injected in 1944 by the RAF with impressive results, so it was logical that hydroplane boats and pylon racing airplanes would take advantage of this tremendous power assist several years ago. Racing planes and unlimited hydros still rely heavily on nitrous for power augmentation.

the nitrous is even more effective on a two-stroke engine than it is on a four-stroke, since the inducted air-fuel mixture must pass through the crankcase before it reaches the inlet port. Here it is subjected to higher temperatures and more room for expansion than a similar charge encounters in the intake manifold and ports of a four-stroke engine. Furthermore, the induction system of a two-stroke is less efficient than that of a cam-and-valve engine, and anything that will help to get a greater quantity of air-fuel into the cylinder in the short time available will greatly improve its performance. Therefore, the cooling effect of the nitrous oxide helps even more on two-strokes than it does on four-strokes. Ron also pointed out that nitrous systems on such engines usually require a slightly greater percentage of extra fuel enrichment in proportion to the N²O.

The manner in which a nitrous system can be employed on such a bike is enlightening, too. The particular motorcycle being tested, a Can Am frame with a Rotax Bombardier engine, is used for 250-cc flat-track competition. It is raced on a half-mile dirt oval, and consequently uses brakes and a transmission (unlike bigger, fuel-burning Speedway bikes which race on shorter tracks). The nitrous oxide is used primarily at the start of the race and coming out of the turns, and the advantage is that it can serve as a substitute for shifting gears. In other words, rather than starting in first gear, the rider can start in second (or even third in some cases), and can use the extra power to get out ahead of the pack. And rather than downshifting in the turns, he can hit the nitrous about halfway through the turn and the bike will accelerate from the slower speed

On the Merlin, a nitrous oxide injector nozzle can easily be inserted in the volute drain between the supercharger and the intercooler.

Enrichment fuel can be injected at the fuel discharge nozzle.

as if he had downshifted. The advantages are obvious. When asked if the nitrous were legal in his class, the rider responded, "We don't ask and they don't tell us we can't use it." The system on his bike is completely exposed, including the nitrous cylinders, and he hasn't been asked to remove it yet.

Not too many dirt bikes are using nitrous systems in competition at this point. But Ron said that he has shipped several similar units to various parts of the country. When asked how the others seemed to be working, he answered characteristically, "After a guy buys one and puts it on his bike for a race—when he calls back Monday morning you can almost see his big smile right on the telephone."

NITROUS ON LARGE ENGINES

In the earlier part of this chapter, while discussing the history of nitrous oxide injection for various racing applications, we mentioned the Unlimited Hydroplane planes. Since these large racing craft have for years relied on the twelve-cylinder Rolls Royce and Allison WWII airplane engines to create their "unlimited" power, it stands to reason that they would be very interested in any type of power augmentation system available for such engines. As far back as the early 1960's some of the front-running hydros were fitted with nitrous oxide systems. One of the most famous of all unlimited hydros, Miss Bardahl, piloted by Ron Musson, was using N_2O in 1962 and the team's chief mechanic, Dixon Smith, is still building nitrous units (with Jim Lucero at Bill Muncey's shop in Seattle) for large boat engines. The Exide Battery Special (driven by Bill Brown), is another hydro that was using nitrous in the mid 60's, and his mechanic, Bernie Van Cleve, is often mentioned with early developers of nitrous systems. The Miss U.S.A. boat was also using N_2O at this time. Unfortunately, however, at the 1966 President's Cup races held on the Potomac in Washington, D.C., three top drivers—Ron Musson, Donnie Ray Wilson, and Rex Manchester—were killed in two accidents occurring the same day, and rumors filtered through the racing ranks that nitrous oxide had something to do with the tragedy. Though these rumors were substantially unfounded, they did set back development of nitrous systems in hydroplanes for a while.

Today nearly all of the Unlimited Hydroplanes racing the A.P.B.A. national circuit are using nitrous oxide injections—which is legal in all classes—and the majority of these are using systems built and designed by Jim Lucero, the chief mechanic for Bill Muncey Industries in Seattle, Washington. Unfortunately, Jim was very reluctant to discuss any of the specifics of his own system, stating only that other types of nitrous injectors being manufactured today were "crude" compared to his. Apparently one of the major advances of his system is the design of the nitrous injector nozzles, which he claims vastly improves the even distribution of the N_2O and fuel in the intake. His system does not use an intercooler, and the N_2O is apparently injected between the supercharger and the intake ports. Most of his units (about fifteen have been installed) are made for the 1650-ci Rolls Royce Merlin. This engine is currently winning about 95% of all races, the next most popular engine being the 1710-inch Allison. A typical nitrous system for such a boat uses about thirty pounds of N_2O, usually contained in three ten-pound bottles similar to those used in automotive applications. The system is employed primarily for acceleration in the turns during a typical fifteen-mile race. Lucero would not give exact horsepower capabilities for his system, stating only that, "You can get as much as you want." But the typical Merlin engine is modified to produce about 2600 horsepower *without* the N_2O. If you want to find out more details than this about Lucero's nitrous oxide injection secrets, you'll probably have to purchase one of his units . . . which costs about $1500.

A guy who is more willing to talk about nitrous injection in large aircraft engines is Dave Zeuschel; but he readily admits that he had more problems than success with the stuff, and he no longer uses it on his engines. Dave primarily builds Rolls Royce and Allison engines for restored World War II fighter planes and for similar modified planes used in pylon racing, but some of his past experience with nitrous might be helpful to our understanding of current systems.

Dave said that he had first seen nitrous used on the large power boats, and that he used Ricardo's book as his initial source of technical information. He relied primarily on the "five-pounds-per-100 horsepower-per-minute" figure noted in the Ricardo account to develop his first system. He arrived at nitrous nozzle sizes by hooking up a line from a bottle to the nozzle, turning the nitrous on, and then noting how many pounds of N_2O flowed through the nozzle in one minute. In this manner he could calculate the flow rates, in pounds-per-minute, of various sized nozzles, and could use them to dial in horsepower increases for the system on the engine.

In actual practice on racing airplane applications, Dave would locate the nitrous injector nozzle between the supercharger and the aftercooler, either in the volute drain of the blower or just ahead of the cooler, and he would add enrichment fuel through the fuel discharge nozzle. Approximately 150 pounds of liquid nitrous oxide would be carried on the plane (total weight of the system was about 300-400 pounds), which would give an extra 200 horsepower charge for about thirteen minutes—the normal length of a race.

The biggest problem encountered by Dave with a system of this size and used under these conditions was keeping the flow rates of both the nitrous oxide and the extra fuel constant, so that their percentages would remain balanced throughout their use. Naturally, if too little fuel or too much N_2O were injected, the engine would have a tendency to blow up (as was proven on a few occasions)—and that's not much fun in an airplane. As Dave tells it, "The key to the whole thing seemed to be the enrichment pump," meaning the pump which would supply the extra fuel when the nitrous was being injected. He found that an engine-driven pump seemed to work the best (similar to the type used for fuel injection systems on race cars). The second major problem was keeping the pressure and the flow rate of N_2O from the tanks to the nozzle constant. Obviously the configuration of an airplane would not allow the placing of three sixty-pound bottles of N_2O very near the engine, so the lines had to be fairly long to begin with. Once the N_2O line was filled and feeding the engine, keeping the nitrous liquified was sometimes difficult. Dave discovered, for one thing, that any "step down" or restriction in the line would act as a venturi, and cause the nitrous oxide to begin vaporizing at that point. A bigger difficulty was maintaining a constant pressure from the large N_2O tanks to the nozzle. With all of the tanks filled to capacity at the beginning of the race, the system might "surge" when the pilot first pressed the button, delivering too much nitrous to the engine. On the other hand, towards the end of the race, as the tanks began to empty, the nitrous delivery would fall off, creating an imbalance of extra enrichment fuel being fed to the engine. To correct the first problem, various types of pressure regulators were tried. To compensate for the second, Dave added a tank of pressurized nitrogen and tapped this into the bottoms of the nitrous oxide tanks to keep a constant source of pressure feeding the liquid out the other end. Another solution to the pressure problem would have been to carry a larger quantity of N_2O on the plane so the tanks would not run low, but they obviously did not want to carry the extra weight of unused liquid nitrous oxide on a racing airplane.

Dave has since given up nitrous oxide projects, being one of the believers of "I can blow up engines

Ron Hammel's daily transportation, a turbocharged diesel-powered Dodge pickup, has run several thousand trouble-free miles with a 10,000 RPM nitrous injector.

without it." *But the problems he encountered—those of maintaining constant correct metering of both the nitrous oxide and the enrichment fuel and of maintaining steady feed pressure in the emptying nitrous bottle—are two of the major areas still open for further improvement in nitrous oxide injection systems today.*

NITROUS WITH DIESEL ENGINES

Ron Hammel has his own ideas about what is fun to drive. Since he has been working with nitrous oxide for so many years, building all sorts of exotic units for every conceivable type of high-power engine, you might expect him to be the owner of a street stormer himself. Yes, his daily transportation is nitrous oxide injected—but the vehicle is not something you would guess.

It's a bright blue (nitrous oxide bottle blue, to be exact) 1969 Dodge four door pickup—powered by a turbocharged Perkins D-354 (354 cu. in.) diesel engine, not your usual sort of hot rod. But the beast is a runner, and from it Ron has learned quite a bit about using nitrous oxide with diesel power. The engine is almost stock (it has a ported head and stronger valve springs), and it is mated to a Torqueflite automatic transmission (since the T-flite was the only readily available automatic that doesn't need engine manifold vacuum for shifting). The Perkins engine is available with a turbocharger option, but Ron added an aftermarket Rajay turbo to his, which delivers fifteen pounds boost at full throttle. The engine's compression ratio is 16:1.

Ron feels that nitrous oxide is of little benefit on diesels unless they are turbocharged or supercharged—"The nitrous works almost like an aftercooler. The turbo heats up the incoming air as it compresses it, but with nitrous oxide the air comes out of the turbo at about 20° F." On Ron's particular engine, he injects the N_2O at the mouth of the turbocharger, and finds this method to work quite well. Presumably the nitrous could be added behind the turbo, where it might be able to retain a denser charge. As a matter of fact, just recently Ron tested a 283 cubic-inch Nissan diesel, to which he had fitted a turbocharger, and found through comparative testing on his dyno that an N_2O injector placed about 12 inches downstream from the turbo produced about 15% greater horsepower than one at the mouth of the turbocharger.

Because of the characteristics of a diesel engine, "leaning" with nitrous is not a problem, as it is in gasoline or fuel motors. Direct cylinder-injected diesels induct only air through the intake manifold and intake valves, and this air intake is not "throttled" as it is on other engines. In other words, the air is in-inducted at full throttle all the time; but the fuel, which is injected through individual nozzles directly into the cylinders precisely at the right moment for combustion, is increased or decreased in volume to control speed. Therefore, a diesel engine compresses relatively the same volume of air on each stroke, whether at part throttle or full throttle. This is why a diesel gives better efficiency than a gasoline engine at slower speeds (the gasoline engine is utilizing very little of the total potential volumetric efficiency until it reaches wide-open throttle). This is also why a diesel can be injected with

straight N_2O, without adding extra fuel at the same time. By the same token, a diesel can be operated on nitrous for a much longer time than spark-ignition engines can. Ron loves to describe how he uses the nitrous oxide to help climb steep grades in his truck. When asked how long he can keep the nitrous turned on at one shot he grins and replies, "As long as the bottle holds out." Ron recommends using a large bottle on diesel applications.

Injecting additional fuel into the airstream along with the nitrous oxide would not work on a diesel engine. Such an engine has no ignition system, and relies on the timed spray of fuel from the cylinder injector to trigger ignition (the fuel immediately explodes because of the heat of the severely compressed air; therefore diesels are known as compression-ignition engines). If extra diesel fuel were sprayed into the intake manifold and allowed to enter the cylinder along with the air, it would ignite too early (causing an effect similar to preignition in a spark-ignition engine). The nitrous can be injected into the air stream at any time since it is not combustible by itself. The only method for properly enriching the fuel charge of a diesel when the nitrous is turned on would be to somehow rework the fuel injection metering system to increase the flow a given percentage on demand—and such reworking could be difficult and expensive to devise. Of course, it is possible to enlarge the fuel injector nozzles so that the engine will deliver a greater percentage of fuel at all speeds—and Ron did this on his engine.

Although he couldn't inject diesel oil or gasoline with the nitrous into the turbo, Ron found that he could use alcohol (methanol) as an enrichment fuel on his diesel. The alcohol has a high enough knock limit that it will not explode in the diesel cylinder until combustion of the injected diesel fuel begins. It is the only fuel Ron found that could be used this way. However, the use of alcohol as an enrichment fuel on a diesel posed problems. First of all, it had to be carried in a separate tank or container (that wasn't too difficult to solve). And secondly, it needed some sort of pump or pressure device to deliver it to the engine. Since the alcohol would only be fed to the engine at full throttle, and since the turbocharger would be creating plenty of pressure in the intake manifold under this condition, Ron simply tapped a pressure line from the intake manifold to the top of the alcohol tank. Since the manifold has nothing in it but air (until the nitrous is turned on), and since it develops only 15 psi pressure, he figured it would be a safe source of compressed air for a tank that wouldn't

The nitrous nozzle is located at the mouth of the turbo (arrow) and the system can be operated without enrichment fuel, or with a separate methanol fuel enrichment system (not shown).

have to be very strong. It works fine. The outlet line from the pressurized alcohol tank leads to what would normally be the extra gasoline solenoid on the nitrous unit, and from the solenoid the alcohol line leads to a jet placed next to the N²O nozzle at the mouth of the turbo.

Ron developed the total system on his diesel over a period of time, and kept track of the improvements as he went. The gains in torque worked out like this:

Stock engine	225 lb/ft
With Turbocharger	250 lb/ft
With richened fuel injectors	350 lb/ft
With N²O and methanol	450 lb/ft

Ron increased the diesel fuel delivery by approximately 30%. He also noted that with the nitrous and alcohol turned on, the exhaust temperature of the engine never exceeds 1250 degrees. Without the N²O, under a full turbo boost condition (such as climbing a grade), the intake manifold temperature would be about 280°. With nitrous added, this temperature drops to 160° and 1½ pounds of manifold pressure and about 40 lbs-ft of torque are gained. With the nitrous and methanol added together, Ron gets another 2 pounds of boost and a total of 100 extra lbs-ft of torque.

Hammel hasn't tried his nitrous/alcohol system on many other diesel engines, but he did learn a lesson on one occasion. A contestant at Bonneville was running a small four-cylinder diesel in a sports car and he asked Ron to add a nitrous-alcohol injection system to his engine. Ron did so, and when the customer hit the button at speed on the salt flats he immediately blew all the pistons out of his engine.

The problem, Ron decided later, was that this small diesel was of the prechamber or "pre-cup" design, which is similar to a stratified charge gasoline engine. Such a diesel usually runs a much higher compression ratio in the main cylinder, and this compression was high enough to ignite the alcohol spontaneously before the timed diesel injection. If the N²O alone had been added to the engine, it probably would have worked fine, but as Ron said, "He wasn't too excited about trying any further experiments." Ron's engine, like most larger diesels, is of the direct injection (D.I.) type, and the system apparently works fine on these. In fact, it is currently being employed by several of the large turbocharged diesels being used in the Midwest for tractor pull competition.

NITROUS OXIDE— FUTURE POSSIBILITIES

Nitrous oxide injection as a turn-it-on, turn-it-off burst of extra horsepower for all types of internal combustion engines sounds wonderful—and it generally is. If used improperly or without restraint, it can lead to some serious problems in your engine. However, when put together and dialed in carefully, nitrous oxide appears to combine the beneficial properties of several potent fuels and performance components, without their drawbacks. It may be both the elixir and the panacea of the high performance engine, in one easy-to-swallow capsule.

Plus, there is plenty of potential for improvement. To reiterate the evaluation made by Jim Lucero, the typical nitrous oxide injection system in use today is relatively "crude." That's a harsh term, maybe "simple" or "uncomplicated" might be more appropriate. But the fact remains that we are still using N²O injection in basically the same configuration used thirty years ago—with even less technical monitoring and data-collecting of in-use systems to guide further development. The current manufacturers of nitrous oxide systems are hot rodders, and their developments have primarily been the result of a trial-and-error approach. They know "approximately" how much fuel will work best with what amounts of N²O; they know what size nozzles

Ron Hammel recently dyno-tested a 327 cid Nissan-Chrysler prechamber diesel to which he added a Rajay turbocharger and nitrous oxide injection. No enrichment fuel was added, and the dose of N²O was limited to about one-fourth that for a similar-sized gasoline engine.

For initial tests Ron placed the N²O nozzle at the mouth of the turbo, but found that a nozzle location several inches downstream from the compressor (arrow) increased the power output by 4%. Total torque gain with nitrous oxide on this engine was 15%.

flow given volumes; they know about how much extra horsepower a set amount of N²O will create; and they know too much N²O will cause an engine to blow. Most of all, they know that dumping N²O and extra fuel into an engine will create an immediate and impressive increase in power. The current state of the art of nitrous oxide injection is similar to the periods when racers discovered that eight Stromberg 97's made a Chrysler Hemi run a lot faster than four did, or when they found out that the GMC 6-71 blower made it run faster than anything.

Consequently, the significant improvements in nitrous systems over the years have been directed primarily at eliminating the mechanical bugs: finding valves that wouldn't malfunction; developing Teflon seats for solenoid valves to insure complete shutoff; creating better methods for filtering dirt particles from the system; and of course, devising more ingenious ways to conceal the whole system. These are practical improvements. They make nitrous oxide injection reliable.

What can we expect from nitrous oxide in the future? Plenty. Some of the foreseeable improvements will be important—such as further experimentation to determine where the nozzles should be located to get the optimum benefit from the nitrous, or developing a better means of ensuring a constant flow and pressure of N²O from the bot-

tle to the nozzles. Beyond trial-and-error progress, which will undoubtedly evolve slowly, we will hopefully see some well-documented engineering studies performed on nitrous oxide and the reactions inside an internal combustion engine. As of this writing, very little technical information exists about the properties of nitrous oxide and its exact chemical/mechanical relationship to combustion engine processes. The studies conducted in the past often disagreed, and the auto enthusiast searching for guidance is pressed to find much about N²O in a handbook of chemistry, physics or thermodynamics. The few values generally listed for the physical properties of N²O often vary (and are almost always expressed in widely-differing units). For instance, five different values for the latent heat of vaporization of N²O can be found, only two of which are closely matched. The table of nitrous oxide properties presented here is culled from several varied sources and some of the values may not correlate with all other references. An effort was made to select the most widely accepted value. At least the available information is set forth here for those interested, and involved, with the subject.

Likewise, readers will undoubtedly notice major discrepancies between the results or the calculations of the British and American WW II testing of nitrous oxide and what we find to be

'the results of such systems in practice today. Much of the reason for differences in early testing was caused by the widely-varying pressure or temperature at which the N²O was injected into the manifold. For instance, the British results would seem to show a decided power advantage when using unpressurized liquid N²O rather than pressurized liquid. However, you will notice that the unpressurized liquid was injected at -88.7°C (-128.3°F), or at the vaporization point, while the pressurized N²O was injected at 0°C (32°F) In practice, the current pressurized nitrous oxide systems (if they are operating as intended), are injecting the N²O at its vaporizing temperature—so the unpressurized figures of the British should be more applicable to the present systems.

A major problem is determining the temperature at which the N²O is coming out of the nozzle. More data should be collected about temperature and pressure changes at different locations in the manifold and combustion chamber when the nitrous oxide is injected at various points. Perhaps someone will also be able to determine what the extra oxygen and inert nitrogen released during the combustion process do to alter that combustion. For instance, at what temperature, considering the pressure in the combustion chamber, does the N²O dissociate (there are three widely-varying temperatures listed for dissociation of N²O at atmospheric pressure). We likewise need to know at what pressures and at what temperatures, in an actual onboard system, the N²O remains liquid or turns to gas. It is surprising that not one of the N²O users or developers (including the WW II researchers) discussed the critical temperature and pressure of N²O. The critical temperature is that value at which a gas cannot be changed into a liquid by pressurizing (no matter how much pressure is applied); and the critical pressure is the pressure exerted by the liquid (its vapor tension) on the container at the critical temp (in other words, the pressure necessary to keep the substance a liquid at that temperature). Considerable research indicates the critical temperature and pressure of nitrous oxide are 102.2°F and 1278.03 psi, respectively. From this it is obvious that considerable attention must be given to the temperatures playing upon the nitrous bottle and all of the lines between it and the injection nozzle. Furthermore, respect should be given to the pressures which can develop in the system—well above the 800 psi under "normal" conditions.

It appears, at this point, that the perfection and refinement of nitrous oxide injection in the future lies in: 1) establishing better guideline data on N²O and its reactions, 2) documenting and optimizing the flow of N²O as a liquid throughout the system, and 3) developing the best combinations of nozzle design, manifold configuration, and nozzle location to maximize both the cooling efficiency of the N²O and the even vaporization, controlled pressurization and distribution of the air-fuel charge. Compared to the power increases already being generated from relatively simple N²O injection systems, these future improvements may not add much to performance but they will greatly improve reliability.

We are no longer on the frontier of nitrous oxide development. The explorers made their initial discoveries decades ago; the pioneers of current systems have many years of experience behind them; now is the time to enjoy the benefits of this fertile new field of engine performance. Over-the-counter systems are now as readily available as superchargers or turbochargers. And, if you are a serious hot rodder, this road to "instant power" may be to your liking. In fact, you may be the one who will solve some of the mysteries of this wonderful potion that puts people to sleep but wakes automotive engines up.

NITROUS OXIDE SYSTEM SUPPLIERS

Marvin Miller Manufacturing
7745 S. Greenleaf Ave.
Whittier, California 90602

   Sales and Marketing
   15611 Product Lane, B-16
   Huntington Beach, California 92649
   (714) 898-9645

Nitrous Oxide Systems
2667 E. 28th. Street, Suite 508
Long Beach, California 90806
(213) 595-7074

10,000 RPM Speed Equipment
22624 S. Normandie Ave.
Torrance, California 90502
(213) 533-9282

ORV Engineering
P.O. Box 813
Azusa, California 91702
(213) 339-6634

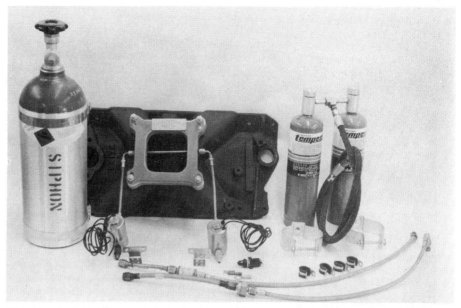

This typical-looking system is actually quite unique. Developed by ORV Engineering, this unit injects propane, instead of gasoline, as the additional fuel. ORV claims the use of propane improves low-speed engine response.

Future testing with nitrous oxide will no doubt unlock further performance potential. As current designers develop better hardware, the systems will be cheaper, more reliable and more easily obtained.

SUPERCHARGING

By LARRY ATHERTON

SUPERCHARGING

The subject is really volumetric efficiency. High lift cams, tunnel ram manifolds, polished and ported heads are a few of the many ways power searchers fulfill this need. When these intricate modifications provide the desired results, they almost always are successful because of the improvement in the engine volumetric efficiency. Therefore, with the exception of special fuels and oxidizers, *volumetric efficiency is the true key to performance.*

What is volumetric efficiency? A textbook definition might be: the mass of fresh mixture which passes into the cylinder in one suction stroke, divided by the mass of this mixture which would fill the piston displacement at inlet density. This sounds like a typical scientific explanation, virtually unintelligible. In simpler terms, one could say that volumetric efficiency is really a measure of how much air-fuel mixture an engine will take at wide open throttle. The more available mixture to burn, the more power the engine will produce. Faced with this fact, it almost seems obvious that more power can be had if we can just force more air-fuel mixture down the engine's throat. This is exactly the purpose of a supercharg-

Some guys think the GMC 6-71 blower is a factory option on Top Fuel Chryslers. In tact, the entire series of GMC blowers has always been used for exhaust scavenging of GMC diesel engines. However, racers have been using them on race engines for over 30 years.

This is what a GMC supercharger looks like before it gets bolted onto a racing engine. These GMC blower cases are being inspected prior to assembly on a Detroit Diesel.

ing system, and in particular the Roots compressor, which is the subject of this chapter.

In order to accomplish our goal of "throat-stuffing," and to have a finished product that will not only provide eye-watering performance, but also make more than one test run down the driveway, we should have a firm understanding of supercharger systems. The Roots-type supercharger falls into the broad classification of a displacement compressor, more specifically a *rotating displacement compressor.* The term displacement refers to the fact that with each full rotation of the compressor elements, *a specific fixed volume of air is pumped from the inlet side to the exhaust outlet.* A very common compressor, of the displacement type, is the internal combustion engine. This is true of both the piston engine and the Wankel rotary design. With each stroke of the piston, on the intake cycle, the displacement of the piston is the sole factor controlling the *volume* of air that will be compressed — the *density* of this volume is determined by the carburetor restriction, cam specs, etc. Compressors of the Roots type act somewhat like a piston moving in a cylinder, providing a pulsing flow of air as the rotors turn inside the housing. *The length and diameter of the rotors determine the volume of air that will be moved through the compressor per rotation of the rotors.*

This GMC-designed Roots blower is the most popular and rugged supercharger for street or strip use. Air is drawn through the two large top ports and "captured" by the rotors as they move in opposite directions. The pocket of captured air is then delivered to the outlet ports on the bottom of the housing.

The most popular type of Roots supercharger is the GMC 4-71 or 6-71 blower. Currently these models utilize a *three lobe rotor*, that is, there are three blades positioned 120° apart on each of the two rotor shafts. The effect of this is to increase the number of pumping cycles and reduce the surging of air on the outlet side — providing a more stable, less restrictive flow. Since each "gulp" of air is less turbulent with a three-vane, versus a two-vane type, the overall efficiency is somewhat greater.

A further example of the excellent engineering in the GMC Roots blower is the use of carefully machined helical-shaped rotors. The smooth twist in each rotor provides an increase in efficiency while again reducing the pulsed flow.

There are several Roots blowers that use a straight vane and/or two-lobe rotors. These designs, although not as sophisticated as the GMC, have proven themselves capable performers. One can even draw an argument for the use of a two-vane rotor. If you consider the three-vane type has four additional mating surfaces that can allow air leakage and that can contact each other when flex and vibration are created by high speed operation, they don't look very good for racing use. Additionally, the elaborate machining techniques used to manufacture a three-vane rotor make it very expensive for a company that wishes to build a Roots blower specifically for high performance use. So, even though there may be a few blowers with the two-vane system, one must look at the entire package and decide if there are other advantages built into the unit that offset the possible disadvantages of the two vanes. Things to consider might be: inlet and outlet ports shaped for

good flow at high speed, stronger end plates, stiffer blower housings, smaller size (if desired), etc.

We have already mentioned efficiency, and since this is so important in relation to supercharging systems, perhaps it would be enlightening to cover a little more ground in this area. Blower efficiency is a measure of the amount of air that the supercharger can pump relative to the amount of energy (horsepower) it consumes. Further, efficiency can also refer to the amount of boost that the system delivers compared to the amount of boost desired at a specific engine speed. The first definition we call the *design efficiency* and the second, the *system efficiency*.

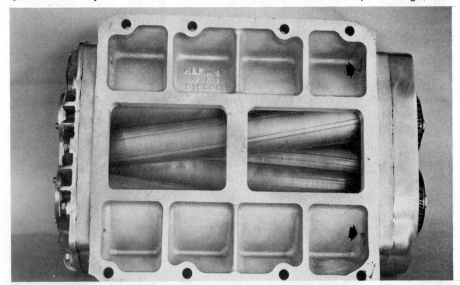

The lower outlet ports deliver the air-fuel charge to the intake manifold. Return leakage is minimized through the use of very close internal clearances. Arrows indicate the ports in the case that must be plugged. These holes allowed oil to circulate in the truck application; if not closed off, lube will drain from the front cover either into or onto the intake manifold.

The design efficiency of the Roots-type blower is good, but certainly not at the top of the pack. This is where the turbocharger really shines. With its exhaust-driven compressor, the turbo is the most efficient (design efficient) system when one considers the amount of horsepower required to drive the unit to a particular boost level (a turbo does not have a direct mechanical link to the engine and does not absorb horsepower during the operation). This advantage becomes greater as the engine speed goes up and as the boost is increased. However, the turbo isn't perfect either, for when one looks at the system efficiency, at least for low speed "off-road" use, the turbo has a few problems. The Roots-type system is belt-driven directly by the engine. This then insures that the blower will respond to the engine demand for additional boost immediately when the rpm goes up. This is not the case with the turbo—since exhaust pressure must first build, then the turbine wheel must speed up as a result of this pressure, and finally the inlet charge will receive more boost. This chain of events results in "turbo-lag," or less system efficiency at lower speed than the Roots type. As the speed and boost levels go up, however, the turbo passes the Roots in system efficiency because the turbo likes speed (it operates efficiently at turbo shaft speeds as high as 100,000 rpm), and is small and very efficient at extremely high constant boost requirements. On the other hand, as the Roots speed goes up, the unit becomes much less efficient (at least when compared to a turbo).

At first examination, it would seem that the turbo really has it over the Roots blower. Well, it does, except for the low- to medium-speed range, and especially during transition from idle to full throttle. And guess what, that's perfect for street and street/strip driving. The Roots design with its direct coupling to the engine will provide horsepower, instantly.

The design efficiency of the Roots type is, as we've said, better at low boost levels, falling off at higher pressures. When the engine is running at idle or light throttle cruise, the engine vacuum tends to help the blower turn over (it is not uncommon for the blower rotors to rotate of their own accord, with the belt removed, under these conditions). The efficiency at this point is very high, probably 90 to 95%, however, no boost is being provided; the entire intake system is operating under normal vacuum conditions. As engine speed increases, along with a corresponding decrease in throttle plate restriction (throttle open wider), the blower will begin to produce a positive pressure boost. With the system providing a pressure level of about 3 psi the efficiency is still very high, 80 to 90%. As boost continues to go up, to say 7 or 8 psi, the efficiency drops to 70 to 80%, still not bad. Beyond this boost level, the Roots type begins to fall on its face, with efficiencies dropping as low as 50% at pressures near 14 psi. Pressure levels over 8 or 9 psi are beyond the scope of this book and not advisable for anything other than an all-out drag car, therefore, 75% efficiency at these moderate boost levels speaks well for the Roots-type system.

All Roots superchargers have two moving elements, or rotors, that rotate in opposite directions. The left element rotates in the same direction as the engine and the right element in opposition. As the air-fuel mix enters

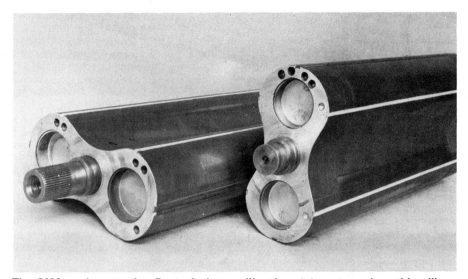

The GMC, and most other Roots designs, utilize three lobe rotors, since this will reduce pulsing of the intake charge. Two lobe designs have been experimented with in search of additional strength while giving up little in pumping efficiency. The creation seen above provided the sought-for rigidity, but the violent pulsing led to incurable tuning problems.

the blower it is "captured" between one of the rotors and the case, then moving in an out-and-down direction, "pushed" to the plenum area beneath the rotors. Due to the design and shape of the rotors, the air mix cannot return to the inlet side except through the small spaces between the rotors or through the space between the rotors and the case end plates. Air is a very slippery critter and will take good advantage of every leak space, no matter how small. However, the smaller the better (for us, not the air). These critical clearances dictate the difference between a new, efficient unit and one that does its job poorly. These leak-space clearances are measured in thousandths of an inch (more on the specifics later) with a total span from

tight to loose of under 0.030-inch. There must be a clearance level between rotating parts that both reduces air leaks to a minimum acceptable level and allows the moving parts sufficient room to operate without contacting one another even at high speeds and high temperatures. These critical dimensions make the Roots blower very sensitive to foreign matter. Dust, dirt, and, even worse, small rocks can tear a blower up quickly. The moral of the story is to *always run an air cleaner,* don't take chances!

The rotors are connected by an angle-cut (on GMC type) gear train that runs in a bath of oil. The gear case, located on the front of the blower housing, is sealed from the air-pump section with special shaft seals. The gear train is also responsible for the precise rotor-to-rotor timing. Excessive play between these gears would allow the rotors to touch and chew themselves to pieces. So, although a Roots supercharger is just a "case with a couple of flappers," flapper size and position are all important.

ROOTS SYSTEM ADVANTAGES

Supercharging an internal combustion engine with a Roots-type compressor will realistically involve some good points and some problem areas. First, let's have a look at the advantages. The most important, at least the first thought of, is more horsepower. Power increases of approximately 30 to 60% are possible. This is with the low octane gas and low compression used in most street engines. An average increase of better than 100 horsepower is certainly a convincing reason to bolt one of these babies under or through (that's one of the disadvantages we'll

GMC blowers, once a very specialized addition to any street or race car, are now available across the counter at a good number of well-equipped speed shops. Phil Lukens, at Blair's Speed in Pasadena, California, can supply ready-to-bolt-on units and drive kits.

get to later) your hood. Along with the performance potential of a Roots blower, there are other reasons to choose a "huffer" over more traditional hop-up techniques or other "super power" alternatives.

The Roots blower is a very simple and straightforward contraption. It doesn't require any pre-oiling after standing still for several days or weeks. There are no wastegates or priority valves to stick open or closed. Along with simplicity, comes reliability, when properly prepared, and many thousands of street miles are not at all unusual. Your first thought when looking at the local hot-dogger's mill, with that 6-71 pumper on top, may be "Oh boy, I bet this turkey is good for one hard pass. I wonder if he'd like to race cross-country. I'd have him then!" Well, there's more than one case on record of a Roots blown engine built just for a cross-country hop. After all, the "Jimmy" was originally designed for exactly that purpose.

The turbocharger requires special exhaust piping that runs at very high temperatures. Also, the turbo is sensitive to camshaft profile. The Roots system suffers from neither of these drawbacks. Although the right cam can "sharpen" the whole package, special cam grinds are not necessary since the blower is not powered by exhaust gas flow. This is not just a minor point. Trying to tune up your supercharger by changing cams is no easy task, and can be very frustrating for those of us that don't have a computer terminal in our garage. This is not to mention that the Roots system just plain blows the doors off any other design in eye appeal. That big box sure looks nasty.

There are also several operational advantages to the Roots system, not the least of which is the generally smoother engine performance. Because of the improved fuel vaporization, due to compressor turbulence, a more uniform distribution of air mix is possible, contributing both to smoother running and a possible decrease in emissions. The direct downward travel of the air mix insures easy starting. Since the rotors turn even during en-

gine cranking and Newton's law of the apple works in our favor, the air mix finds its way to the intake valves with very little difficulty. But you say, "What if the blower belt fails, especially in the middle of the boonies?" Guess what, you can still drive your iron horse home! The straight shot once again pays off. Engine vacuum will generally turn the blower rotors slowly, even without a drive belt, while gravity does the rest. The very worst case, however, would be if the blower seizes due to bearing failure, or if a small rock found its way between the rotors. After removing what's left of the drive belt, your rod can still be started and driven; admittedly you'll be a bit shy on power, but it will run. Why? Remember those small clearances we mentioned earlier. Well, as small as they are, they will leak enough air mix by to fire the engine, and get you by in an emergency. There was one case reported to us of a hot rodder that experienced just such a problem (probably didn't read this book before he prepped his blower). Unfortunately, this seizure occurred

Blower drives evolved through several stages of development. The V-Belt was the predecessor to the Gilmer drive. Although V-Belts are rarely used today as Roots compressor drives, there are a few diehards willing to endure the fabrication problems for the furtherment of "uniqueness."

The Gilmer belt brought reliability to Roots supercharging. Their capacity for heavy loads, high speed, and vibration absorption, insures their continued use for many years.

The rotor geartrain drive is responsible for maintaining precise rotor-to-rotor timing (or phase). The angle-cut gears operate in an oil bath, and will provide high reliability as long as ample lube is present and a minimum of foreign material enters the blower.

several hundred miles from home. He first thought about hitching it 50 miles to the next town hoping to find a blower belt (probably the only one there would be too short), and he feared his pride and joy would be missing when he returned. After that mental terror, he decided to see if it would start and run long enough to get him to the next phone. It not only started, but he

was able to drive it all the way home, at better than 50 mph, no less! The Roots system is a forgiving one with many practical advantages.

The blower is normally driven by a toothed Gilmer belt arrangement. The upper and lower pulleys are easily changed to modify the overdrive or underdrive percentages, and although we will go into this in more detail later, this

system will assist you in final tuning the boost to the proper level to maximize the performance while minimizing detonation or preignition. Merely by swapping pulleys, the entire boost curve can be altered to suit your own requirements. Also, the Gilmer drive system is one of the most reliable power transmitters. A properly designed pulley setup will give many thousands of trouble-free miles, and since spare drive belts are neither expensive nor hard to store, it's not a bad idea to carry a spare. In just a few minutes with the right wrench, you can be back on the road again.

Finally, the last advantage of the Roots system that we will cover (there are undoubtedly more we have not mentioned) is the blowers' resistance to damage from backfire. We are assuming that the fuel being used is gasoline, not alcohol or nitro, since both of these will cause severe damage if a backfire occurs. Gasoline, however, will generally leave things in good condition, providing a blow-off valve has been incorporated on the pressure side. The specifics of the blow-off valve will be discussed later in the sections covering the nuts and bolts of the Roots installation.

At this point you may think that the old Jimmy is a sure bet, but before you run amuck looking for a 6-71 and some bolts, read on as we take a close look at some of the disadvantages of the Roots supercharger.

The GMC blower is a very simple device, however, the few parts that it contains operate in very close proximity to one another. Many areas must be checked for correct clearance and alignment. The arrows indicate a few of the important places that an expert must carefully check to insure long life and efficient operation. Shown are: A) Rotor-to-case lower clearance, B) Rotor-to-case upper clearance, C) Front cover-to-case pin (to adjust A and B), D) Rotor balance, E) Rotor-to-rotor clearance, F) Rotor-to-end plate clearance, G) Rotor phase, H) Cover support O rings, I) high precision bearings.

DISADVANTAGES OF THE ROOTS SYSTEM

Like most really good things, there are some "cons" that come with the "pros." Probably the first obvious disadvantage to the Roots blower is size. Most street rods (unless the engine has been drastically lowered) and all normal "door-slammers" will find that an abnormally large hole is required in the hood for clearance. Usually all of the carbs and air cleaners, plus most of the top drive pulley, are "in the wind." This makes the blower a very evident modification, and one can expect the normal crowd of good-looking girls, curious onlookers, degenerate racers, and local authorities to gather within short order after parking at your local hamburger stand. If you think this is a lot of attention for just sitting in a parking lot, just wait until you start that thumper up. You will soon learn that Roots Blowers are nearly as loud as they are big. Both the blower and the belt drive kick in to generate plenty of that well-known "blower scream." If you're the mild-mannered bookworm during the week, and you've had the desire to let it all hang out on the weekend, just bolt a blower on your '57 Chevy and you've got it!

You'll have it, that is, if you manage to overcome another problem area, connecting the throttle shafts to your right foot. The carburetors sit about 6 or 7 inches higher than stock and this can make linkage hookup difficult. There are two common methods of solving this problem and they both will

Stock GMC blowers can be found tucked away in the corners of many shops; these are fine "bargains," but remember they must undergo much modification if you expect reliable performance on the street or strip.

work well. Installing a cable throttle is the most straightforward approach since there are usually many lengths that can be purchased through your local dealer. The throttle cable and accelerator pedal used on all later Chrysler product cars are very good choices. Your local Mopar parts department can usually provide all the needed parts right from stock, and at a reasonable price. Cable lengths can be had from about 3 or 4 inches to over 5 feet (used on vans); all you need to find is a sharp parts man to order the right numbers. The cable bolts to the firewall with one bolt and requires two small

holes (about ¼-inch) to complete the installation. On the carburetor end, a small mounting bracket can be made without much trouble from virtually any stock Mopar throttle cable bracket.

Another common approach used in the design of carburetor linkage is the bellcrank and link rod system. Making all the brackets and rods, plus the drilling, taping, and bending, is no easy chore, even if you are well-versed in the techniques. The end result, if the proper care was taken, however, is usually more appealing to the eye, though probably no more functional, than the cable method. The link rod system will also provide more adjustment latitude of throw and ratio than can be found in a cable linkage, although once the right setting is found there is rarely need for additional correction.

In the advantages section, we mentioned that the blower has good resistance to damage during an engine backfire. Now we will take a look at the other side of the coin. The complete story is that you can never completely eliminate the possibility of damaging the supercharger if the engine "sneezes." The blowoff valve is a step in the right direction and will exhaust excessive pressures that would cause internal damage or cause rupture in about 95% of the instances. The other 5%? It was perhaps best explained by an expert in the field who said, "Using a pop-off valve is like throwing a hand grenade in a phone booth and leaving the door open. If it's a good grenade, good-bye phone booth." Most engine backfires are not of sufficient strength to flatten your phone booth, however, you can bet money that if an intake valve hangs open at 6 pounds of boost, look out. Under a positive intake pressure, most

The Roots blower installation may be more visual than a turbocharger, however, it is more of a "bolt-on" installation, since it requires no exhaust system modifications.

The Roots blower can easily be removed and replaced by a normal four-barrel intake. Providing the water pump is driven by a conventional V-belt, the throttle linkage, gas line, and radiator connections are the only other changes that need be made. This swap can be accomplished in less than one hour with a little practice.

backfires will cause damage. The cough during cold engine start-up is a common low-or-no-boost backfire, and thankfully is almost always handled by the pop-off valve with no serious consequences. We have come to a point where we must emphasize that all systems must be properly designed if you expect to run a Roots blower without a lot of maintenance and repair. There is a right way to do it. We will cover all areas that are essential to reliable operation, and we will do it thoroughly. If you set up your puffer right, you will be very happy with the results. The wrong combination, like many projects that are not undertaken carefully, may be one big headache.

A final note, while on the subject of engine backfire, is that it can be induced by driving without considera-tion for the supercharger. Specifically, this means that getting on and off the throttle in rapid succession can result in a severe lean condition. Carburetors have a rough time keeping the air-fuel ratio correct during normal throttle transition. A lean condition, caused just as the throttle is released, will be boosted into the cylinders if you then stab the throttle immediately. If a back-fire results, it will occur with high boost and raw gas in the blower, and the end result can put you out of business. The moral of this story is, a Roots blown engine is not a toy. Rather, it is a sophisticated power plant that demands respect. It is not unnecessarily troublesome, but specialized, and requires a certain discipline to be adopted in driving. This need not affect your free "expression of thought" once the basic ground rules are understood.

The addition of a supercharger, of the belt driven type, will usually result in a decrease in gas economy. This is not because superchargers are inefficient, but because they are capable of increasing horsepower. The large improvement in power is often well used by the driver, resulting in increased gas consumption. However, if one uses a light foot in driving, it has been demonstrated more than once that Roots blowers will not severely reduce gas mileage. Some increase may even be possible as a result of the improved mix between air and fuel, generated by the turbulence of the blower elements, this can help the fuel distribution and result in improved efficiency and gas economy. More often than not, there will develop a balance between hard acceleration and "featherbedding," usually providing similar or slightly less economy than the pre-supercharged engine supplied.

There are drive and blower kits available from several sources (more on this later), however, there just isn't a complete package with a multi-page instruction sheet. It will be up to you to more or less engineer your own system. You will have to decide who will prepare your blower, which drive kit you will use, whether or not to use water injection, the appropriate percentage of under- or over-drive, and the like. There is at least one complete turbocharging kit that uses a step-by-step approach, and is complete with nuts, bolts, gaskets, etc. The Roots system will be more of a challenge. Fortunately, there are many sources of good additional information; take a look at the list of suppliers at the end of this section. Most of these shops will be happy to answer your questions. We can honestly say, after doing a good deal of research, that all are knowledgeable and concerned about superchargers working correctly (either for street or for racing) and not only about selling all the parts they can. If you run into problems, contact one or more of these people; they have all had a great deal of experience with Roots-type supercharging and will put you on the right track.

Supercharging isn't as easy as bolting on a trick carburetor or ignition, but these methods won't double your horsepower either. If you're still with us, let's go into some detail about the nuts and bolts of the Roots supercharging system.

THE BLOWER

By far, the most common Roots blower used for automotive performance is the GMC 6-71. GMC rated this blower by the amount of air (volume) displaced relative to the engine

The pop-off valve will usually prevent any damage to the blower during engine backfire. Even with this protection, there is still a possibility of backfire damage. With a moderate level of care, though, backfire problems can be virtually eliminated.

The turbo system has a definite advantage of lower noise (at least in the method of drive). The Gilmer belt and pulleys have ribs that interlock with one another, and at high speeds they produce the distinctive "blower sing."

The GMC blower, with the noise it produces, the performance it produces, and the ready visual identification, just seems to be the right way to go on a street rod project. This eyeball popper (still in preparation) is the result of several "billion" hours of effort on the part of Larry Bowers. Larry, an expert on the intricacies of the GMC, will undoubtedly have a real "runner" when the project is completed.

size for which it was intended. The four most common sizes found in the automotive world are the 3-71 (originally designed for a three-cylinder engine, in which each cylinder displaced 71 cubic inches), the 4-71, the 6-71, and the 8-71. The 4-71 and the 6-71 are most suited to supercharging the modern V-8 engine, while the 8-71, although sometimes used for racing, is rather expensive for other than all-out drag cars. GMC utilized these blowers to scavenge their diesel engines which are of two-stroke design. Used as de-designed, they compress air only, no fuel is drawn through the rotors. This results in a very high air temperature after compression and dictates loose clearance requirements for long life. The aluminum alloy used for the rotors and case expands rapidly with heat, and as the parts expand, they come closer to touching. If the rotors contact one another, or the case, the wear rate will increase rapidly, further reducing efficiency while introducing aluminum particles into the engine. Lots of rotor and end clearance is required on diesels, and that's just the way GMC likes them. This just won't do for our requirements; we must custom tailor the blower to live in a new environment.

The single most important reason the GMC blower works well in a high performance application is that it compresses not just air, but an air and fuel mix. We are all aware of the cooling effect brought on when a volatile substance (one that easily evaporates) escapes as vapor. A familar example is the coolness of rubbing alcohol. This, in scientific terms, is called the latent heat of vaporization. When the supercharger draws both air and fuel droplets, the high turbulence will contribute to better fuel vaporization. This vaporization lowers the mix temperature to an extent (this effect is more pronounced with fuels like methanol than with "straight" gasoline). As a result, the internal clearances can be reduced and the efficiency increased. If the fuel charge was not cooled during

Preparing a GMC blower for racing or for street use is a very straightforward and simple job, but some of the work requires fairly complex machining (at least for the backyard mechanic). Unless you have access to such machinery and know how to use it, leave your blower preparation to one of the experts listed in the appendix to this chapter.

This late-model street machine uses a complete 6-71 blower installation, including a Hilborn racing fuel injection system. Even though the machine is operated on pump gas, this setup can be difficult and uneconomical for day-to-day driving. Nonetheless, it is possible.

Two of the weak points in the GMC blower (at least when racing/high performance is considered) are the end plates. They are designed with very little metal around the bearing bores. The additional loads generated by higher rotor speeds will cause cracks to develop and the bearings to shift in the bores.

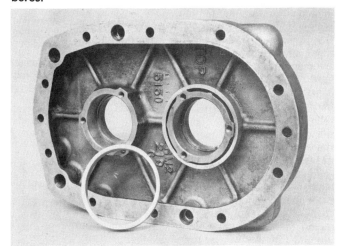

To prevent bearing trouble, the plates should be "O-ringed". This involves press-fitting a steel or aluminum ring around the bore after it has been machined for proper contact.

Left - here the end plate is being machined to accept the support ring. This special fixture, designed and built by Mert Littlefield, centers the cutter by locating on the bearing bore.

induction, the supercharger would be less effective as a performance device. Preignition and detonation would limit boost to lower levels, perhaps no more than 3 or 4 lb.

Further cooling of gasoline blower systems can be accomplished through water injection. This doesn't alter the air-fuel ratio but does provide a greater amount of liquid that can evaporate. We will cover water injection in detail later, since cooling the intake charge

103

The support rings can be either steel (left) or aluminum. Testing has indicated that both work just fine, the problems start when you don't use either.

A sturdy arbor press is used to push the support ring over the bearing bore. The ring only contacts three spots on the housing, so the press fit is very tight.

The steel plates anchored to the bearing bosses by three small flat head screws will keep the support rings from working their way off the covers and retain the bearings in the bores.

will directly improve performance, efficiency, and blower-engine reliability. The addition of a liquid to the inducted air also tends to improve the seal of the rotors and thereby improve efficiency.

Finally, an air-fuel mix allows the blower to operate at a much higher shaft speed, which is important if boost levels are to reach those required for racing (sometimes over 25 psi). Since the GMC blower will be running under conditions other than those for which it was originally designed, there are many areas that require modification for reliable operation. A closer look at these alterations is in order.

Critical areas that require modification or inspection will be covered in the next several pages. The purpose of this discussion is not to provide a step-by-step instruction sheet so that you can modify your own blower. We strongly feel that attempting to prepare your own Roots blower can cause more trouble than it is worth. There are many shops that specialize in the made-to-order GMC blowers. Use the services of one of them! The cost is relatively

A strong, inexpensive rear end plate can be had by O-ringing the bearing housings and installing rear caps. Grease fittings are NOT a good idea, since they usually lead to excessive lubrication and damage of the rear seals.

low and they have the equipment on hand to do the job properly (a precision lathe and vertical mill with special fixtures are required).

Why, then, should we even go into the specifics of blower modification? The reason is simple. By understanding the inner workings you will be able to intelligently discuss the preparation required and double check the modifications to insure that they have been properly done. Also, if problems develop, you will be able to troubleshoot the causes. If, however, you have lathe and mill experience, you will find all the information required in this section to do the work yourself.

More often than not, you will be starting with a used blower. It may have come directly from a diesel truck or it may have been used on a race car. Even if it is a brand-new unit, it will still need a thorough going over. Stock GMC blowers have identical front and rear covers, more specifically called *bearing supports.* These supports are designed to last for hundreds of thousands of miles in diesel application. For street use the stock end plates will work just fine if the bearing support areas are reinforced. This is done by machining the covers for a press-fit steel or aluminum ring to support the bearing and to prevent cracks around the bearing bores. If the cover is already cracked, as many are, it can still be saved by adding the support rings, providing the cracks are caught early and have made little progress.

Additional clearance for the distributor can be had by using *bearing caps* over the rear bearing bores on the stock cover, rather than using the large cover plate. You can get even fancier (and more costly) by using one of the special cast aluminum rear covers available from several of the blower shops. Although they are designed for racing and are unnecessarily strong for street or mild racing use, they do add that look of professionalism (they look trick!). After the covers are beefed up

Special cast rear plates are a necessity in high-rpm drag use. They are not necessary for the street, but they can add that extra bit of class to your supercharger. Here are two examples of well-designed covers that will help prevent splitting of the bearing bores.

The best choice for rotor drive gears is the 30° cut gears. Those cut at 45° will self-destruct when exposed to high loads. The gears on the right are the cast iron, compared to the steel. The cast iron set are wider and will work just fine on the street or for mild racing. They will even provide more precise rotor-to-rotor timing since they are cut to closer tolerances. The steel set must be used in an all-out drag car, since the iron just doesn't have the load-carrying ability.

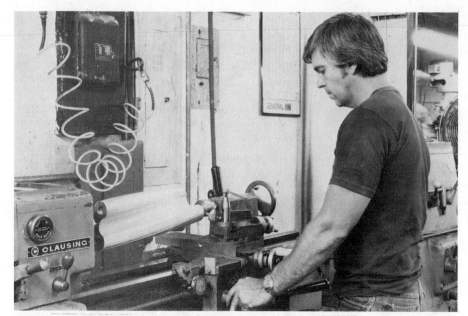

Rotor-to-case clearance is controlled partially by the end plates, and also by the rotor diameter. If sufficient clearance exists, a high-precision lathe must be used to machine material off the top of the lobes. There is certainly no one better qualified to "turn the knobs" than Larry Bowers.

with support rings and carefully checked for any additional cracks or warpage, many shops will blanchard grind the covers to insure an optimum seal at the rotor ends.

The stock GMC gears, located under the front cover, are either cut on a 45° or 30° angle. The additional end thrust exerted by the 45° gears can cause premature bearing failure and offer no advantages in backlash reduction. All 45° gears should be avoided. The 30° gears are available in either cast iron (wider) or cast steel (stronger). The best choice for the street is the cast iron set. They have a wider contact surface and are machined to closer tolerances, reducing rotor backlash. If the blower will be used for all-out racing, the steel gears are the best choice, since they will handle more power than the cast iron design. The gears should be looked over for any signs of galling or discoloration on the teeth. Check the spline area for cracks. If there are any of these indications, replace the gears; don't take chances in this department.

The rotors should also be carefully checked for any signs of cracks. Nicks, dings, and scratches don't necessarily mean that they are junk, but cracks usually do. The addition of teflon strips to the rotors is not uncommon in full-race blowers to insure the best seal possible. Although teflon is not recommended in street blowers to reduce operating clearances, they can be used to repair badly worn rotors, providing the same street operating clearance is used.

Double pinning the rotors to the short steel shafts that are pressed into each end of the rotors is not a bad idea (a single pin is used in each end of stock rotor assemblies), although for street use, it shouldn't be considered essential. For all-out racing, you bet! The operation is really very easy; all that's involved is drilling the rotor through to the shaft center, and driving a steel pin in place, followed by peening the hole over to prevent the pin from backing out. Applying a little green Loctite (Loctite sleeve Retainer fluid) to each pin and mating hole before assembly is another good idea.

The rotors should also be trued on the ends (a machine cut on the rotor ends to insure that they are perpendicular to the shaft centerline). The longest rotor of the pair should be machined to the shorter rotor length. Both of these machine operations are of less importance on a street blower, but to build a "right on" puffer, they're certainly valuable. Plus, trueing cuts will simplify clearance checking since high spots will be eliminated.

The rotors are supported in the front and rear end plates by ball bearings. The preferred bearing for use in the front housing is a new high-precision double-row roller bearing assembly. The tight fit between the rollers and the roller guides increases the stability of the rotors, preventing contact during operation. The stock bearings are of a single row design and allow more

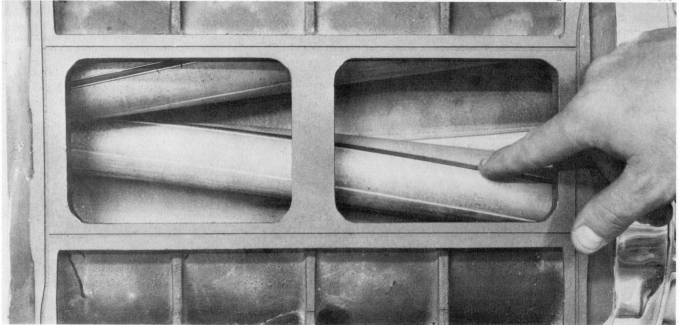

Teflon inserts are often added to the lobe edges of racing blower rotors. This will increase efficiency of the blower and increase possible boost levels. However, such techniques are expensive and really not necessary on a street blower.

movement (vertical and horizontal) between the rotors and the case, not advisable even for a street-only blower.

The case is one part that cannot be repaired if it is found to be cracked. Inspect the housing bores for deep scratches or gouges, because they will allow air leakage and reduce efficiency. If you find a lot of small fine scratches along the bearing bore, chances are the blower will be fine for street and probably race use. It's the deep ones that cause trouble. We mentioned that blanchard grinding the end plates was a good idea, the same applies to the blower case. Trueing the ends and the bottom will assure not only correct end plate alignment but also reduce the possibility of the blower drive belt "walking" off the top drive pulley from poor parallelism with the crank centerline. If the blower you are rebuilding has been run on a race car, take a good look at the case for expansion (bulging) that might have been caused by a severe backfire. Cases that suffer from this are better left alone.

The rotors and case operate, by de-

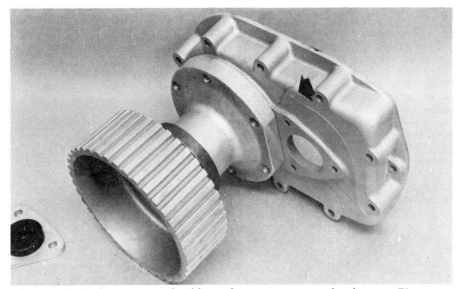

It is tempting to buy an ex-racing blower for a street setup—but beware. Blower explosions are normally the reason a huffer is retired. Note that this front plate has been cracked and though it can be repaired by welding, this may be more expensive than you bargained for when you bought the blower.

sign, in very close proximity, and with the addition of heat, deflection due to load, and dirt particles, they occasionally clash with one another. Both are made from a relatively soft material and mutual contact generally results in surface scratches. There is a technique, involving a chemical treatment, that can be used on aluminum parts leaving a hard surface only 0.002-0.003-inch thick. Called hard anodizing, this process will help prevent scratches from lowering the pumping efficiency by reducing the depth of most scratches to a very shallow level. It has been said many times that hard anodizing does not change the size of the part. This is not true. Hard anodizing usually affects about 0.003-inch of material at the surface of the part. Most often, 0.002-inch of the surface is a hard layer penetrating the surface, but the other 0.001-inch is a hard layer built up on the surface. This will vary depending on the amount of hard anodize the part is subjected to, but a good rule of thumb is that one-third of the hardness has been built up on the surface and will result in a dimensional change. Also, once a part has been hard anodized, it is difficult to machine. Be on the safe side, ask the people that will anodize your parts how much they will "grow," and make allowances before it's too late. Finally, hard anodizing is not an essential process. It's a nice "extra" if you want the deluxe setup and can afford the expense. Properly done, it can't hurt.

To prevent bearing oil from entering the compressor box and thereby entering the engine, lip-type shaft seals, supported by the end plates, ride on each end of the rotors. The seals are usually installed so that the lip portion faces the outside of the case. This pre-

For positive oil control inside the front cover, the air space above the drive gears and oil bath must be vented. This will insure proper oil control and prevent undue failure of the rotor bearing seals. Note on this street machine that the cover is vented directly to the engine crankcase.

vents oil from running into the blower from the gear train. However, this will allow the cover over the gears to become pressurized by the boost generated in the blower. On all-out drag cars, there is often a pressure release valve installed in the top of the front cover. This valve is opened after each run, releasing the trapped pressure that would otherwise leak back into the main case, drawing oil along with it. For the street or for occasional racing, venting the cover externally works just fine. If the vent is not properly baffled, however, oil will be blown out with the exhausting air and can not only make a mess, but also may eventually cause the gear compartment to become dry of oil. The vent may be connected through a small line to the engine sump via the valve cover or cylinder head drainback passage. A small plug placed at the proper oil level, similar to the fuel level sight holes in a Holley float bowl, will facilitate checking the gear oil level in the front cover.

Some drag racers install the seals in the reverse position, that is, with the lip towards the inside of the blower. This method prevents pressure from entering the end housing, however, the seal is less effective in preventing oil from entering the oil blower housing and the engine. Blowers used for drag racing only are much more suited to this type of seal installation since they are almost always providing positive boost. Under boost no oil can enter the case, although when the engine is idling with manifold vacuum, there is a tendency to draw oil from the end covers. Since

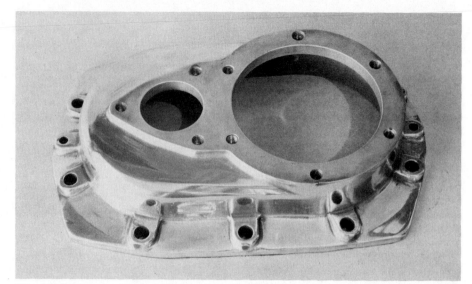

The GMC front cover houses the rotor timing gears. Its main function is to retain the oil bath used to lubricate the gears. The shaft seals which isolate the interior of the case from the front cover space will allow blower pressure to collect inside the cover. It is, therefore, essential that some sort of venting be provided to bleed this pressure out of the cover.

The bearing cover caps in front gear housing. Several different models are available from the various manufacturers. This one from Larry Bowers also incorporates a mounting post for the drive belt idler pulley.

When the front cover and bearing plate are properly mounted on the case, there should not be any trouble with the rotor drive gears, bearings and seals. It is also important that the manifold is properly aligned with the block and that the blower is properly mounted on the manifold.

idling is not the plan in all-out racing, reverse seal installation works. The covers must still be vented, for as the oil is heated, pressure will build in the end cover, possibly to a level higher than boost pressure. Seals installed in the reverse position only assure oil-free air during boost. We suggest you play it safe; install all seals with the lip to the outside.

Tuning a GMC blower for the intended application is more or less a question of clearances. The space between the moving parts will determine if the blower will be more suited for operation at near 15,000 rpm while pumping nitro, or running at 6,000 rpm and supplying gasoline for a street hot rod. The important aspects of tuning

are: 1) rotor *end clearance* with the front plate, 2) rotor end clearance with the rear plate, 3) rotor-to-case clearance at the top and bottom, 4) rotor-to-rotor clearance, and 5) rotor timing or *phase.* Each one of these must be properly adjusted to get the most from your blower. Improper adjustment of clearances can induce the blower to tear itself to pieces. Make no mistake, this is the most important part of your installation. Taking these critical areas one-by-one, we will explain how the unit can be modified to gain proper clearance, and how you can check or verify that your blower has been properly prepared.

The space between the rotors and the front plate is called the front rotor

Proper internal clearances are the secret to long life and good performance. Rotor-to-rotor clearance is being checked here by an expert at Bowers Blowers. This is just one of the many all-important internal checks that must be performed.

A completely polished blower is a good-looking "piece." This blower unit is ready for a new customer. The measured clearances are recorded by Bowers for future reference.

clearance or, more often, just *front clearance.* Long strip or "feeler" gauges are used to measure this and other internal clearances. Insert the strip between the rotor and front plate—the largest strip that will fit will show present clearance. GMC recommends 0.007-inch for a new blower. However, most out-of-the-box units measure a lot closer to 0.012-inch. The desired clearance for all-out racing will be between 0.005- and 0.007-inch. A street puffer should be set no closer than 0.008-inch. The clearance may be increased by machining the end of the rotor, and decreased by machining the bearing shoulder on the front shafts. The clearance is set relatively tight on the front because the rotor shafts are "located" in the front bearings, and as the rotors grow with heat they will reduce rear clearance since they are allowed to slide within the bearings. If the rotors were not allowed to freely expand in length, they would bulge the case and surely destroy the bearings.

The rotor-to-rear plate clearance will, as we mentioned, decrease as the blower heat builds. This necessitates that it be greater than the front clearance. GMC recommends that rear clearance on new blowers be set 0.014-inch. For all-out racing 0.014-inch is a little tight, but acceptable. On a street setup, 0.015- to 0.017-inch is

acceptable. Most new GMC blowers will measure about 0.020-inch, which is a bit too loose. Excessively tight rear clearance will let the rotors contact the rear plate and badly gall the surfaces or, if it's too tight, the blower may seize. Too much clearance will allow a large air leak, substantially lowering overall efficiency. To increase the rear clearance, a machine cut is required on the rear of the rotors (to shorten them). Decreasing the rear clearance necessitates a machine cut on the rear of the case. This may be done on a mill or the required amount can be removed by blanchard grinding.

Though many rodders look upon blowers as "race-only" equipment, they can provide many miles of reliable street performance. Street preparation of a blower is very simple and relatively inexpensive, though the novice is best advised to leave the prepping details to a reputable rebuild shop.

The rotor-to-case clearances, measured between the rotors and the top and bottom of the case, are most often referred to as *top and bottom clearances*. On a good blower the clearances will be 0.016-inch on the top and 0.005-inch on the bottom. The tight clearance on the bottom is required to seal the high pressure developed on the lower side of the rotors. This clearance is the most difficult to modify since it requires moving the front and rear end plates. The plates are pinned to the case by GMC and in order to raise or lower them, the dowel pin holes in the case must be offset bored on the desired center to accommodate a larger pin. This is not an easy job nor can it be done in a slipshod manner. The holes in the end plates must be reamed to match the larger pin size. For example, if the bottom clearance is 0.007-inch and the desired clearance is 0.005-inch, the end plates must be lowered 0.002-inch. We are assuming that the clearance of 0.007-inch is uniform on the front and rear of the case. The stock GMC pin diameter is 0.309-inch. If we select a pin that measures 0.312-inch and bore the new 0.312-inch hole in the case on a 0.002-inch lower centerline, the end plates will sit 0.002-inch lower on the case. If all was done with precision, the new rotor bottom clearance will be 0.005-inch as desired.

The top clearance is not as critical as the bottom. Adjust rotor position for the correct bottom clearance. If the case and rotors are in good shape, the top clearance will generally be acceptable. If there is excessive top clearance, the only cure is another blower—but before you toss anything in the trash, give one of the blower shops a call and check to see how bad things really are. *Street use will allow almost any top clearance,* only race use requires exact clearancing.

After you have set the correct top and bottom clearance, drill and ream the end plates and case to accept two additional dowel pins. Choose a location, at about the 11 and 5 o'clock positions, that has a good deal of material adjacent to the original holes. The additional load applied to the front end of the case by the belt drive may move the end plates, reducing the bottom clearance. Metal-to-metal contact will result, so buy some insurance. Two extra pins in each end plate will do the trick.

The GMC blower has proven to be the most reliable method of supercharging the modern drag racing engine. Considering that the blower was originally designed to operate at 5,000 rpm and pump air only, it is a true engineering feat—one of many that racers have to their credit—that racing versions are consistently turned to 15,000 rpm while pumping nitromethane at better than 2

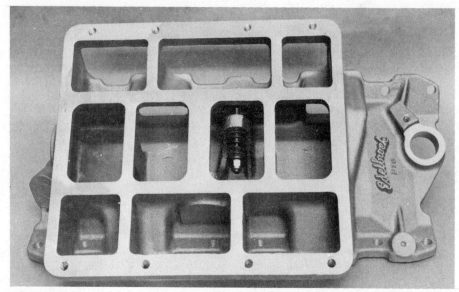

More often than not, a used race manifold will be the choice for your project. If you are building a smallblock Chevy, however, take a good look at this super manifold built by Edelbrock. This late design is available only through Isky cams, as a complement to their street blower kit.

atmospheres (28 psi) pressure. Blower builders, almost to the man, were or are racers. They have modified every internal clearance, added teflon to the rotors, made special seals, cast their own end covers, made their own cases, and a few are involved in building special rotors. For many years blood, sweat and experimentation was used by hundreds of racers throughout the country to unlock the secrets of racing a Roots blower. Success did not come cheaply. Mistakes usually resulted in damage to or total destruction of an expensive racing engine. This knowledge, experience, and technique are the commodities that people like Larry Bowers, Mert Littlefield, Phil Lukens, Don Hampton, Isky, and many more are selling. Considering the costs that

went into finding the right answers, what they charge is a real bargain. It took years for the professionals to find the answers. How long do you think it would take you by yourself? A professionally-prepared (or at least a professionally-inspected) GMC blower is like a doctor, you can't afford not to have a good one.

BLOWER MANIFOLDS

The blower manifold performs two important functions. The first is obvious—it must direct the air-fuel mix exiting the blower into the cylinder head intake port. All intake manifolds perform this function. However, normally-aspirated engines will achieve best performance from a manifold

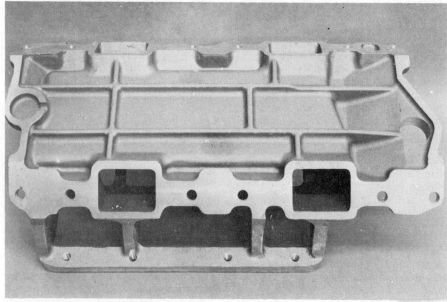

This Edelbrock-Isky manifold features siamesed intake ports, a blocked heat riser, rigid design for sturdy blower mounting, and a unique pop-off valve.

"tuned" to the power curve of operation. Blower manifolds are oblivious to such efforts. Ram tuning, or similar effects, are canceled by positive manifold pressure. Therefore, the best runner design for a blower manifold is one with direct passageways, the shorter and straighter the better.

The second function the blower manifold performs is to form a firm foundation on which to mount the supercharger. The loads developed by the drive belt can be considerable. If the manifold allows the blower to tip forward under load, the belt can move forward on the tipped pulley. The result will be either a thrown belt or one that is rather short-lived.

Obviously, the best intake manifold for a GMC-blown car is one that was originally designed to mount a blower. An old drag race manifold is an excellent place to start. If you are able to locate one, check it out carefully. Those that have cracks or imperfections should be avoided like the plague. Chances are they suffered these wounds at battle (during a blower explosion) and are badly warped. Use your straightedge to check the flatness of all surfaces: blower face, and intake port sides. If you find one that has a small crack and the owner says that it can be easily fixed by any competent heli-arc welding shop, be aware that welding over the crack is simple; but note that welding an aluminum manifold will usually cause some degree of warpage. This requires a milling machine, along with a good deal of setup time, to correct. If you happen to have a mill in your garage, great! If not, we suggest avoiding the deal. Don't buy a broken manifold on someone's assurance it's really not that bad; chances are it is.

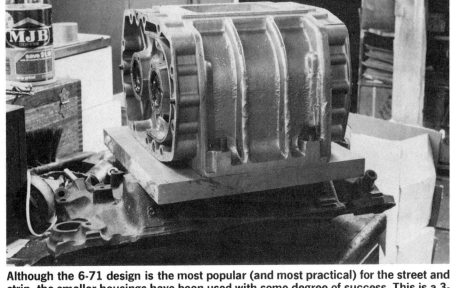

Although the 6-71 design is the most popular (and most practical) for the street and strip, the smaller housings have been used with some degree of success. This is a 3-71 that is being built for a special cross-country event. The 1-inch adapter plate allows the use of a stock Chevy intake manifold.

If you are planning to put a blower on something other than a Chevy or Chrysler Hemi, the biggest headache involved is finding a manifold. There are excellent manifolds available for the big and small Chevy and for the early and late Chrysler Hemi. Beyond that it gets pretty scarce. As a result, there are quite a few street blowers mounted on adapted four-barrel manifolds. There are a couple of disadvantages to this system. Such a manifold was never designed to flow the amount of air that a blower can supply, and is, therefore, often restrictive. Also, the adapter plate used to mount the blower may not provide a firm base, and may allow the blower to tip forward. All is not lost, however, as one can buy a modified manifold complete with adapter plate and installed pop-off valve. Complete modified manifolds are available from Gary Dyer at 8807 78th Ave., Bridgeview, Illinois. We will take a closer look at Dyer's equipment later.

Larry Bowers, at Bowers Blowers, suggested a possible alternative to the four-barrel manifold. Edelbrock makes a series of manifolds called *STR manifolds* (Street Tunnel Ram). These are two-part manifolds. The base is designed similar to the factory short-ram manifolds of the mid-sixties. The large top, available in single- or dual-carburetor designs, is attached to the base by several small bolts around the perimeter. By making another top, or possibly modifying the stock one, to provide an inlet hole matching the blower outlet, most of the restriction can be eliminated. Some of the manifold tops are not parallel to the crank centerline, but angle milling the top of the base or putting a wedge plate beneath the blower would get the blower drive centerline parallel to the crank centerline. The disadvantages of this method, aside from the obvious fabrication required, is that fuel distribution may be a problem, although the thorough mixing provided by the blower may offset this. The wide flat base of the STR will certainly provide a solid foundation on which to mount the blower. Like all adaptations, it has good points and bad; but when properly done, it would make a very unique installation.

Whichever manifold you finally choose for your hot rod, use a fiber gasket to seal it to the blower. Some blower housings are cut for an O-ring. These cases are OK, just ignore the O-ring groove and use a gasket. A light coating of oil on both surfaces will facilitate easy removal and eliminate the

The adapter plate is located to the intake manifold with the four stock carburetor bolts. This adapter has been relieved to facilitate air flow. The adapter plate must be very thick material to provide a sturdy flat surface for the blower to transfer belt loads, and to prevent case distortion, which will lead to rotor wear.

The pop-off valve on the Edelbrock-Isky Chevy manifold is a modified intake valve. A sturdy spring holds the valve against the seat in the blower plenum and alignment is insured by a built-in guide boss. This design is adequate for street use since it will produce good sealing and virtually eliminate leaks, however, the cross-sectional area of the valve is rather small and a healthy full-throttle backfire at the strip would probably do it under.

This Mickey Thompson manifold uses a four-bolt blow-off valve that incorporates a rubber gasket for positive seal. This type of seal can cause problems if the rubber comes loose from the valve or is blown out. Also note (arrow) that this manifold has been weld-repaired. This is the kind of thing to look for if you are in the market for a used manifold. This small area has been prepared professionally and no distortion to the neighboring casting was noted. This is usually the exception, generally welding that is not followed by complete re-machining is to be avoided.

need for scraping the old gasket and possibly damaging the surfaces. Both the blower and the manifold must be clean. Don't use a gasket sealer. The large contact surfaces will really stick together and you will have one hell of a time getting them apart.

Pressure relief valves seem so simple that they are often overlooked. As a result, they have driven many a racer right square up a wall. As the blower is running, it is delivering air in very strong pulses. These surges will sometimes push the valve off the seat allowing a leak. With the valve percolating,

the engine will act very strangely, possibly leading the owner on an extensive wild goose chase. The valve requires much more spring pressure than you may think necessary. For example, the typical blowoff valve may measure 2½ by 4 inches, with an effective surface (inside the seal area) of 4.5 square inches. During operation, it has been shown that pressure pulses on the order of 30 psi can be created (a good deal higher than this in an all-out race package). This means that at least 135 pounds of spring pressure is required just to keep the valve closed

during normal operation. A good starting place might be 300 to 400 pounds. This will provide a release when manifold pressure reaches 65 to 85 psi, well below the pressure that would destroy parts.

Some relief valves are sealed to the manifold with a rubber gasket or O-ring. These work just fine until a good healthy backfire. After which it is not uncommon to find them slightly "tweaked," and no longer providing a positive seal. The best way to avoid this is to lap the valve plate to the manifold with valve grinding compound. The two

This Edelbrock blower manifold for the late Chrysler Hemi is a popular design. The four springs nearly eliminate the valve hang-up problem. The springs on this manifold are adjusted for all-out competition on nitro. Do not use this high seat pressure on the street.

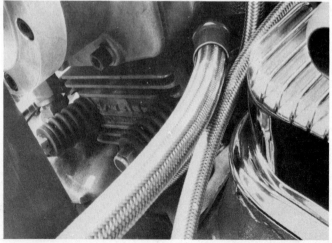

This Weiand blower manifold will function well at the drags or on the street. The blow-off valve is a twin-spring design that can hang open; if the engine runs rough after a backfire, this is a place to look.

metal-to-metal surfaces will seal adequately, and be leak free. Another point to remember, as the backfire is occurring and the pop-off valve is off the seat, it rises on two guide studs. If these guides are threaded on the portion over which the plate will ride, the valve may wedge against the rough threads, hang open and allow one heck of a vacuum leak. The guides should be smooth across the distance the plate may move, and the holes in the valve plate should be at least 1/16-inch oversize. These measures will prevent most problems, however, if the engine begins to act unresponsively, or backfire a great deal, check the pop-off valve first; it may save you a lot of time.

Bolting the GMC to your manifold may seem like an easy job. And easy it is, but here's another place you can get into trouble if it's your first time. Most

up, take the time to rotate the blower slowly to find any possible "tight spots." If there are some, loosen all the bolts and try it again. Also, inspect the gasket and make sure that it's flat and hasn't picked up any dirt. If the rotors still seem tight, check the surface of the manifold once again, as it may require a surface grinding. If all this fails, take two aspirins and see a professional in the morning.

BLOWER DRIVES and DRIVE RATIO

When drag racers first began to discover the tremendous performance improvement that could be had with a supercharger, there were some strange methods concocted to drive the blower. Multiple V-belts were used in the early

was a very solid connection, and that was one of the drawbacks. Engine harmonics were transferred to the blower and with no rubber connection to absorb or reduce this resonance, the blowers would shake to pieces. Also, the long distance the air-fuel charge had to travel, from the blower to the manifold, caused additional restriction. The very long boost tubes also caused a problem in the event of a backfire. Filled with explosive mixture, they would blow up like a keg of dynamite. In the late 1950's, the Gilmer belt was introduced to racing. The impact was tremendous and it is still obvious today. The Gilmer belt provided a flexible coupling, cancelling harmonics, and a non-slip toothed surface, insuring a 100% coupling.

There are several drive kits on the market today, and most of them are

The Gilmer belt has become the heart of all drive kits currently available. It is well known for reliability and is less expensive than matched V-belts. The Gilmer setup shown drives an 8-71 on top of a 392 Chrysler Hemi, and after several hundred ¼-mile runs the belt is still in service.

The 8-mm belt has deeper grooves and more internal strength than the previous ½-inch pitch design. The 8-mm belt can be used on the street with no adverse effects, although the additional cost and strength are not necessary. The ½-inch belt will give many thousands of miles of reliable street performance.

manifolds have either 7/16-inch bolt holes or 7/16-inch studs. The typical 7/16-inch bolt is torqued to 65 foot-pounds. Blower bolts are not typical, and they require special attention. Beginning from the inside and moving out (on each side of the blower), start at 5 ft-lb and increase in 5 ft-lb increments, until you reach 20 ft-lb. Then stop! More torque will distort the blower housing and change those internal clearances that you spent so much time checking and resetting. Before you attach the blower belt and fire it

drive systems, but as higher blower speeds were required, a more positive method of connecting the engine and blower was needed. The chain drive provided a solid hookup and for a while was considered the ultimate. It had a few drawbacks, though, it was rather noisy, it would throw oil in the mechanic's face, and when it broke many felt the chain must have gone in orbit, because it sure never came down nearby. The direct drive, with the blower mounted in front of the engine (and driven directly by the crankshaft),

very good. They all employ the Gilmer belt and include belt tensioners, accessory drives (when applicable), crank hub connections, and sprockets. Since the Gilmer drive is commonly used in drag racing, there are plenty of pulleys available to adjust the overdrive or underdrive ratios. By varying the tooth count of the belt pulleys on the crank or the blowers, the drive ratio can be varied to turn the blower slower than the crank (underdrive) or faster (overdrive). And the faster you turn the blower, the more boost pressure it will

The standard ½-inch drive and the new 8-mm drive pulleys can be obtained in a wide variety of sizes to underdrive or overdrive the blower as desired. Selecting the proper drive ratio is one of the most important aspects of any Roots blower installation.

develop (up to a point). There are a few drive kits available that are specifically designed for street or street-strip use. They include provisions for driving the stock water pump and usually require no alteration to the radiator or accessories. These street kits sometimes include a special steel front hub. The stock vibration dampener has a cast hub and cast outer rim. Those with a heavy, lead right foot, should consider a steel drive hub to eliminate the problem of splitting the hub through the keyway (caused by the extra strain of the blower drive). If you are a more conservative driver, the stock dampener will work fine. Modern technology has refined the Gilmer belt to a point that it will very seldom require replacement on a street blower. With one of the modern, well-engineered drive kits, there is no reason for belt failure at less than 100,000 miles.

The blower drive ratio that you select is an all important factor affecting the driveability and performance of your supercharged engine. It is very closely related to the engine compression ratio, the fuel you will be using, and whether or not the engine will be driven on the street.

Engine lead (total ignition advance at speed) is another very important factor affecting reliability and per-

formance. Many of you street enthusiasts will believe that the recommendations on compression ratio, blower speed and ignition lead we make in the next few paragraphs are too conservative. Let us assure you that they are not conservative. They are correct. It is the mistaken belief of some that a street blower can be run at race track specs — forget the race stuff if you want a street blower to work properly.

A blown fuel (nitro) engine can handle as much as 30% overdrive speed and up to 50 degrees ignition lead. The enormous amount of nitro and alcohol drawn through the blower cools the charge greatly; nitromethane is a fuel that resists detonation. Gasoline, on the other hand, will detonate very easily, and remember, an engine that runs while detonating is beating itself to death. The octane rating of pump gas is slowly getting lower and lower. A normally-aspirated engine can no longer run with high ignition lead on today's gas with 10 to 1 compression. Even at 8½ or 9: 1, most engines will knock severely on anything but the very best premium fuel. It just stands to reason that a supercharged engine must run an even lower compression. If you are going to run a street rod with a Roots blower *don't use more than 8½:1;* that's maximum. You're even better off with 7 or 7½:1. At wide open throttle, with 15 pounds of boost, an engine running at the point of detonation will live only a few seconds. The result will be melted or collapsed pistons, or, at least, damaged compression rings. If it

Larry Bowers has designed a street blower drive kit for the small and big-block Chevrolets. The front cover is an offshoot from his drag race design and carries the belt tensioner arm from a special cast front snout. The top pulley is driven through a unique split-collar drive hub, located with three allen head bolts.

BLOWER DRIVE PERCENTAGE CHART
courtesy of Mert Littlefield Blowers

½″ PITCH	TOP PULLEY				
(BOTTOM PULLEY)	40	35	34	33	32
40	80 / 0	75 / 14.2	74 / 17.6	73 / 21.2	72 / 25.0
41	81 / 2.5	76 / 17.1	75 / 20.5	74 / 24.2	73 / 28.1
42	82 / 5.0	77 / 20.0	76 / 23.5	75 / 27.2	74 / 31.2
43	83 / 7.5	78 / 22.8	77 / 26.4	76 / 30.3	75 / 34.3
44	84 / 10.0	79 / 25.7	78 / 29.4	77 / 33.3	76 / 37.5
45	85 / 12.5	80 / 28.5	79 / 32.3	78 / 36.3	77 / 40.6

8 MM PITCH	TOP PULLEY						
(BOTTOM PULLEY)	52	51	50	49	48	47	46
63	115 / 21.1	114 / 23.5	113 / 26.0	112 / 28.5	111 / 31.2	110 / 34.0	109 / 36.9
64	116 / 23.0	115 / 25.4	114 / 28.0	113 / 30.6	112 / 33.3	111 / 36.1	110 / 39.1
65	117 / 25.0	116 / 27.4	115 / 30.0	114 / 32.6	113 / 35.4	112 / 38.2	111 / 41.3
66	118 / 26.9	117 / 29.4	116 / 32.0	115 / 34.6	114 / 37.5	113 / 40.4	112 / 43.4
67	119 / 28.8	118 / 31.3	117 / 34.0	116 / 36.7	115 / 39.5	114 / 42.5	113 / 45.6
68	120 / 30.7	119 / 33.3	118 / 36.0	117 / 38.7	116 / 41.6	115 / 44.6	114 / 47.8
69	121 / 32.6	120 / 35.7	119 / 38.0	118 / 40.0	117 / 42.7	116 / 45.6	115 / 50.0

The crank drive incorporates a special drive hub, and a machined V-belt pulley sandwiched between the hub and Gilmer pulley. Since specific requirements will change from car to car, Larry will custom tailor the drive package to meet your needs.

The Bowers lower hub is a very strong steel piece that will completely eliminate splitting through the keyway, a common problem with the stock vibration dampener. A V-belt groove is also machined in the front to allow the user an additional accessory drive.

seems like we are trying to scare you, we are. Play it safe!

While on the subject of detonation, it must be said that oil mixed with the inducted air-fuel will cause detonation. This will be true even in very small quantities. Oil that leaks by the seals in the blower, or that leaks by the piston ring or valve guides, or is introduced into the induction system from any other source, will either limit engine output or will damage internal parts. A small amount of oil may not affect a normally-aspirated engine, but will cause some "hard knocks" when the engine is supercharged.

Considering these possible problems, we will attempt to make some recommendations on blower drive ratio. Almost all street-driven engines utilize a 6-71 GMC puffer. Because of this, the drive ratio discussion will concern 6-71's only. The 4-71 is very limited in air flow capabilities, and requires more speed to produce the same boost level. However, the increase speed also increases the pressurized air temperature. This means that an engine with a 4-71 will detonate sooner than one with the more efficient 6-71. Bear this in mind if you wish to apply this information to a 4-71 supercharger.

A properly-built street engine will have a compression ratio of 7 or 8:1. If you have a neat set of pistons that you plan to run in your pride and joy, a set with, say, 10 or 10½:1 compression, DON'T DO IT! Have the pistons machined to the right ratio for a supercharged engine. This means not more than 8½:1 maximum. This bears repeating because this is the place that most people get into trouble. All right, now that we have the correct compression ratio, we recommend that you underdrive the blower 10 to 12% less than crank speed. We know that a lot of you are thinking, "Oh boy, these guys are really out to lunch. If I build it this way, it probably won't even start." Not true; it will not only start, but it'll run great. We admit that it might put out more power with more blower speed, but the question is, how long? If you are looking for a reliable supercharged street engine, you will have one if you follow the rules. Break the rules, and you will probably break an engine.

Another rule of importance is: be conservative with the ignition lead. We recommend that total ignition timing not exceed 28 to 30 degrees in a wedge-chamber engine (like the smallblock Chevrolet). If you run more lead, the risk of creating high-speed detonation is very high. At this point, you should realize that detonation is the biggest killer of supercharged street engines. It is the limiting factor

The Gary Dyer street drive is designed just for street operation. This does not mean that the drive system isn't strong. This means that the system was designed to fulfill the need for a blower drive built to overcome the problems of high cost, accessory drive limitations and additional bulk that can cramp working space. The Dyer front cover is a one-piece unit that carries the front bearings and seals, and also supports the belt tensioner arm.

The front cover also carries a slight glass (arrow) that indicates at a glance the correct oil level. The Dyer cover is a well-finished and engineered design that will complement any street puffer.

The Gary Dyer drive package uses a clever three-piece lower drive pulley, allowing an adjustable number of accessory drive belt grooves.

The Dyer lower pulley, shown here disassembled, illustrates the three-piece construction. The Gilmer drive is on the left, the V-belt pulley pack fits in the center, and the centering adapter on the right keeps all three in alignment when bolted to the stock vibration dampener.

of performance, and must be avoided like the plague. Nonetheless, even with an engine that has been prepared properly, detonation will sometimes strike. It could be due to a bad tank of gas, very low humidity, or high air temperature. If you are building your engine from the ground up, keep this in mind, for a little extra time and money spent on premium parts can help it through hard times.

Detonation causes a very high pressure to "hammer" the piston domes. This load is transferred to the rods, bearings, crank, and block. Heavy-duty parts will resist failure during this pressure pounding. Forged pistons are, of course, a good choice for a high-output engine. They are not essential, unless the engine will be used for racing at high boost pressures or high rpm levels. Factor cast pistons, with thermal expansion limiters (steel struts added to the piston around the pin bosses), are a very good choice for the street. They are able to withstand high heat, fairly high engine speeds (under 7000), and substantial loading, but not detonation. Cast pistons will crack, while those of forged construction will take the punishment longer (though only a little longer). Connecting rods should be the strongest forging available from the factory. Use good rod bolts that are Rockwell-tested, and have everything Magnaflux inspected. This includes the crankshaft, main caps and bolts. These are a few things that must be checked when building a blown street engine. If you intend to bolt a GMC on a stock engine, with a compression ratio of 8.5 or less, realize that you do not have the extra protection of these special heavy duty parts; all the more reason to play it conservatively.

The supercharged engine will ingest more air and fuel than a normally-aspirated engine. This will produce more heat in the combustion chambers, and will possibly require a colder heat

The Isky drive kit is one of the strongest units that you can buy. The front cover is a casting of high-strength aluminum alloy, and the front drive hub and pulley are forged aluminum.

The front drive hub and bearing assembly is a super strong aluminum forging. If you are considering a few all-out passes down the strip, this is just the ticket.

range spark plug than stock. Speaking of plugs, here's a neat little trick that can save an engine. If you use extended tip plugs, they will act like a safety valve if detonation occurs. The high heat of detonation will melt the plug tip, shutting that cylinder off before damage is incurred. It's better to burn plugs than pistons.

The supercharged engine will demand a little more from the valvetrain. As boost builds, there is a greater tendency to force the intake valve open (due to air pressure on the backside of the valve). A two-inch valve with a ⅜-inch stem will receive better than 75 pounds force at 15 psi boost. This force will reduce the effective valve spring seat pressure by 75 pounds. We suggest that you run at least 125 lbs spring seat pressure for a street-driven engine, and 180 for an all-out drag motor. Hydraulic lifters will work very well on a supercharged street engine, providing enough seat pressure is provided. A stock valvetrain might have only 80 pounds of seat pressure. When this low pressure is combined with hydraulic lifters and the blower pressure, the stock lifters may "pump-up," holding the intake valve off the seat. If this happens at high speed and boost, a backfire and blower damage can result. With hydraulic lifters, it is essential to run ample valve spring pressure and keep the engine speed below valve float. In any street engine, aluminum valve spring retainers should be avoided. Also, don't waste your money on titanium, chrome moly steel retainers are your best bet. Since drag racing involves short duration running,

The Isky idler pulley is another example of the finest in engineering for a street drive kit. Little need be said regarding the strength. This drive kit, although the ultimate in strength, is suited for everyday driving, with the added features of the ultimate in reliability and a close resemblance to the drag race drives.

it's possible to get by with aluminum. However, in this case we recommend titanium because of the high tensile strength of this material. Street engines should use cams of under 300° duration (measured at 0.015-inch lift), while racing engines can go the limit.

The additional heat in the combustion chambers will increase the intake and exhaust valve temperatures. To keep the valves cool, this extra heat must be dissipated. Wider valve seats are a step in the right direction. Wide valve seats would normally reduce in-

take flow and engine performance, but this is no longer a problem with a supercharger. With a blower the problem is not flow, but heat. What is not dissipated through the seats will travel up the valve stem, creating additional expansion and requiring additional stem clearance. This is even true of bronze-wall guides. In a normally-aspirated engine, bronze-wall guides can be set up for a palm press fit, when supercharged, however, they must have at least 0.001- to 0.0015-inch clearance. If intake and exhaust seats

The complete kit illustrates the unique water pump pulley that Isky claims is just the ticket to increase water pump life on a hot street engine. The pulley allows a small degree of slip at high speed, an important advantage. A 100% solid hookup with the pump can ruin the bearings and seals when the engine turns over 7000 rpm. The slight slippage doesn't affect engine cooling.

The Isky drive kit is complete with all hardware and even the cover plates for the front cover and rear cover of the blower. T. Willey at Isky can even supply a street-ready blower with the drive kit, so all you need is tools.

are cut to 0.050-to 0.060-inch wide, they will control the valve head temperature and prevent the stems from galling and sticking in the guides. Hard chrome applied to the stem in a thickness of less than 0.001-inch will improve the frictional coefficient and prove beneficial with both cast iron and bronze guides. Take the time to polish the stems after the chrome has been applied to eliminate the surface irregularities that remain after plating. This rough finish can cause excessive guide wear before the stem has worn smooth.

To maintain good top end integrity, cylinder head or block O-ringing is a very good idea. With the advent of lower and lower compression ratios, stock head gaskets have become less efficient. In an attempt to save money, most of the car makers are no longer

producing the "good" head gaskets used on older, high-compression engines. These older gaskets might work adequately on a blown engine without O-rings, but it is better to be on the safe side—use a good hi-po gasket and O-rings. Since the O-ring position will vary with the gasket you choose, try to obtain several high performance gaskets and find the best one available. Choose a gasket with a metal piece that wraps around the combustion chamber circle. Try to find a gasket that measures at least 0.025-inch thick, for if it is thinner than this, the O-ring won't have enough material in which to imbed itself. This will cause the head to stand on the O-rings, letting the water and oil passages leak. This can be reduced or eliminated by using silicone rubber sealant. A very thin film should be applied to the water

and oil passages on the deck and head surfaces before assembly. This sealer (silicone rubber) should be used to prevent seepage, even if an adequately thick head gasket is used. We don't recommend solid copper head gaskets for the street, unless they are the only high-performance gaskets available. Head gasket seal is essential for reliability, top performance, and proper cooling. Keeping your supercharged engine cool is not difficult; it's just a matter of using the right parts, and that's the subject of the next section.

THE COOLING SYSTEM

The GMC supercharged engine is considered impractical for street use by a great number of people. They claim that poor reliability and overheating are the plague of the Roots supercharger. We have already explained that if the system is properly designed and assembled, reliability is not a concern. The same is true of the cooling system. On most supercharged engines it will be necessary to modify the stock cooling system, since the blower either sits on top of what used to be the water outlet, or the blower manifold has no provision for a radiator hose. An efficient cooling system need not be plumbed exactly to factory specifications, however, there is little room for improvement. Rather, we must try to duplicate their design as closely as possible with additional provisions for the blower.

There are four essential factors that must be a part of every cooling system if it is to function efficiently. They are 1) adequate coolant flow, 2) complete coolant flow, 3) sufficient radiator core surface area, and 4) adequate air flow across the cooling cores at idle and at

The Isky lower drive hub is machined from 4130 chrome-moly steel and is fully degreed to aid in setting engine timing. It is secured to the crankshaft with a special washer and bolt.

Mert Littlefield uses a small vent in the front cover to eliminate any internal pressure from forcing oil into the main blower housing. Mert likes working with street enthusiasts, and is willing to help if you run into problems, or supply any blower or blower-driven parts that you may need.

When the blower manifold doesn't have a front water provision, one can be fabricated or built up with heli-arc welding. This does involve a good deal of skill and the proper equipment, but a very clean, stock appearance can be the result.

Effective engine cooling can only be accomplished if an adequate supply of water is flowing through all important areas of the block and heads. Larry Bowers decided to add extra water fittings to the radiator, allowing more flow volume if necessary (see arrow).

speed. These four factors form the criteria for all water radiator cooling systems. Discussing these points one by one, the remainder of this section will hopefully supply enough information to guide you through the proper design and construction of all cooling systems, regardless of their individual peculiarities.

The first essential on our list is adequate coolant flow. In order for any cooling system to effectively remove heat from the engine, a sufficient amount of cool water must flow through the internal passages. There is

no such thing as too much water flow through the block (there can be too much flow through the radiator, but we will go into that later), as long as the water entering the engine is sufficiently cool to absorb enough heat from the cylinder walls. A typical characteristic in inadequate water flow is overheating at high speed, while keeping fairly cool at moderate and low speeds. Though other problems may also create this symptom, inadequate flow is the most common (since there is such an interrelated dependence among parts of a cooling system, it is im-

possible to diagnose problems with complete accuracy).

The amount of water flowing through a cooling system is controlled by the drive ratio of the water pump, the number of pumping fins cast into the water pump impeller, and the internal passage restrictions. First, we must remember that the water pump speed and the number of impeller fins are related. Cars that are equipped with air conditioning are usually fitted with water pumps that have fewer pumping fins. The reason behind this is not to pump less water, as is often thought,

Hot water must exit the cylinder heads at the front of the engine. Some blower manifolds have a water outlet, making the hookup much easier. This is a Weiand manifold for a big-block Chevy.

Water inlets in an other-than-stock position can cause heat pockets and possibly lead to steam pressure in the system. This can force water vapor to be pushed past the radiator cap despite the 14 or 16 psi relief spring.

If no provision for water outlet is provided in the manifold, the best place for water connection is the front of the cylinder heads. This roadster uses two small lengths of hose without a thermostat for calibrated restriction. This can work fine if some experimentation is done with hose and fitting size to prevent excessive water flow.

but rather to pump the same amount of water. Pumps with fewer impeller fins are fitted with a smaller water pump pulley, causing the impeller to spin faster. All this may sound pretty strange, except for the fact that the fan is attached to the water pump shaft. *The system will now pump the same amount of water while spinning the fan faster.* This results in additional cooling at idle, just where it's needed with an air-conditioned car. From this we can conclude that if you have a heating problem only at idle, it's not a water flow problem, but an air flow problem.

Excessive water flow can also cause problems. When water flows at high volume through the cooling system, it does not remain in the radiator long enough to release the heat that it picked up while in the engine block and heads. Hot water then returns to the engine, keeping the engine heat at a higher level than desired. It is safe to say this will never be a problem if you use a standard thermostat in the system. Aside from being responsible for quickly heating up the engine, the thermostat is a calibrated restriction to control water flow, allowing enough time for the water to give up a good portion of the heat it has absorbed. Therefore, don't eliminate the thermostat! The only times removing the thermostat will prevent overheating is on those rare occasions when it has malfunctioned (stuck closed). If a stock water outlet and thermostat cannot be used, Offenhauser makes an aluminum casting that duplicates the stock thermostat housing in the intake manifold. This unit is connected to the engine block with short lengths of heater hose; this closely parallels the factory system.

Inadequate water flow may be caused by the water pump running too slowly, or restrictions in the plumbing, radiator, or cylinder block. As long as these problems are avoided, there should not be coolant flow inadequacies even when the engine is supercharged. While on the subject of restrictions, in the last section we suggested you use silicone rubber seal on the head gaskets to prevent water leaks. Use the sealant sparingly. An excessive amount may ooze into the water passages connecting the block and heads, forming silicone rubber plugs that will be impervious to damn near anything. The plugs will restrict water flow, and at the very least cause hot spots in the heads (promoting detonation).

The second cooling system essential is complete water flow. The typical water flow pattern begins as the coolant leaves the radiator, through the lower radiator hose, and enters the water pump. The pump forces the coolant to enter the cylinder block at the front, usually just below the deck surface. As the coolant flows around the cylinder bores, some is allowed to take a short cut through small connecting water passages into the cylinder heads. This insures that the hotter areas of the head will receive more coolant in an effort to equalize internal temperatures. As the coolant enters the head, it begins a return trip toward the front of the engine, finally exiting at the front of the head casting where it enters the intake manifold (on a stock engine), passes through the thermostat housing and reenters the radiator via the upper fitting.

This is a complete coolant circuit. Moving coolant has passed over all internal casting surfaces. If any part of this flow were allowed to stand still, the coolant might overheat and boil, resulting in steam and forcing coolant out of the radiator. And, aerated coolant (resulting from boiling or excessive water pump speed) is a poor conductor of heat. All special or custom cooling systems must duplicate this flow pattern as closely as possible. Remember this when using a special water outlet such as the Offy external thermostat housing. The small hoses leading into the housing must exit the heads at the front of the engine. This will assure adequate coolant flow.

The third essential in a good cooling system is supplying enough radiator to do the job. This may sound fairly obvious, but you would be surprised how many times, for some unknown reason, a 6-cylinder radiator will be

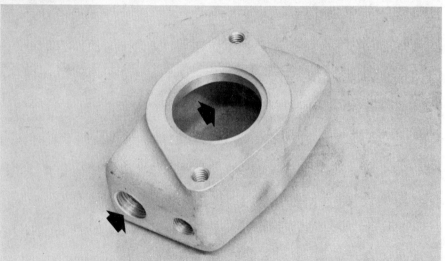

This water junction block is the best way to connect water flow from the cylinder heads to the radiator, since it allows the use of the stock thermostat. Water inlets from each cylinder head are indicated by the arrows. The small tapped hole is for a temperature sender.

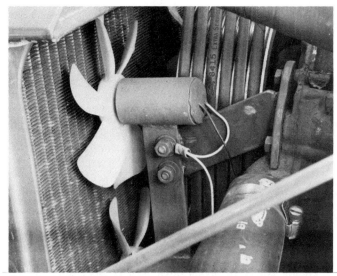

Electrical fans are a super idea even if a standard fan is practical. They will provide constant cooling at all engine speeds and can often eliminate any overheating tendency during long periods of idling in traffic. They can also be left on after the engine is shut down to aid post-operation cooling.

In most cases it is possible to use a standard fan belt and fan to assist cooling. In some cases, as with this Hilborn-injected induction, a standard fan is impractical. In these cases an electrical fan(s) is a good bet.

hooked to a 454 cubic inch street screamer. The results are very predictable—constant overheating. Many radiator shops can install a more efficient core (they are rated in the number of fins per inch). This means one that has more fins per inch or more rows of tubes, or is physically larger, or uses a combination of these factors. All existing cores should be "rodded out." This involves forcing a specially-shaped rod through all the cores making sure that they are open to flow. Often factory radiators will have as many as 30% of the tubes plugged with solder when they are brand new, and if it has been in use for a while, another 20% could be become clogged with rust or other foreign matter. This doesn't leave much left to cool the

water. A street supercharged engine can only be enjoyed if it stays cool and doesn't boil over; a large, efficient radiator is an essential part of a well-designed cooling system.

The last, but not least, factor that must be considered in efficient cooling is adequate air flow through the radiator at all times. Plenty of air is available at speeds above 30 or 40 mph; getting it through the radiator may sometimes require ducting, or baffles. Most street rods and late-model super cars have sufficient frontal area to capture plenty of wind. However, if your engine stays cool at idle and slow speeds, but tends to heat when the car is at a fast cruise, give a close look at the sheetmetal under your hood ornament. As we mentioned earlier, addi-

tional air flow through the radiator at idle and slow speed can be had by increasing fan speed or installing a fan with more or more deeply fluted blades.

The best setup we know is spinning the water pump faster with a smaller pulley, and installing a fluid drive fan to let the fan coast at high engine speeds, virtually eliminating fan noise (at some slight sacrifice in cooling). Electric fans are a very tricky animal. They can help as auxiliary cooling units, but more than two are usually required if they are to replace the stock fan. Just open the hood of your pride and joy, and while your head is in close proximity to the air cleaner, rev the engine to a mild 1000 rpm. You will soon see that a lot of air is moved by that windmill. Can

The use of electric water pumps (instead of the belt drive stocker) can work if you are willing to suffer the frustration of getting the bugs out. A normal system will usually require two pumps and even with both running, the engine may still overheat at high speed. For a drag car they work super, but for the street, stay with the Detroit design.

This is one of the few GMC blowers that has a water jacket built into the case. Water would provide cooling and help eliminate wear caused by excessive temperatures. Most agree that this is not a sought-after case unless the intended use is marine performance, where an unlimited supply of cool water is available. Although, even with cool lake water, only a very slight cooling effect will be imparted to the intake charge.

electric fans do the job? Sometimes yes, sometimes no. Often they can be more trouble than they are worth.

WATER INJECTION AND AFTERCOOLING

We have done a lot of talking about detonation. It is obviously our enemy, and any method that can be employed to eliminate or at least reduce this bugaboo is very useful. We have mentioned that oil, high boost, and low octane gas are some of the causes. Another important cause of detonation is heat. With high boost (13 to 15 lb) and load, the air temperature inside the manifold may be higher than 500°F, a sure cause of detonation. Cooling the intake charge will reduce the detonation point and produce more power.

There are several ways that this can be done through the use of aftercoolers. An aftercooler system involves components similar to the engine cooling system; a heated element, a fluid to transfer heat, and a radiator. When aftercoolers are used with GMC blowers they usually include a radiator (more properly called an absorber) installed just below the rotors in the manifold. A coolant, often antifreeze, is pumped through the absorber core into a remote-mounted radiator through which outside air flows. A system like this will heat the coolant to above 200°F., therefore, the usefulness is generally very limited. Since the intake mixture spends such a very short time moving through the absorber, the inlet charge temperature is lowered only slightly, if at all.

Another approach, perhaps more effective, is to use an air conditioning compressor to pump freon through the absorber (now more properly called an evaporator), where it turns to a gas (the latent heat of vaporization cools the evaporator and the air-fuel charge passing through it). The gaseous freon is then pressurized and forced through a radiator mounted in front of the engine radiator, where it returns to a liquid state releasing the absorbed heat. An efficient air conditioning system can lower the evaporator temperature to near freezing. This may keep the door closed on detonation, but at the expense of higher engine temperature (air entering the engine radiator is hotter), additional pulleys and belts, and more plumbing.

Aftercooling is particularly well-suited to marine applications, since the lake or ocean provides an endless supply of cool water to pump through the heat absorber. As in all aftercooling applications, the efficiency is limited by the surface area of the heat absorber. There just isn't a lot of room to put a large absorbing unit on a GMC blown engine. In marine use, however, it is possible to raise the blower a few

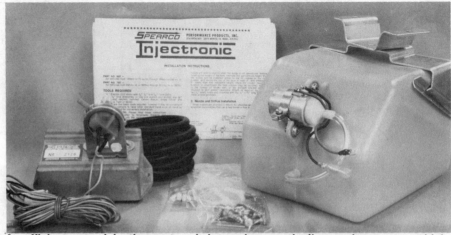

An efficient water injection system is becoming practically mandatory on any high-performance street machine. As the gas quality continues to decline those who wish to maintain reasonable engine efficiency levels must turn to this technique. The Spearco Injectronic system, though designed for naturally-aspirated engines, will work fine on a blown street machine.

inches, requiring a longer drive belt, in order to install a custom aftercooler. Aftercoolers, often called heat exchangers, are widely used on turbocharged marine engines. In these instances, there are no drive belt problems and the heat exchanger is not limited in size as severely as with Roots superchargers.

Another very effective method of aftercooling, although not often referred to as such, is water injection. This is an easily accomplished technique of spraying water through the carburetor when the engine is under boost. Most often a windshield washer bottle is used as a water reservoir and pressure is provided by a small electric 12-volt pump that can be activated at the flip of a switch. In some cases the

switch will be a pressure diaphragm that senses intake manifold boost. When the pressure level reaches a point at which detonation might occur, the diaphragm closes an electrical contact, starting the pump motor. Water is then supplied through a hose to the carburetor air horn, where it is sprayed through a nozzle into the air stream. The water particles begin to evaporate as they move downstream. This cools the mixture, tending to offset the heat generated by the supercharger. The air-fuel and water mixture then enters the combustion chamber and the water turns into steam. The steam vapor performs two important functions. The first is, it tends to inhibit detonation (through some not completely understood process), and the second is the hot

Probably the most common carburetor used on street blown engines is the Carter (Competition Series). This is not an iron-clad rule; good performance and driveability can be had with the Holley 600- or 650-cfm (when used in pairs). Avoid center-squirters or double-pumpers for the street, these carburetors are much better suited for all-out racing.

steam will clean the pistons and chambers eliminating a good portion of the built-up carbon that can cause pre-ignition and detonation by glowing hot spots. The miracle fluid, the super solvent, the liquid that we all think little about (until we run out), has once again demonstrated another means by which it can serve man.

Water injection kits are available from several manufacturers. Rotomaster (the turbo kit people) supply a water injection system that will work very well with a Roots blown engine. Their kit includes a plastic bottle with an electric pump, a preset pressure switch, sprayer nozzle, and a small needle valve that is installed in the water line to provide an adjustment in water delivery volume. It's just a matter of opening the valve until your detonation problems are over.

It's so simple, that it sounds impossible. Take our word for it, though, it works! A most dramatic example of this was the chassis dyno testing of a newly-supercharged street machine. With the water injector turned off, the engine was brought to speed (about 3500 rpm). At this point the engine was receiving 10 pounds of boost and detonating badly. The dyno operator reached over and opened the water valve a couple of turns, and the result was truly remarkable. The engine smoothed out and began to run quietly. Plus, the rear wheel horsepower readings showed a definite increase. All that from water! Amazing!

The effects can be increased slightly by adding a percentage of a volatile liquid, such as methanol, to the water. The alcohol helps the water evaporate and assists in charge cooling. Methanol, however, is very prone to preignition and when mixed with water in stronger than a 50% solution, the re-

sults can be undesirable.

Spearco manufactures a water injection kit, designed primarily for normally-aspirated inductions that is probably the most sophisticated unit on the market today. The unit is controlled by a "brain box," similar to a transistor ignition system, that decides when to inject water into the engine. The brain senses the engine speed and manifold vacuum and gives a squirt just when the engine needs it. With some modification this system would be the ideal choice for a supercharged engine. It would supply water only during boost, and also during high-speed low-vacuum conditions.

SUPERCHARGER CARBURETION

A properly-functioning carburetion system on a normally-aspirated engine must perform a wide variety of tasks in order for the engine to run smoothly and economically at different throttle positions and engine speeds. The separate circuits of the carburetor (idle, off-idle, part throttle lean, part throttle enrichment, full throttle) are all designed for an engine that is normally-aspirated. When a Roots blower is installed, some of the engine requirements will change. Additionally, the engine will work as if it is of "normal" size at idle and light throttle, but when the supercharger is working, the engine will draw fuel as though it were twice the original displacement.

A carburetor that is set up for a non-supercharged engine will deliver 12-13.5 to 1 air-fuel ratio at wide-open throttle. This ratio will provide best all-around performance output when there is no boost on the induction. When the engine is supercharged, it will produce more horsepower when the fuel mixture is enriched. The additional

fuel will provide more cooling to the intake charge, and this, plus the increased fuel density, will delay the power robbing detonation. As the fuel mixture is additionally enriched, more boost may be added to the induction without detonation. There is a point (about 60% richer than part throttle) at which a richer mixture will increase detonation. With the use of a water injection system, however, a good portion of this additionally rich mixture can be replaced with water. When you consider that water is cheaper, "burns" cleaner, and steams clean the combustion chambers, water injection looks better than ever.

The carburetor must meet the radical air flow requirements of a supercharged engine. At low speed, we want a small carburetor to provide good throttle response; at wide open throttle, a large carburetor is required to keep up with the additional demands of the supercharger. The transition from small to large must not be abrupt, for this could lead to lean spots, resulting in backfire. The best choice in carburetion will be a design incorporating small primaries and large vacuum-operated secondaries. The vacuum control may require modification of the opening rate to eliminate backfire or stumble. The secondary jetting will usually need enrichment for two reasons: 1) the carburetor will be supplying air and fuel to an engine that will appear to be twice as large as the same normally-aspirated engine, and 2) the richer mixture will help prevent detonation.

A very popular choice for GMC blower carbs is the Carter competition series. These units have mechanical secondary throttle plates. Above these plates, however, are vacuum-operated flaps that open as the engine require-

Super strip or marine performance can be had with this special dual 4500 Dominator setup. This casting, available from Mert Littlefield Blowers, will run as good as it looks, and that's plenty good.

The Dominator carb is a race-only design incorporating low restriction throttle shafts, double accelerator pumps, and huge throttle bores. The combined air flow on this twin-carb induction is 2,200 cfm.

123

Some street blower fans have experimented with Hilborn injection for pump gas use. The Hilborn unit was designed for race use and has little provision for part throttle metering. This system has been modified to improve part throttle performance, but builder Pat Coyle still threatens to yank it off in favor of a normal carburetion system.

Running a blower means moving the carburetors up, and requiring a new throttle linkage. There are virtually endless techniques that can be developed to provide a positive hook up. The rear blower end plate is a natural for bellcrank mounts. This very clean linkage is the result of a good design that was well executed.

Pat's Hilborn setup does have some strong points. The "visuals" are something else. The Hilborn system bypasses a large amount of fuel at idle and low speed operation. As the throttle is progressively opened, more and more fuel is directed to the nozzles. For this system to function, a high-volume fuel pump that is directly connected to the engine (insuring twice the fuel at twice the rpm, etc.) is a necessity. Pat utilized the rare-type cam drive fuel pump, adding even more authenticity to this very impressive street machine.

ments increase. Carter also makes a carburetor commonly called the "air-valve" carb. This model has a large air flap above the secondary throttle bores. This flap, utilizing an adjustable tension spring, is well-suited to rapid throttle transition, and should not be overlooked when searching for the ultimate street blower carb. If you decide to run a Holley, do not use double-pumpers or center-squirters. It is possible that these carbs would work well in a drag racing situation, but steer clear of these for the street, even when normally-aspirated.

When you are running "foot-to-the-wood", don't run out of gas. This may sound so obvious that you say, "Tell me something I don't already know!" Well, you may already know that running out of gas is not a good idea, but don't forget to do something to prevent it. With all the throttles standing on end, you're not in a gas mileage contest. The engine will be using better than 3 to 5 gallons per mile, not miles per gallon. An additional electric fuel pump is virtually a necessity if you are to avoid the dangers of lean-out. Both Holley and Carter manufacture very good electric fuel pumps. Supplement one of these electric units with a high volume mechanical engine-driven pump (also available from Holley and Carter). Then top the whole thing off with at least one high-flow fuel filter, and a fuel pressure gauge. One final note, do not use Corbin-type hose clamps (of the spring wire variety), stay with the stainless steel screw clamps, as they will not slip or allow the hose to pop off, a decided problem with 6 psi and a high volume pump.

Larry Bowers, owner of Bowers Blowers, operates a very complete shop specializing in drag race blower preparation. Bowers may be the first company other than GMC to manufacture rotors. These special units, designed for racing, will withstand greater loads than the stock "diesel" rotors, and just may be responsible for the next broken barrier in elapsed times.

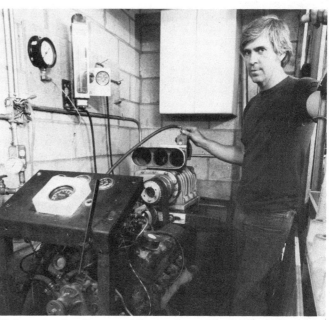

Unique to the Bowers shop is their blower dynamometer. Powered by a 301 Ford engine, this fixture can test GMC's under actual operation conditions.

SOME OF THE SUPPLIERS

Bowers Blowers, Larry Bowers

Bowers Blowers' well-equipped shop specializes in the manufacture and preparation of aluminum and magnesium GMC racing blowers. Larry's shop supplies complete blowers and parts to many of the major names in drag racing, including Don Garlits. His shop can also supply excellent street blower preparation. This can include parts inspection, parts replacement, clearance checking and setting, special rotor machining, and complete assembly. The Bowers company has a virtual encyclopedia of knowledge gained from many years of racing and blower building. Larry is more than willing to help any rodder with blower problems, just give him a call.

Bowers also makes a blower drive kit for the small and big-block Chevrolet engines. Based on his race package, this unit incorporates both strength and simplicity. Larry feels that each street combination will have special requirements, and therefore he builds each drive to the customer's specifications.

Larry utilizes a unique fixture to test and evaluate new ideas, and insure the highest in blower efficiency. Powered by a 301-inch Ford engine, his supercharger "dyno" will run the blower at any desired operational speed and measure the air pumped, the air temperatures, the overall efficiency, and functional reliability of any GMC supercharger. During the operation of this fixture, ear protection must be worn by all in the shop for the noise generated by the supercharger is thunderous. Water is injected into the inlet side of the blower to duplicate the effects of fuel and to provide the cooling necessary for nondestructive operation. This dyno test fixture is just one example of the complete dedication that the company has for top quality.

The Bowers shop has been involved in many special projects for street use. Cross-country supercharging, adapting 4-barrel manifolds for blowers, and the like, have broadened the viewpoint of this thriving company. Larry is also personally involved in building his own pet street project—a sano smallblock street rod, supercharged, and equipped

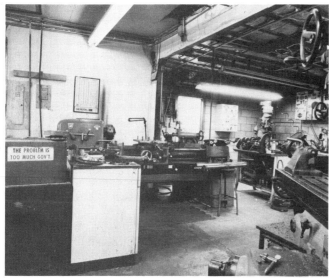

The preparation of blowers for either drag racing or street use requires a high degree of experience and no small amount of high-precision equipment.

Mert Littlefield Blowers specializes in building a blower to the customer's needs. Mert has developed many ways to save a puffer owner money and still supply a highly-durable product. Mert is willing to help any street blower enthusiast, even if he is supercharging one of those rare ones, like a Ford.

This V-8 drag bike belonging to Russ Collins is a perfect example of the de-design-to-customer's-specs blowers that Mert is famous for. Russ Collins must be congratulated for the tremendous engineering that went into this incredible machine.

Russ Collins' supercharged drag bike uses a pair of Honda fours connected like a V-8. The Roots blower is positioned between each engine and draws air from the bottom of the bike. The first set of injectors are located at the inlet and the second set (port injectors) are located in a special manifold that was hand-built, as are most of the pieces on this outstanding machine.

The special blower manifold uses two blow-off valves that each have triple hold-down springs. The valves are hand-lapped to have the manifold for a leak-free fit. Additional allen screws (indicated by arrows) were added to each end of the manifold to prevent a severe backfire from blowing the top off and throwing shrapnel at the driver.

with everything under the sun, including a CB radio.

Mert Littlefield Blowers, Mert Littlefield

There are few people lucky enough to be able to work at their hobby. After many years of racing experience, Mert Littlefield made the decision to fill a need in the racing market. Mert Littlefield Blowers is a small company that reflects the best qualities of the small business man. A dedication to quality, a personal pride in his work, and almost never-ending energy are a few of Mert's attributes. He has a refreshingly direct attitude and can provide any service the street puffer fan could want. He realizes that many enthusiasts have a very limited budget and prefer to repair, rather than replace, blower assemblies. Mert can also provide all the usual "higher dollar" parts that are required for all-out drag racing. He manufactures his own end plates, covers, blower cases, and can supply Dyer's street drive kit, as Mert Littlefield is the west coast distributor of this fine product.

Mert stocks many of the unusual and hard-to-find parts required by street blower enthusiasts. He has a very nice twin Holley Dominator manifold that is just the key for maximum performance on a boat. Designed to bolt on a GMC blower, this ultimate induction will also find a place on the street for those that are willing to make a very large hole in their hood. Mert is also willing to help those that may be interested in supercharging an oddball engine for which blower parts are not readily available. This can be worth a great deal to those diehards working with Mopars, Olds, or whatever.

Blair's Speed Shop, Phil Lukens

Phil Lukens owns Blair's Speed Shop, and it couldn't be in better hands. Phil is one of the most knowledgeable people in the racing parts field. Why? Because he is an avid, active drag racer. He is more than a drag racer, in that he believes in and practices doing things "right". His race car is a blown fuel Altered, and it reflects immaculate preparation. Phil has had a good deal of experience with blown engines and can supply more information than you ever thought existed. His shop specializes in installations of turbochargers and superchargers, and can provide any or all parts that one may need.

Blair's Speed is one of the very few original speed shops that still exists today. Virtually a legend in the Southern California area, this shop has shelves and tables on which you may find such things as flat head cylinder heads, used intake manifolds for just about everything, old GMC blowers, 4-speeds, automatics, parts of blower drives, etc, etc, etc! The total feeling of Blair's is racing and performance. The most important concern to Phil is supplying good parts and service at a decent price. If you would like the advice of a true professional and perfectionist, give Phil a call.

Iskenderian Racing Cams, T. Willey

If you mention a supercharged Studebaker, a GMC-blown, or a turbocharged street hot rod, you will immediately get the attention of one of the friendliest people at Isky Racing Cams. Isky cams has been around as long as drag racing, and T. Willey has been with Isky since the beginning. He has seen it all, and he is willing to talk about it. Isky manufactures a super-strong forged aluminum blower drive that works very well for the street. T. Willey will be more than happy to talk tech with you about the drive, street blowers, race blowers, or any other problems that you may have.

We know of no other single individual that has more first-hand experience than T. Willey. He has a very sensible approach to supercharging, all based on successes and failures in his own projects. That's right, he is one of the few people that will admit to making a mistake at one time or another. If you want some "straight-from-the-hip" help, give Isky a call. Oh yes, and ask for T. Willey!

The following companies manufacture GMC blower parts, and can supply complete race or street blowers:

Bowers Blowers
17430 Parthenia Street
Northridge, CA

Mert Littlefield Blowers
2773 E. 19th Street
Long Beach, CA 90804

Hampton Blowers
13620 Dunrobin Avenue
Bellflower, CA 90706

Dyer's Blower Service
8807 78th Avenue
Bridgeview, Illinois 60455

Isky Racing Cams
T. Willey
16020 S. Broadway
Gardena, CA 90248

The following companies can supply parts and help in blower installation.

Blair's Speed Shop
Phil Lukens
2771 East Foothill Blvd.
Pasadena, CA 91107

Ted Brown
2765 East 19th Street
Long Beach, CA 90804

T. Willey
Isky Racing Cams
16020 S. Broadway
Gardena, CA 90248

R/C Engineering (Motorcycle Supercharging)
Russ Collins
16216 S. Main
Gardena, CA 90248

Experience is the all-important factor in the modification of equipment for performance or racing. Phil Lukens, owner of Blairs' Speed Shop (left in photo), is one of those lucky few that has spent most of his life involved with designing, building, and racing cars. He believes in doing things right, as in sano. This turbocharger installation recently completed at his shop is an example of the "superworkmanship" that can be expected at Blairs.

FUEL INJECTION

By JIM MCFARLAND

INTRODUCTION

To most people, fuel injection systems are associated with the various forms of racing or high-performance engines. Actually, this is not an accurate consideration of how such systems compare with conventional carburetion methods of supplying air and fuel to today's internal combustion engines. But because it is relatively simple to contact the manufacturers of contemporary fuel injection systems and receive information about how different approaches are designed and function, the purpose of this section is to study the reasons why fuel injection may or may not be superior to carburetors, provide you with some mathematical means for determining what sort of fuel injection system you might need, and an analysis for determining the design criteria for related engine parts such as intake manifold and exhaust system design. You'll find discussion of the more popular versions of fuel injection systems, with particular emphasis on the current status of electronic fuel injection development. Aside from the benefits that such systems may provide relative to fuel economy, outright race engine performance stands to benefit from these improved methods of fuel control and delivery.

What we'd like for you to keep in mind is that this section is not a collection of "catalog" material. Rather, it is intended to dip into some of the basics and related areas that affect both normally-aspirated and supercharged internal combustion engines, with the

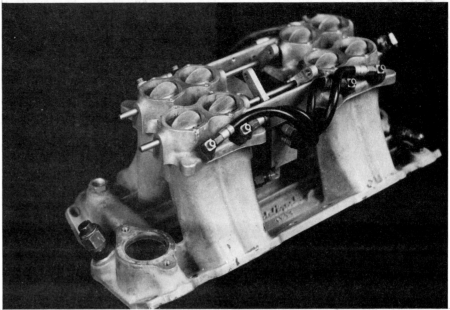

To take advantage of contemporary intake manifold designs, some injector systems have been fabricated using throttle plate clusters and port nozzles situated as shown. Nozzle location is critical and often requires experimentation for best power. Manifold shown is so-called Tunnel Ram base.

hope that you will be able to understand the advantages and limitations of fuel injection—regardless of how it may apply to the engine of your choice.

By itself, gasoline will not burn. If you could dip a burning match into a bucket of gasoline, the liquid would extinguish the flame. But just above the gasoline, there exists a mixture of air and fuel (owing to vaporized fuel in the air). The fact that this mixture stands between your burning match stick and the liquid fuel will probably prevent you

from attempting such an experiment again. Even so, the point is that air and fuel must be mixed before combustion can be accomplished. And with respect to the internal combustion engine, something needs to be provided that will serve this purpose.

Mixing valves, as they once were called, actually "mixed" air and fuel before entry into the combustion chambers. Exactly how this was accomplished in early times is pretty much the way it is done today, but there are some variations that should be understood. One of them is fuel injection. But to fully understand the principles of operation and advantages (or disadvantages) of this method of fuel delivery, the basic "carburetion" of air and fuel should be discussed. The following paragraphs are intended to lay this foundation with the hope that a more complete understanding of fuel injection can result.

First, air moves through an engine as a function of engine crankshaft speed and the total piston displacement of the engine. The larger the engine, the more air it will displace in a given period of time. While the *rate* of air movement (in a given intake or exhaust cycle) is related to such things as stroke length and connecting rod length, the point to remember here is that any type of induction system (fuel injection or carburetion) is tied to the amount of air that is passing through the engine. Since air-fuel ratio (the amount of air per amount of fuel) is related to the amount of power output, any induction system must provide the proper air-fuel ratio for the demands of the engine. We must also keep in mind that this air-fuel ratio varies as a function of

Fabricated injectors (using carburetor intake manifold parts as shown) require circular throttle bores to provide adequate idling and low throttle blade angle engine operation. Due to flow velocities within the injector manifold runners, fuel delivery is often best accomplished on the "short side" of the runners (roof area as shown).

129

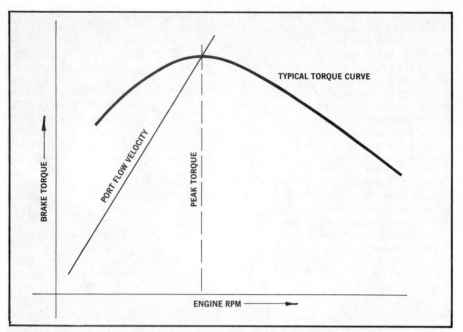

As engine speed increases, so does port flow velocity on the intake side of the engine. Since critical "flow velocities" dictate where torque peaks are developed, there is a point at which max torque is produced, above which rpm there is no increase in torque production for subsequent increases in flow velocity within the injector manifold.

how the engine is being used. Engines required to provide high levels of fuel economy operate more in a range of air-fuel ratio of 14.5-16.0:1. Those for which maximum power is required fall in a range of 10.5-12.0:1. And it is a requirement of the induction system (injection or carburetion) to provide the correct mixture ratio.

It has been said that when the perfect fuel injection system is designed, the result is a carburetor. Even though this may or may not be true, both systems must accomplish about the same thing: air-fuel delivery to suit the demands of the engine. So in an attempt to develop the air-fuel requirements of an engine, the following model is offered. At low speeds, air flow through the engine is relatively low. Normally, this means that very little throttle blade opening (or near maximum induction system flow restriction) is provided. As a result, high manifold vacuum conditions exist. Since the air flow rate is low, the amount of pressure drop across the "mixing valve" is also low. Keeping in mind that atmospheric pressure (force) is the only thing that causes fuel to flow into a normally-aspirated engine, low engine speeds do not allow much atmospheric pressure influence to be felt by the engine. Consequently, a system that is sensitive to low engine speeds needs to be provided so that the proper air-fuel ratios can be established. In carburetted engines, this becomes the idle circuit and amounts to a combination of air-fuel mixture enrichment screws (or adjustments), idle air and fuel bleeds, and a general system of providing limited quantities of fuel

for very low engine rpm. Fuel injection systems, depending upon intended design, must also accomplish this function.

Once an engine begins to operate in higher rpm ranges, more air will be displaced (passed through the engine). As a result, more fuel is required to maintain the proper mixture ratio. Depending upon operating conditions, this fuel is provided by a so-called intermediate circuit (in carburetted engines). Since the engine is not yet in a "full on" operating mode, maximum fuel delivery is not required, so a middle-of-the-

road circuit is necessary to maintain the correct air-fuel ratio.

It is this portion of the fuel supply function that many carburetors do not properly handle. The problem stems from incorrect "overlapping" of the idle and power circuits, whereby the engine does not receive adequate fuel supply. And even though accelerator pump circuits (fuel shots that are intended to cover up the lack of fuel delivery upon sudden opening of the throttle blades) cure much of the problem, quick throttle operation after an engine has reached a given rpm does not have the benefit of such fuel delivery. The reason for pointing out such deficiencies in carburetted induction systems is to establish a frame of reference so that the advantages of fuel injection can be directly compared later in this section.

Carburetors are also sensitive to atmospheric pressure. Since fuel delivery depends (among other things) upon the difference in pressure between the intake manifold and atmospheric pressure, changes in environmental conditions affect fuel flow. For example, when less atmospheric pressure is available, less fuel will pass into the engine (unless some change is made to fuel flow orifices such as jets, etc.).

And there is another problem seldom discussed. Given a fuel flow orifice (jet) of some size, the amount of fuel it will pass depends upon the pressure drop across it. Let's say that a particular jet is in a particular carburetor (and this is going to relate directly to fuel injection, believe it or not). If the pressure drop "across this jet" is only 70% of what the jet can flow,

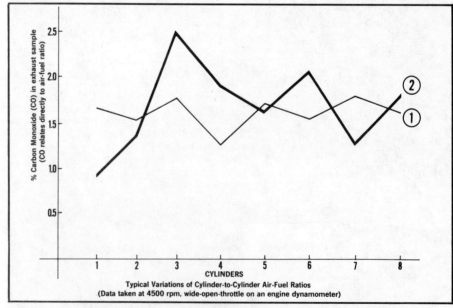

Typical Variations of Cylinder-to-Cylinder Air-Fuel Ratios
(Data taken at 4500 rpm, wide-open-throttle on an engine dynamometer)

Trace #2 shows how air-fuel variations result from improper intake manifold design. Such cylinder-to-cylinder variations reduce net engine power and make injector fuel delivery setting difficult at best. Trace #1 is more desired and results in improved engine performance and/or fuel economy.

its total opening is not being used to full capacity. With more air flow (under these conditions), there would be an additional 30% of fuel flow, until the jet reached what we shall call its "total fuel flow capacity." Herein lies some of the answer to why both fuel injection systems (and their jets or "pills") and carburetors can deliver more or less fuel without a change in metering. And although this is at the risk of oversimplification, the underlying fact is that *it is not always necessary to increase the jet or pill size just to get more fuel to flow.* Additional *air* flow can produce an increase in flowed fuel.

In this respect, there is one major difference between a carburetted system and a fuel injection system. It is how each reacts to what is called "reversion" or back-flow into the induction system. Because this particular phenomenon is commonplace in just about any internal combustion engine (normally-aspirated or otherwise), it might be worthy of some brief discussion.

Simply stated, it could go as follows. At the time the intake valve opens, pressure in the intake manifold is less than that in the cylinder. If it were not, flow through the exhaust system would not be taking place. Because of this, some residual exhaust gas (or by-products of combustion) are passed back into the induction system. This happens whether the engine is carburetted or fuel injected. At this point, the engine doesn't know the difference. Any combustion residue that finds its way back into the intake-side of the engine can contaminate following intake charges and reduce net power. From the standpoint of reduced oxides of nitrogen (NOx), this may be beneficial. But in terms of what it takes to optimize horsepower, it is subtractive to engine efficiency. Therefore, it is important to prevent as much reversion influence in an engine (intended for optimum output) as possible. Engines that are fuel injected, consequently, have the benefit of "timed" fuel delivery (a feature to be discussed at length a little later). This feature reduces the chance that fresh fuel will be "blown back" into the intake system during the reversion period, resulting in less contaminated and more accurately controlled air-fuel mixtures at the time of combustion.

While all of this may sound like something less than "How I planned to make my car go quicker with fuel injection," it is part of the basis for understanding what fuel injection is really all about. And then there is the subject of how fuel injection systems contain fuel versus how carburetted systems contain fuel. The problem here is angularity. In a carburetor, there is typically a fuel bowl in which fuel to be delivered to the engine is held. Associated with the fuel bowl is a float and some sort of check-valve that is designed to stop fuel flow into the bowl when the fuel reaches a certain level. If, for some reason, the carburetor is tilted, this "fuel level" indication is altered and more or less fuel will flow into the bowl, resulting in possible disruption in the air-fuel ratio delivered to the engine.

In vehicles used for racing, sudden changes in acceleration or direction often cause problems in the handling of fuel (in carburetors, fuel tanks, etc.). For this reason, fuel injection is superior to carburetion and, if it did not provide any other benefits, eliminates the problems associated with "keeping the jets covered" during severe operating conditions.

In particular, versions of electronic fuel injection systems, deal with so-called "dry-flow" mixture control. These systems do not provide fuel for the engine until well after the piston has passed the top dead center (TDC) position and/or they inject fuel very near the intake valve. In both cases, there is a reduced chance for fuel to be blown back into the intake system during the reversion period. And the more fuel that can be provided (under controlled conditions) to the engine, the better the engine will produce power.

To a large extent, the air-fuel mixture "problem" can be reduced by providing the proper air and fuel to an engine *under a wide variety of operating conditions.* But to properly do this, any injection system should be tailored to those other engine parameters that are affected by an injection system ... namely the intake and exhaust systems.

TUNING THE INTAKE AND EXHAUST SYSTEM TO AN INJECTOR SYSTEM

First, there are so-called critical flow velocities in a piston engine. This

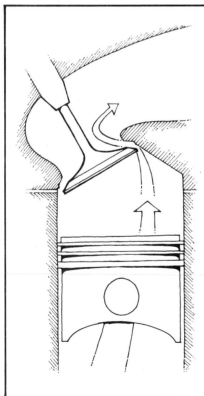

"Reversion" is a term often discussed but just as often misunderstood. As discussed in the text, it amounts to reverse-flow into the combustion chamber as a result of cylinder pressure being higher than intake manifold pressure when the intake valve opens. The location of such flow is often along the "short side" of the intake port (as shown).

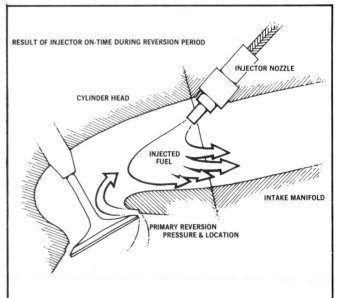

RESULT OF INJECTOR ON-TIME DURING REVERSION PERIOD

INJECTOR NOZZLE

CYLINDER HEAD

INJECTED FUEL

INTAKE MANIFOLD

PRIMARY REVERSION PRESSURE & LOCATION

In continuous-flow injection systems, reversion pressures are more of a problem than in systems that are timed. Should the injector be flowing fuel when the reversion "cycle" begins, some amount of fuel will be "blown back" into the injector manifold, resulting in possible lost power.

means that there are engine speeds at which the "energy conditions" or resonance characteristics of the engine lend themselves to more gains in net power than at some other engine rpm. Since most fuel injection systems employ intake manifolding of the "individual runner" design, there is less influence (reversion, adverse pulsation, etc.) from one runner to the other. Basically, there is no air cavity (plenum chamber) connecting all runners of the inlet manifold. So there is no communication of adverse pressure pulsation among the intake manifold passages.

It has been proven that the induction system of "collected" runner engines will produce two distinct "torque boosts" at two different engine speeds. Since most fuel injection systems employ inlet manifolds designed without a "collector area" or plenum chamber, such "double boost" torque increases are not possible. However, in fuel injection systems that incorporate intake manifolding with a collected runner volume (plenum chamber), low-rpm torque increases are possible . . . given the proper attention to plenum chamber design. The point to remember here is that low-rpm torque improvements are a function of plenum chamber volume. Torque increases above this point depend upon the cross-sectional area of the actual port branches themselves (manifold runners). This, in fact, even applies to the design of exhaust systems. But this will be discussed later.

Because fuel injection systems typically employ isolated intake port runners, particular attention should be paid to the cross-sectional area of these runners. And while the length of the inlet manifold runners will affect the torque output of an engine, such changes do not alter the point at which peak torque is developed. The "torque curve" is merely "rocked" about the point at which the peak value takes place. Inlet manifold runners that are longer enable the engine to make more low-rpm torque while shorter passages cause higher-rpm torque output. But regardless of the amount of torque produced throughout the rpm range, peak torque remains at the same point until the cross-sectional area of the inlet passages is changed.

The same theory applies to exhaust systems. Here, the pulses that generate flow are different in that the piston is in a different position during maximum flow, as compared to the induction-side of the engine. But the conditions of "tuning" remain the same. Exhaust plenum chamber (actually the exhaust header collector(s) as may or may not be joined by a cross-over tube) tuning is no different than that applied to the induction-side of the engine, and "collected" exhaust systems

act as "single-plane" systems when the collectors are joined by some sort of an equalizer tube. In any event, the induction system (in particular an injection system) will respond to such changes in the exhaust system.

Typically, as the intake and exhaust system are "tuned" more closely to each other (resonant at about the same rpm), a given fuel injection system needs to be calibrated (for fuel delivery) more accurately to the requirements of a given engine. And while engine dynamometer testing will provide such fuel requirements, at-the-track tests will indicate the same sort of calibration (in general terms of "richening" or "leaning" of the fuel metering).

A major point to consider in the selection of any fuel injection system is the type of intake manifolding that will be incorporated. If we can define intake manifold development improvements as gains in induction system "technology," it is safe to say that fuel injection manifold air flow technology has not kept pace with that of carburetted induction systems. Why this has taken place remains a point of discussion, but the fact remains that intake manifolds typically used with fuel injection systems are not state-of-the-art with comparable carburetted systems.

Factors to be considered in the selection of a particular fuel injection system are: 1) engine rpm range and 2) basic dimensions of the exhaust system. Since both of these have specific effect on the net power output of a given engine, both should be considered in the selection of engine pieces.

For example, let's assume that a flow rate of 245 feet/second is critical to a given engine's torque output. This is

said to hold true for either the intake or exhaust side of an engine. If you accept the fact that it is at or about this flow velocity that torque peaks are produced, and the fact that runner cross-sectional area governs much of the capability of a particular intake or exhaust system, then selection of good intake and exhaust manifolding for an engine becomes very critical. Actually, there has been considerable experimentation whereby carburetted intake manifolding has been used in combination with some fuel injection pieces, such that the end result is an induction system that provides the best of two worlds; controlled fuel delivery through the best available intake manifolding.

The "bottom-line" of all this tuning stuff is the fact that both the intake and exhaust systems contribute to an engine's ability to make horsepower or torque. Under the assumption that so-called "critical flow velocities" are reached as a function of engine rpm (and total piston displacement), either the intake or exhaust portion of an engine will be "resonate" at some rpm. If the intake and exhaust systems are designed (or selected) to be resonate at the same rpm, maximum torque production can be expected at that rpm. Should they be designed to be resonate at different rpm points, less peak torque will be produced while a broader torque range will result. The point of all this is that since most fuel injection intake manifold designs are of the "plenum-less" design, you should decide at what high rpm point peak torque should be produced and then select an intake manifold capable of producing a peak at this rpm. Consultation with the fuel injection

For utmost performance it is important to tune the intake and exhaust tracts to the engine-fuel injection requirements. Single "uncollected" induction stacks require careful tuning to these requirements, but benefits can be derived from "collected" intake systems utilizing a plenum to gain "double boost" torque increases.

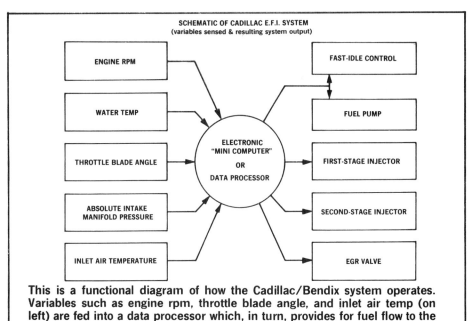

SCHEMATIC OF CADILLAC E.F.I. SYSTEM
(variables sensed & resulting system output)

ENGINE RPM
WATER TEMP
THROTTLE BLADE ANGLE
ABSOLUTE INTAKE MANIFOLD PRESSURE
INLET AIR TEMPERATURE

ELECTRONIC "MINI COMPUTER" OR DATA PROCESSOR

FAST-IDLE CONTROL
FUEL PUMP
FIRST-STAGE INJECTOR
SECOND-STAGE INJECTOR
EGR VALVE

This is a functional diagram of how the Cadillac/Bendix system operates. Variables such as engine rpm, throttle blade angle, and inlet air temp (on left) are fed into a data processor which, in turn, provides for fuel flow to the engine.

manufacturer of your choice should do one of two things: 1) nail down a unit that will satisfy the needs of your particular engine or 2) prove to you that your choice of manufacturer was wrong in the first place. Just remember that no fuel injection system will be complete unless the proper induction and exhaust system are chosen for the rpm range in which the engine will be operated. A mistake here could cost you the entire benefits of almost any fuel injection system.

STATE-OF-THE-ART IN FUEL INJECTION SYSTEMS

Most of us remember the Rochester system that was used on smallblock Chevrolet V8 engines in the mid-1950's.

Actually, this system was a compromise between pure carburetion and true fuel injection. There was no carburetor, but its replacement was not truly what you would consider to be a "classroom" fuel metering device. Today, fuel injection is heading toward systems that utilize some sort of injector nozzles and fuel supply controlled by electronic delivery. In most cases, solid-state electronics are employed to analyze air-fuel ratio requirements (under a variety of engine operating conditions) and provide the necessary input to fuel control devices (nozzles, pumps, etc.) to maintain such fuel flow.

Utilizing electronic feed-back systems in conjunction with the sampling and consolidation of various engine

operating variables (such as intake manifold vacuum, engine rpm, inlet air temperature, coolant temperature, etc.), these contemporary systems generate "signals" to mini-computers that provide just exactly the amount of fuel required to meet the demands of various engine conditions. For example, if an engine is under acceleration, the conditions that indicate this is the mode of operation are fed to the electronics portion of the system and fuel flow is regulated accordingly. As the power demands are reduced, these same operational variables (as previously mentioned) change, resulting in a subsequent change in fuel delivered. Gone are the "by guess and by golly" approaches. Where previous fuel injection fuel delivery was based upon engine rpm and/or throttle blade position, these current-day systems (some available, some in development) "study" the state of the engine and provide fuel accordingly.

Some systems, such as the Continuous Fuel Injection System (CIS) as used on late-model Porsche and Audi Fox engines, monitor air flow (by way of a so-called air flow sensor) and regulate fuel flow in accordance with the air-fuel ratio such air flow requires. In this particular system, air flow measurement is sensed at the entry to the inlet manifold. Based on the amount of air passing into the engine at this point, a fuel distributor regulates the amount of fuel delivered and associated pieces such as a cold-start valve, fuel pressure regulator and a fuel accumulator that both damps pump noise and helps maintain fuel line pressure when the engine is not operating.

Depending upon the manner in which fuel is admitted into the engine, there are both timed and non-timed systems based upon electronic controls. The system, for example, that is used on late-model Cadillac engines is of the so-called "batch" design. Here sufficient fuel for four cylinders is injected into the inlet manifold. While such systems could be defined as "timed" systems, it is not timed so that fuel is delivered into the inlet manifold or ports *during each intake stroke*. But by definition, all electronic fuel injection (EFI) systems provide an ability to control, much more precisely than with either mechanical injection or carburetion, the amount of fuel delivered to the engine for a wide variety of operating conditions.

Actually, an EFI system employs electrically-operated solenoid valves that operate under constant (or relatively constant) fuel line pressure. At the specific time fuel is to be delivered to the engine's inlet ports or manifold, the solenoid is given an electrical signal (actually an electronic "pulse" of predetermined duration), and the

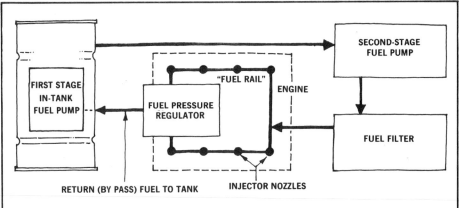

SECOND-STAGE FUEL PUMP
FIRST STAGE IN-TANK FUEL PUMP
FUEL PRESSURE REGULATOR
"FUEL RAIL"
ENGINE
FUEL FILTER
RETURN (BY PASS) FUEL TO TANK
INJECTOR NOZZLES

CADILLAC SEVILLE FUEL DELIVERY SYSTEM

This schematic layout shows the relationship among the various fuel delivery pieces of the Cadillac EFI system. Note that there is a first-stage pump in the fuel tank that is boosted by a second pump just ahead of the "fuel rails" or injector nozzles.

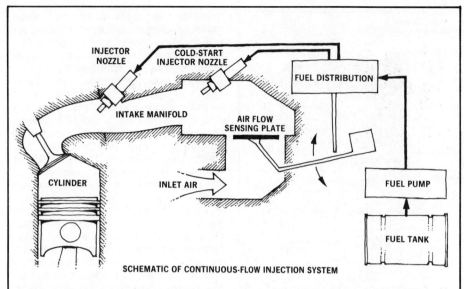

Labels on schematic: INJECTOR NOZZLE, COLD-START INJECTOR NOZZLE, FUEL DISTRIBUTION, INTAKE MANIFOLD, AIR FLOW SENSING PLATE, CYLINDER, INLET AIR, FUEL PUMP, FUEL TANK

SCHEMATIC OF CONTINUOUS-FLOW INJECTION SYSTEM

Here is a schematic of the Continuous Injection System (CIS) such as those found on the Porsche Audi and 911T Porsche engines. Note how variations in position of the "air flow sensing plate" regulate the amount of total fuel flow into the engine. This plate acts much like a conventional "throttle blade" in a carburetor.

solenoid opens the valve and then shuts it. The actual amount of fuel delivered is a function of how long the valve stays open. It does not necessarily follow that the injector timing (relative to crankshaft or piston position) will vary for different engine load or operating conditions. Typically, all injectors are turned on at the same point relative to piston position. But it is the period of time they are left on that governs how much fuel is delivered.

Some of the more critical factors of such EFI systems are: 1) good atomization of fuel as it leaves the injector nozzles, 2) provisions in the system for the handling of hot fuel once the engine has been run and is subjected to hot restart, and 3) inlet manifolding that provides a range of inlet vacuums that are sensitive enough for proper electronics control input. But regardless of how these particular features are accomplished, a major difference among the various types of EFI systems is the pattern of injector "on-time." There are three: Continuous Injection Systems (CIS), where fuel is delivered by the entire set of nozzles releasing fuel all at one time; Batch Injection Systems (BIS), where fuel is injected by sets of injectors alternately operating throughout the engine's firing order (like the Cadillac that feeds cylinders 1-2-5-7 at one time and 3-4-6-8 the next); or Sequential Injection Systems (SIS), in which injector nozzles are turned on to follow the engine's firing order exactly.

For example, in the latter case, if the firing order happens to be 1-8-4-3-6-5-7-2 (as in the case of most General Motors engines), each injector nozzle

will open and close in accordance with this order. Thought by many to be the more efficient in terms of fuel control, sequential (SIS) systems offer the ability to develop intake manifolding that is essentially "dry flow" to the extent that many of the problems associated with wet-flow manifolding (including carburetted engines) are substantially reduced. Of special note is the fact that air-fuel mixture separation (one from the other) is significantly reduced in SIS designs, and fuel economy improvements result.

In order to better understand the overall EFI function, consider the

following example. It is typical of such systems as they are currently being produced both domestically and abroad. Fuel is supplied to the injectors by some sort of fuel "rail" that is under constant pressure. A common pressure range would be from 25-40 psi in the rail. Such pressure levels help establish good fuel atomization during the injector on-times. Depending upon which system is in operation, there will be a time when fuel goes into the engine. Normally, this point of entry is at or very near the intake ports.

A number of engine operating variables, such as inlet air temperature, intake manifold pressure (depressions), engine rpm, ignition advance, coolant temperature and comparable conditions are constantly monitored and fed into what we shall call a "mini computer." This portion of the system is designed to generate an electric signal which, in turn, is sent to an injector nozzle to control its operation. As engine demands vary (load, speed, etc.), more or less fuel is required, regardless of the air-fuel ratio desired. Based on the fact that the monitoring portion of the system (the one picking up the operating variables) is constantly updating the injector on-time data (typically at the rate of about 1000 times per second), it is virtually impossible to "get ahead" of the system. Just as soon as some small changes take place in the mode of engine operation, the mini-computer has noted it, changed the signal going to the injector nozzle and the increase or decrease in injector on-time has happened . . . at the rate of 1000 corrections per second! Compare this with the up-dating sensitivity of a conventional carburetor and you can be-

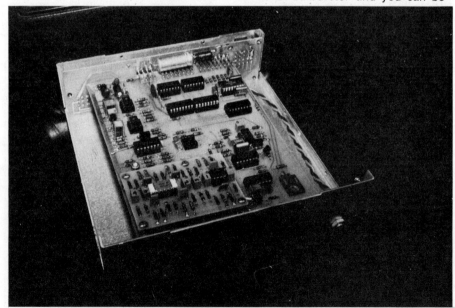

The electronics of the Edelbrock EFI system incorporate a so-called "mini-computer" and an injector "drive board" that provides injector-on and injector-off data to the electrically operated injectors. A pressure transducer produces intake manifold vacuum data which is part of the computed fuel signal data (injector instructions).

gin to see some of the advantages an EFI system offers over just about anything else.

Perhaps the heart of any EFI system is its ability to sense intake manifold pressures (actually, we are here speaking of absolute pressure). Expensive pressure transducers are situated such that even the smallest change in the absolute pressure conditions of the inlet manifold can be read. This is necessary because the degree of air-fuel ratio control required of EFI systems is far more critical than with conventional carburetted systems. To maintain cruise mixture ratios truly in the 15-17:1 range, precise fuel delivery timing, good fuel atomization (and atomized particles of relatively the same size), and system repeatability under a wide range of operational temperatures are absolute necessities.

The fact that EFI systems employ dry-flow intake manifolding is an obvious plus (air-fuel separation within the manifold is reduced), but it has been found that torque improvements from velocity-flow-only manifold designs are not necessarily the same as for carburetted engines. In other words, the high rate of system updating available from EFI does not require high velocity flow in the intake manifold. For a carburetor to be efficient (atomization, particle size, correct fuel delivery, etc.), it must "see" some amount of inlet air flow velocity. At low engine speed (rpm), such velocity through the carburetor is low and fuel delivery efficiency is also low (fuel particle size is varying rather widely). As engine speed is increased, the carburetor begins to become more efficient, and its operation is enhanced by an intake manifold design that contributes to the flow velocity of the wetted flow passing through it (air and fuel mixed). As a result, the fuel required by an engine at any particular moment will be supplied slightly later, since the carburetor cannot react quickly enough. There's a little "Kentucky windage" in the system, or lag in fuel flow. Intake manifold design that improves flow velocity at low engine speeds helps generate fuel flow "signals" in the carburetor more quickly than internally larger manifolds.

However, in EFI there is far less "lag" in the system. With updating of fuel flow data every 1/1000th of a second, fuel is delivered almost exactly when the engine demands it. So inlet manifolding that previously added low rpm velocity to the system is not required—resulting in slightly larger volume designs that aid in damping out unwanted pulses that might "confuse" the pressure transducer portion of the system and cause more fuel to be delivered.

As you might expect, ignition timing and the relation of fuel delivery to in-

An electronic "chopper" or rotor is used in such systems as the Edelbrock electronic fuel injection system. This part of the ignition distributor triggers the primary ignition circuit much like a set of ignition points in a typical Kettering system. A similar magnetic pickup rotor delivers timed signals to the injector nozzles.

jector timing (phasing) is also critical in EFI. Depending upon the time (relative to piston position or crankshaft angle) at which fuel is to be released from the nozzle, the point of spark in the combustion chamber becomes very important. This is especially true in lean-burn engines (those operating above stoichiometric air-fuel ratio, leaner than about 14.7:1). Consequently, good EFI design includes ignition systems (high energy or HEI) that will work with both lean-burn and precise injector timing. Interestingly enough, some SIS (sequential) systems incorporate injector on-times that are well into the inlet cycle. For example, injectors may not be turned on until the piston is past top dead center and several crankshaft degrees into the intake stroke. In this way, inlet air is already passing into the cylinder when fuel is released in the stream. It's somewhat like pouring a bucket of water into a flowing river; there is little chance for reversion pulsation to prevent fresh fuel from passing into the combustion chamber.

And then there is the question of whether such systems can be designed for positive intake manifold pressures such as you would find in supercharged or turbocharged engines. The answer is, yes. Typically, what is required is a positive pressure sensing portion in the mini-computer and a set of circuits establishing a fuel curve (amount of fuel delivered as a function of engine operation) compatible with the amount of inlet air flow supercharging or turbocharging provides. Actually, and this is especially true with SIS, the system knows only what the status of the sensed variables

are (inlet air temperature, rpm, etc.) and how much fuel it should provide *based on a predetermined fuel curve or set of curves*. It does not care what the engine is doing beyond the scope of these variables. And the amount and degree of fuel control offered for non-normally-aspirated engines is both significant and an area under particular study today, since electronic fuel control appears to be the next level of technology for the internal combustion engine . . . regardless of how it is used.

THE BASIS FOR PREVIOUS FUEL INJECTION SYSTEMS

Obviously, fuel injection is not new. Diesel engines have been fuel injected for many years, as have certain aircraft engines. But in domestic, new-car market, there have been only a limited number of designs.

Perhaps one of the better-known systems was the Rochester FI unit released in the mid-1950's for smallblock Chevrolet V-8 engines. Known as a "drool" or continuous-flow port-injection system, this design had three basic pieces: an intake manifold, a fuel meter-injector assembly, and an air meter. A conventional fuel pump supplied fuel to a high-pressure, gear-type pump that was located in the fuel-metering cavity. Two outlet lines for fuel came from the metering chamber, one feeding the fuel injector lines and the other a return line to the fuel tank. As a function of intake manifold vacuum, a plunger in the fuel-metering chamber operated to vary fuel flow through the injector nozzles. Excess

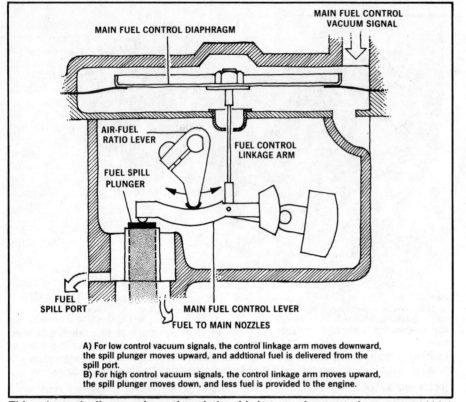

MAIN FUEL CONTROL DIAPHRAGM

MAIN FUEL CONTROL VACUUM SIGNAL

AIR-FUEL RATIO LEVER

FUEL CONTROL LINKAGE ARM

FUEL SPILL PLUNGER

FUEL SPILL PORT

MAIN FUEL CONTROL LEVER

FUEL TO MAIN NOZZLES

A) For low control vacuum signals, the control linkage arm moves downward, the spill plunger moves upward, and addtional fuel is delivered from the spill port.
B) For high control vacuum signals, the control linkage arm moves upward, the spill plunger moves down, and less fuel is provided to the engine.

This schematic diagram shows the relationship between low control vacuum and high control vacuum signals in the Rochester FI system. Fuel delivery is through the spill port as it is affected by manifold vacuum and movement of the fuel spill plunger.

fuel returned to the tank by way of the bypass or return line.

The injector nozzles were situated in the intake manifold right where the manifold joined the cylinder heads. It was almost like direct port-injection. Under pressure as high as 200 psi (at times), fuel was injected into the inlet ports. A particular feature of the Rochester unit was the fact that fuel was injected continuously into the intake manifold, resulting in air-fuel mixtures (vaporized fuel) standing constantly in the manifold and intake ports, waiting for the intake valves to open and vaporized fuel to flow into the cylinders.

Net engine air flow was controlled by an air valve arrangement, but overall air-fuel mixture ratio was governed by intake manifold vacuum (or pressure). Actuated by a vacuum line connecting the fuel injection air horn to a diaphragm controlling the metering plunger, the metering device "read" engine conditions much like its contemporary electronic counterparts. A second vacuum line was attached to the air horn just above the throttle and extended to a second diaphragm. This second diaphragm actuated a plunger which metered engine fuel during wide open throttle or acceleration conditions.

The usual fast-idle control and an electric choke were added for convenience and smoothness of operation. But one of the more controversial

features of the system was a fuel shut-off control during high intake manifold vacuum (such as deceleration modes of operation) whereby fuel flow was stopped momentarily. While this is a feature of some EFI systems today (electronically controlled), concern over exhaust emissions did not exist back in the mid-1950's. The reason the Rochester FI incorporated such a feature was for improved fuel economy.

One other feature of note was the type of inlet manifold used with the Rochester FI system. Called a "dog house" because of its rather boxy and A-shape design, this manifold lead the way for what was later to become the high-rpm so-called "Tunnel Ram" manifolds. The dog-house design incorporated relatively vertical runners (inlet passages) which were connected (collected) in a common air space (plenum chamber). Active in the development of the Rochester system was Zora Arkus-Duntov, who needs little introduction in the field of performance engines and cars. Since the Rochester unit was offered as a performance-improving option, the tuned-length runners (also featuring slight taper from runner entry to exit) further enhanced the mid- and high-rpm potential of the 283 cid Chevrolet V-8 engines on which it was first offered. But basically, early versions of fuel injection addressed most of the fundamental areas involving fuel condition and control. Some discussion of these ele-

ments is in order so that further study of the benefits and disadvantages of previous and present-day systems can be more easily understood.

First, there is the area of fuel spray characteristics. The problem here is that we are concerned with the mechanical breakdown of liquid fuel. It must be atomized, and it should be atomized to as small a particle size as possible. Carburetion, typically, is not efficient enough to provide good levels of atomization at relatively low engine speeds, so it becomes apparent very quickly that fuel injection can aid fuel economy in these low levels of rpm. Essentially, there are two ways by which fuel can be atomized: 1) delivery of fuel into a moving stream of air (typical of carburetion) and 2) delivery of fuel under pressure conditions that are higher than that of the air stream into which it is passed. In case one, fuel of relatively high volatility is commonly used. Here, the effect of the relative motion between the moving air and slower-moving delivered fuel is to form "threads" or "streamers" of fuel which collapse because of surface tension characteristics and form into small droplets. Since there can be considerable variation in the initial sizes of such streamers or threads, there can be considerable variation in atomized particle size. This can be a problem in developing maximum engine output for a given amount of fuel.

The second method, sometimes called "solid injection," also depends somewhat upon the relative motion of the delivered fuel and air, but here the fuel is being sprayed into the air stream under pressure conditions that are higher than those in the air stream. This allows atomization efficiency much improved over case one in that injector nozzle design begins to play a more important role, also enabling good design to produce both small and relatively equal fuel particle size—which is an aid to good power versus fuel delivered.

In years past, combinations of the two methods (as suggested by Diesel) have been used and called "air injection," but regardless of the method used, the degree of atomization becomes a critical factor. Here we are talking about not only the actual size (or smallness) of each atomized fuel particle, but also the variation in *size* among a given volume of atomized fuel. It seems, all else being equal, that fuel velocity is the most critical factor in affecting good fuel atomization, which depends upon injector pressure. Mathematically, injection pressure is a function of the square root of the difference between injection pressure and combustion pressure. It should also be noted that there is a relationship between injection, insofar as

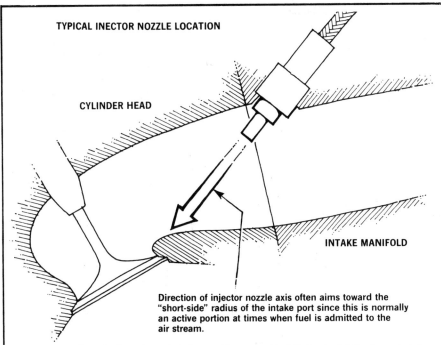

TYPICAL INECTOR NOZZLE LOCATION

CYLINDER HEAD

INTAKE MANIFOLD

Direction of injector nozzle axis often aims toward the "short-side" radius of the intake port since this is normally an active portion at times when fuel is admitted to the air stream.

Since low-lift air flow location is on the so-called "short side" of an intake port, injector nozzle "aiming" is usually toward this portion of the port. Improved air-fuel mixing (fuel atomization ahead of the combustion chamber) can result, especially if this freedom is available in nozzle location.

these relate to how far fuel has passed from a nozzle before actual atomization begins . As you might expect, high injection pressures are good for quick fuel atomization.

There is also the point of how injector nozzle opening (orifice) size may or may not affect atomization. It has been found that small orifices cause large surface-to-volume relationships for the stream of fuel being injected. But this, stated another way, simply means that the smaller orifices will produce the smallest fuel particle size. There is evidence, and this point should be remembered, that the ratio of nozzle length to flow opening (orifice) size has little effect on atomized particle size, Rather, this seems to relate to the "depth of penetration" of the injected fuel stream. Also a factor is air density. While there is still some indecision on the specific relationship between the degree of fuel atomization and combustion chamber air density, there is data showing that increases in air density tend to support smaller fuel droplet size. Actually, at least in theory, air density in the combustion chamber is fixed by mechanical compression ratio, so there should be little (if of any significance) variation in combustion chamber air density.

The amount of injected fuel penetration into the inlet air depends upon injected fuel velocity, orifice size, and combustion chamber air density. The viscosity of the injected fuel seems to have little effect on penetration. In terms of what it takes to arrive at

suitable orifice sizes (tip diameter to length ratios), for injectors intended to see maximum air penetration, ratios on the order of 4-6:1 (length to orifice diameter) have been shown to work well. And for cases where minimum injected fuel penetration is desired (for short inlet paths), length-to-diameter ratios in the range of 1-3:0 seem to work very well.

All of this should not be confused with a term called *dispersion,* which we will define as the shape of the "spray cone" of fuel as it leaves a given injector nozzle. For example, fuel spray dispersion that is relatively shallow will result from a spray cone that is short and wide. Deeper dispersion results from cone shapes that are narrow and long. Such nozzle designs as imping- ing jet, helical groove, annular, slit, and

comparable designs have been and are still used to set up the desired type of dispersion pattern and penetration. Since it is often desired to produce dispersion patterns that are of the large discharge cone type, small nozzle length-to-diameter ratios are commonly used.

Regardless of nozzle dispersion patterns, flow through nozzles can be either turbulent or laminar. It is generally agreed that turbulent nozzle flow improves dispersions patterns, such as you might find in a typical spray can of paint. Through use of higher injection pressures, sharp-edged orifices, or divergently tapered orifices, such turbulent injection flow characteristics can be achieved.

SOME DESIGN CONSIDERATIONS AND TERMS

As mentioned previously, there are essentially two types of fuel injection systems: air injection and solid injection. The more common of these two is the solid injection system in which liquid fuel is injected as opposed to the air system in which fuel *and air* are injected under high velocity pressure, normally requiring the use of an air compressor.

Solid injection systems are produced in a variety of forms, often employing fuel measuring and pumping devices along with single-point or multi-point injection (nozzles) that operate electro- mechanically or mechanically to satisfy a variety of engine operating fuel requirements. Such timed injection systems require fuel pumps that maintain a relatively constant fuel pressure. These systems also inject fuel well into the intake cycle, normally after the exhaust valve has closed, but not past about 115° beyond top dead- center piston position on the inlet stroke.

Direct injection into the combustion chamber (or cylinder head) is believed to be superior to injection farther up-

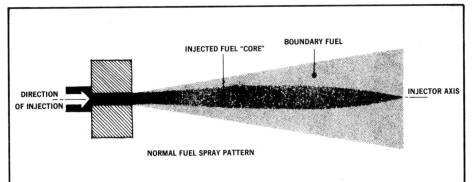

Normal fuel "spray" patterns from an injector nozzle include the injector fuel core (center portion) and boundary fuel located outside the core fuel. Actually, there is a distinct difference between fuel density in these two areas.

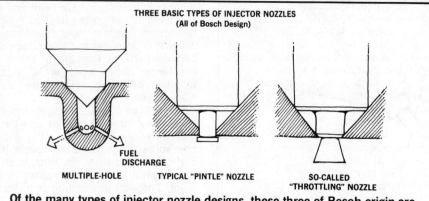

THREE BASIC TYPES OF INJECTOR NOZZLES
(All of Bosch Design)

FUEL
DISCHARGE

MULTIPLE-HOLE   TYPICAL "PINTLE" NOZZLE   SO-CALLED "THROTTLING" NOZZLE

Of the many types of injector nozzle designs, these three of Bosch origin are often used. From left to right, they are the multiple-hole, so-called "pintle" nozzle, and throttling nozzle. Note that the throttling nozzle uses a secondary fuel deflecting cone that extends beyond the exit of the nozzle.

stream of the cylinder, since improved volumetric efficiency (cylinder filling) and the use of fuel of lower volatility can be used with injection point located as close to the combustion chamber as possible. The farther away the point of injection, the more difficult it is to maintain suspended fuel in the air stream. Consequently, more volatile fuels must be used to maintain the required amount of vaporization in the combustion chamber. Recent studies have indicated that while a substantial percentage of fuel is vaporized in the cylinder after both intake and exhaust valves are closed and compression begins (some reports indicate as much as 80%), it is still desired to keep as much fuel as possible suspended in the intake track and ahead of the combustion chamber.

Just exactly how much fuel is injected depends largely upon the load requirement of the engine (with the maximum amount of fuel depending upon the net amount of air passed into the engine). This amount of air, among other things, depends upon such factors as rpm, piston displacement, and normal artificial aspiration conditions (blown or unblown). And since volumetric efficiency usually decreases as a function of rpm (once the high rpm torque peak has been reached), there is less time for combustion to take place at the higher engine speeds. A good feature, therefore, of an injection system would be an ability to *decrease* the amount of fuel injected as a function of rpm, not to increase it.

Duration of injection (regardless of system type) is also worth some comment. Here, we should consider that the combustion of all injected fuel should take place at or near top dead center (TDC) piston position on the compression stroke. Since there could be catastrophic results from a simultaneous burning of all combustible fuel and air exactly at TDC piston position, some amount of time must be provided for combustion to take place. This,

typically, will be in a span or range of piston movement that we can relate to degrees of crankshaft travel. For full-load, wide-open-throttle operating conditions, this period should range from around 25° before TDC and continue until about 25-30° after TDC. Consequently, injector timing will fall in the 25-55° range, with the beginning of the injection period advanced slightly to compensate for ignition lag or, possibly, retarded some amount to dampen combustion pressure rise harshness and produce a smoother running engine.

Obviously, the amount of fuel for part-throttle engine operation will be less than that required for full-load operation. In continuous injection systems (CIS), this can be accomplished by reducing the rate (or frequency) of injection. In systems such as the SIS design, part-throttle reduced fuel delivery can be performed by shortening the time a given injector remains "on." More commonly, the same rate of injection is continued, but the duration of injection is decreased.

As an integral, and critical, part of just about any fuel injection system, the fuel pump must satisfy several requirements. First, it must maintain whatever fuel pressures are required by the system over a wide range of engine operation. Pumps that are driven mechanically by the engine (thus varying in speed and output proportional with engine speed) usually deliver more fuel volume than that required by the engine, with excess fuel being returned to the tank by way of bypass valving.

Electrically-driven pumps, typically running at a constant rpm (or near it), also normally deliver an overly-large volume of fuel, the excess of which is bypassed back into the fuel tank. Exceptions to this, however, are those systems (frequently the electronic designs) that maintain a certain level of fuel pressure at all times, leaving it up to the periods of injector on-time to de-

termine exactly how much fuel is injected.

One problem with many high-speed, high rate of discharge fuel pumps of the type found in racing engines (and frequently those mechanically driven by the engine) is pump cavitation. This can be caused by inadequate pump inlet pressure, excessive fuel temperature between the pump and the injector nozzle fuel rails at the engine, hot fuel in the pump, or combinations of all these conditions. In cavitation, pump efficiency is markedly reduced, resulting in a drop in fuel flow volume to the injectors and altered engine performance, since the system controls (especially those that are electronic) depend upon the fuel delivery system to maintain a relatively constant volume of fuel at the nozzles at all times. Should fuel pressure drop at the nozzle, less fuel will flow for a given injector on-time, and a leaner air-fuel mixture will result in the combustion chamber. There is also a chance that the atomization of injected fuel will not be proper (at least insofar as the design of a given injector should provide under proper pressure conditions) and engine performance will correspondingly decrease.

Additionally, there is the case of "hot soak" conditions. During vehicle operation (or heat build-up during periods after running) inline fuel may be

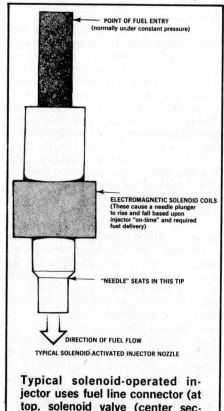

POINT OF FUEL ENTRY
(normally under constant pressure)

ELECTROMAGNETIC SOLENOID COILS
(These cause a needle plunger to rise and fall based upon injector "on-time" and required fuel delivery)

"NEEDLE" SEATS IN THIS TIP

DIRECTION OF FUEL FLOW

TYPICAL SOLENOID-ACTIVATED INJECTOR NOZZLE

Typical solenoid-operated injector uses fuel line connector (at top, solenoid valve (center section), and needle and seat from which fuel is delivered into the inlet air stream.

brought to a critical temperature and begin altering both pump and injector performance. Contemporary injection systems (especially the system employed on the Mercedes-Benz and Cadillac Seville models of EFI) have special temperature control features and special routing of fuel lines to help retard the effects of hot fuel (or heated fuel), not so much while the vehicle is in operation as for times when the engine is stopped—temperatures build in the engine compartment—and the engine is subjected to restart within 20 to 40 minutes after shutdown.

While race-car injection systems do not appear to be as sensitive to such conditions, it points out the fact that there are certain "fixed" pieces in injection systems (namely, the injector nozzles) which rely upon comparatively stable pressure and volume flow conditions. Since injector nozzle efficiency depends largely upon such pressure-volume criteria, overall engine performance is going to be related to how well the nozzles are allowed to function. This is a consideration completely outside the control of what the remainder of a particular system may have over the performance of the engine. In some circumstances, it is possible to have too much line pressure (or flow) just as it is possible to have too little. So it is wise to follow the fuel system delivery specifications provided by the manufacturer of whatever system you may be working on.

SOME THOUGHTS ON INTAKE MANIFOLDING AS IT RELATES TO FUEL INJECTION

As pointed out previously, there are some classical differences between an intake manifold designed for carburetors and one intended for use with fuel injection. Even disregarding, for the moment, the location of injection nozzles in the inlet path, we can assume that as flow velocity (kinetic energy in the air-fuel mixture stream) decreases, atomized fuel particles begin to change in both size and direction within the intake ports and passages. In addition to losses in flowing energy, the condition of the air-fuel mixture when it arrives at the combustion chamber also depends upon the amount of heat absorbed during the time from point of injection to arrival in the cylinder. In conjunction with heat absorbed and flow velocity, intake manifold design plays an important role in determining the status of the mixed air and fuel delivered to the combustion chamber.

In multi-cylinder engines (inline or V-type, it doesn't matter), equal or relatively equal distribution of air and/or air and fuel is necessary to optimum engine performance. In other words, a good manifold designed for use with fuel injection will include not only the proper amount of air to each combustion chamber, but the ability to reduce separation of air and fuel mixed upstream of the engine's inlet ports, including wet-flow through the intake manifold (if this happens to be a feature of the system as in single-point injection methods).

Accomplishing these features is, at best, extremely complicated. If an engine were to be operated at a constant load and rpm, then the problem would be far less complex. This is not the case with most automotive engines, and such factors as variation in combustion pressures, liquid separation of air and fuel somewhere along the inlet path, and changes in air-valve throttle positions can all contribute to uneven air-fuel mixtures among combustion chambers. What must be remembered is that an inlet manifold that provides relatively equal *air* distribution will not necessarily provide equal *air-fuel* distribution, owing primarily to the problems of atomized fuel particle size and the tendency of larger droplets to form liquid "tracks" or "traces" inside the manifold as flow progresses toward the cylinders. Such mixture separation tends to upset intended air-fuel ratio and alter engine performance. And performance, at this point, includes both fuel economy capability, outright horsepower, and exhaust emissions. Internal manifold dimensions (size of passages and volume of any collected or plenum areas) directly relates to resonant or "tuning" characteristics of a given design. At wide-open-throttle (w.o.t.), flow velocities through a given design of intake manifold are a function of the engine's piston displacement, volumetric efficiency (cylinder filling), engine rpm, and the size of the intake manifold in terms of internal dimensions (runner size and plenum chamber or air cavity volumes).

In four-stroke engine designs, a typical equation for the computation of these variables is often presented as follows:

Intake manifold runner cross-section area =

$$\frac{\text{rpm x vol eff x disp}}{2 \times \text{manifold vel}}$$

where, *manifold vel* is the mixture charge velocity through the manifold, *rpm* is engine rpm, *vol eff* is volumetric efficiency, *disp* is total piston displacement at that rpm, and runner cross-sectional area is the average (assuming runner taper) or actual (assuming no taper) cross-sectional area of the manifold's runners.

Perhaps the most important factor at this point is mixture velocity. Using simple algebraic operations on this equation, manifold velocity can be solved for by the following:

manifold velocity =

$$\frac{\text{vol eff x rpm x piston displacement}}{\text{runner cross-sectional area} \times 2}$$

Since, especially in wet-flow manifolds, it is necessary to maintain a high percentage of suspended fuel particles in the air stream, higher flow velocities tend to aid the delivery of fuel all the way into the cylinder. As fuel and air separate somewhere along the line, if they should happen to do so, there will be some unwanted alteration of the net air-fuel ratio at the cylinder, and engine performance will suffer accordingly.

However, in fuel injection systems employing "dry" flow (port injection)

The fuel pump is often the most important ingredient in a fuel injection system. It must supply a constant and adequate supply of fuel to the injector nozzles. Problems may arise from electrically-driven pumps that deliver excess fuel at low engine speeds or with mechanically-driven pumps that encounter cavitation problems at high crank speeds.

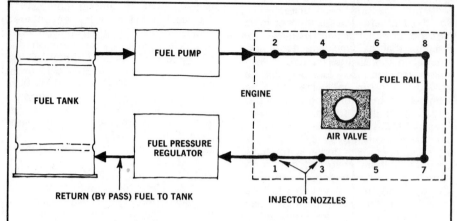

Schematic of Edlebrock EFI system shows relationship among injector nozzles and fuel rails, fuel pump, tank, and fuel pressure regulator. Note that there is no in-tank fuel pump and that by-passed fuel to the tank is regulated by the fuel pressure regulator.

such problems of air-fuel separation do not seem to be as prevalent. Even so, the conditions of flow velocity versus volumetric efficiency (cylinder filling capability as a function of engine rpm) still hold. For example, if you consider that an inlet flow velocity of 240 feet/second is critical to achieving good volumetric efficiency at a particular rpm (actually, this will produce a torque "peak"), then inlet manifold runner sizing must be adjusted accordingly. Consequently, the points in a given engine's power range where torque increases are desired become subject to proper manifold design.

Insofar as fuel injected engines are concerned, high inlet flow velocities tend to produce good low rpm torque characteristics just as in the case of carburetted engines, but there are not the customary problems of air-fuel separation. Larger intake manifold runners (cross-sectional area, not length) are associated with high rpm power output simply because the larger passages require more air rate (rpm) to achieve the velocities necessary for torque "resonance" within the induction system. Wet flow manifolds, thus, become more of a problem at the lower engine speeds (large runners) and lend themselves more to dry flow injection systems where actual fuel regulation is not dependant upon a pressure drop across some form of mixing valve (carburetor).

There is one other point to consider. Mixture velocity would be just about constant for some given throttle position (opening) and rpm if an engine did not have any amount of clearance space (combustion chamber). The previously-mentioned reversion phenomenon again enters the picture here, since with more reversion pressure (es-

pecially at the lower engine speeds) there is a reduction in net volumetric efficiency and intake manifold velocity as the throttle is closed during deceleration of the vehicle. This condition is further aggravated by the use of high performance camshafts that employ very early intake valve openings (much earlier relative to top dead center piston position than with stock camshafts). As a result, the smaller intake manifold runners (cross-sectional area) tend to dampen reversion pulses and make both engine start-up and low rpm operation much smoother, sharper, and cleaner . . . all else being equal.

Also, since a major restriction in the intake track is the intake valve head and valve seat/pocket area, some con-

sideration is typically given to including these areas in manifold design. Keep in mind that it is the flow "opening" or window that exists between the valve head and valve seat (like a transparent cylinder) that is the smallest passage in the entire intake path, until such time that valve lift causes this opening to be equal to or greater than the smallest cross-sectional area existing elsewhere in the path.

Injection systems that employ dry flow, or totally gaseous mixtures, seem to work well with larger valve sizes and intake manifold runners. Since fuel delivery regulation is not a function of flow velocity, it makes sense to remove any flow restrictions (such as the valve head and valve seat) as quickly as possible. Consequently, dry flow systems (especially for engines operated at relatively high rpm) are comparatively insensitive to such problems as getting fuel to accelerate into the engine (a common problem in wet flow manifolds). Engines employing smaller intake valves and areas tend to help atomize fuel in and around the intake pocket and valve head. Fuel injected engines operating with dry flow fuel delivery (those relying on such pieces as port nozzles or comparable injectors) also benefit from small intake passages and valves, providing the engine is not operated in a high rpm range.

Much has been said about intake manifold runner shape. Actually, there is sufficient documentation in support of the fact that the least resistance to flow is a circular cross section, providing the flow is in a straight line and there are no sudden changes in sectional area. This would cause quick changes in flowing energy (acceleration and deceleration of the air or

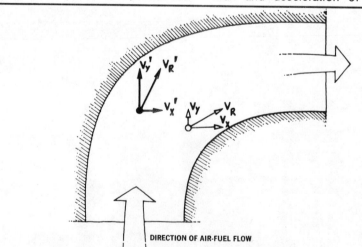

In wet-flow injection systems, some thought should be given to the differences in how air and fuel behave during flow. Vr indicates how air negotiates a flow turn vs. how heavier fuel (Vr') does. The stronger Vy' component of fuel vs. the Vy component of air shows why air can change direction more easily than heavier fuel.

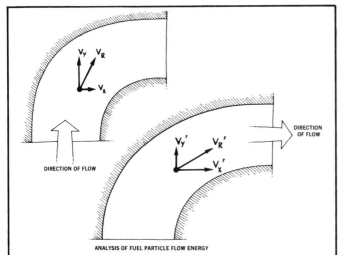

ANALYSIS OF FUEL PARTICLE FLOW ENERGY

An analysis of centrifugal forces on liquid fuel in a curved flow path shows that sharp turns cause more Vy forces (thus air-fuel separation) than in bends that are less severe turning radius. For best air-fuel suspension, the Vy component should be as great as possible.

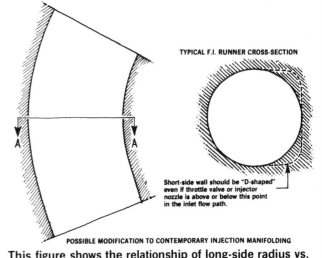

POSSIBLE MODIFICATION TO CONTEMPORARY INJECTION MANIFOLDING

This figure shows the relationship of long-side radius vs. short-side radius. Short-side radii should incorporate flat turning surfaces (or so-called D-porting) to reduce the amount of boundary layer separation and subsequent air-fuel disturbances.

mixture charge), resulting in some amount of loss in volumetric efficiency.

We know, however, that air or air and fuel cannot pass directly into an engine without undergoing some sort of directional or flowing energy changes. The manifold must be designed to provide relatively equal amounts of either air or air and fuel to the engine or cylinder-to-cylinder power potential will vary accordingly. If fuel is caused, for whatever reason, to be separated from the incoming air stream (even if this happens around the valve head area, which it can), it is important that the intake manifold do whatever it can to get this fuel back into the inlet air.

Of the various types of air-fuel separation that have been observed, most often such separation is a result of a sudden change in the relative velocities of the air and fuel such that the air will respond more quickly than the fuel (obviously, since it is lighter in weight). As a result, the air "bends" and the fuel tends to go "straight ahead" (or in whatever direction it was originally moving). Therefore, a property of a well-designed injector manifold would be to aid the suspension of wet flow into the engine by reducing the amount of sudden energy change that a given air-fuel mixture will see.

Surface texture or finish of the inlet manifold is also worthy of some comment. In injection systems employing wet flow, where some amount of mixture separation or "wet out" can be expected, very smooth flow surfaces seem to cause separated fuel to wander at random through the manifold, causing "rivulets" or "stringers" of fuel to collect and enter the cylinders neither atomized nor controlled from the standpoint of specific air-fuel ratios.

Consequently, there seems to be some merit to providing slightly

roughened surfaces for wet flow systems. This tends to increase the activity of the boundary layer of the flow (that thin film of air flowing directly against the inside of the passage) and aid the return of separated fuel back into the air stream. While some might argue that such rough surfaces will reduce the net mixture flow into the engine, actual calculations have shown "pumping losses" attributed to rough intake path walls is at best negligible, unless such surfaces contribute to severe turbulency within the passages. Conditions like this are both rare and difficult to solve simply by reducing surface "roughness."

For injection systems that utilize dry flow techniques, mixture or inlet air heating ahead of the cylinders is not considered a significant problem. However, in wet flow systems, heat to the

incoming mixture is often required just to get the heavy ends of the fuel vaporized before entering the cylinders. Even though there is recent data that suggests a high percentage of fuel is atomized in the cylinder *after the intake valve closes,* some amount of heat is usually necessary to provide cold engine operation. An interesting point is the fact that too much vaporization of the fuel ahead of the cylinders tends to reduce volumetric efficiency and net engine output.

Actually, an air-fuel mixture temperature of about 100-110°F is required for complete vaporization of common pump gasoline (a temperature of about 100°F is frequently found in carburetted gasoline engines), but such temperatures do not appear to be as critical in engines equipped with fuel injection. In such systems as the Edelbrock EFI, the

Edelbrock EFI system includes throttle brackets that will enable re-installment of all factory linkages for "carburetion" and transmission kick-down. Cable throttles all mount in "stock" position.

addition of exhaust heat to the induction system proved detrimental, during development stages. Owing in part to the fact that the heated inlet air reduced both volumetric efficiency and air-fuel mixture control at part-throttle engine operation, this feature was dropped in favor of "cold flow" to both increase charge density and reduce unburned hydrocarbons at the tailpipe.

In a fuel-injected racing engine, cooler inlet air (almost regardless of where fuel is admitted to the air stream) increases engine output, where wide-open-throttle mixture temperature can be observed as low as 80-95°F. Also of value in fuel-injected engines (with respect to inlet air or air-fuel mixture temperatures) are inlet manifolds that provide quick response to changes in heat or temperature. Reduction of this so-called "flywheel effect" enables a given manifold to react more rapidly during engine warm-up or times when cold operation is unavoidable. What should be kept in mind is the fact that heated inlet air and/or fuel can hamper proper fuel delivery to the cylinders. While it is true that some recent experimentation has been performed to show that certain gains in fuel economy are possible with fuel heated to a specific level (and controlled at this level), it does not follow that "generally" heated fuel will show comparable results. Heating of fuel ahead of the cylinders can lead to the loss of some of the more important "light end gasses", resulting in a reduction in combustion heat and lost power.

In fuel-injection manifolding intended more for street use than race applications, this factor becomes even more critical since material losses in fuel economy and vehicle driveability

Injector nozzle location for the Edelbrock EFI system (and a guide for comparable systems) is such that discharge direction is aimed at the short-side radius of the intake port passage. Although discharge atomization patterns for this system are particularly good, delivery direction is still critical.

can result. It is also true that where heated fuel is used (compared to fuel admitted at ambient or "systems" temperature), the actual metering of such fuel through nozzles, jets, or other fuel control passages can be upset, which offers variations in system calibration.

Actually, the amount of heat that should be provided to the incoming air or air-fuel mixture depends largely upon the characteristics of the fuel in use, the amount or percentage of fuel evaporated during delivery to the cylinders, and the air-fuel ratio required. While this heat value can be determined mathematically, it is normally on the order of 9-15 BTU-ft^2-hr-°F. This simply relates to the amount of

heat that exhaust gas cross-overs offer to incoming air or air-fuel mixtures. As effective exhaust gas temperature increases (and it can vary both with the amount of engine power produced and the volume of gas exposed per unit of surface area exposed to the inlet flow), there is the chance that more fuel will be vaporized ahead of the cylinders, possibly reducing horsepower production.

The bottom-line of all this suggests a dry-flow injection system in which very little inlet air temperature increase is provided. By the use of efficient injector nozzle "spray" patterns, less reliance is placed on fuel vaporization prior to arrival at the cylinders. Consequently, cooler inlet air can improve net air-fuel mixture density in the cylinders and contribute to higher engine output.

If an injector system (and accompanying intake manifold design) were to use wet flow properties (such as the Rochester design of the mid-1950 Chevrolet vintage), some consideration should be given to the exhaust heat provided for vaporizing (or helping to maintain vaporization) inlet fuel. A term, called the "mean temperature difference", has been applied to the difference between inlet air-fuel mixtures and exhaust gas. Since there is a wide range of exhaust gas temperatures (depending upon engine speed and load), there will be a resulting range of variation in the amount of heat available to the incoming air-fuel mixture.

Experimentally, it has been shown that one square inch of heating surface (exposed to the intake charge) per each 4 cubic inches of piston displacement will completely vaporize a

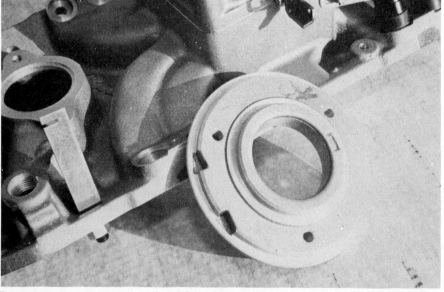

To accommodate both 2-barrel and 4-barrel carburetor air cleaners, the Edelbrock EFI air valve unit is "notched" to accept both air cleaner bases. Note the single and double slots for the air cleaner base. Rotation of the air valve "flange" accommodates both cleaner bases.

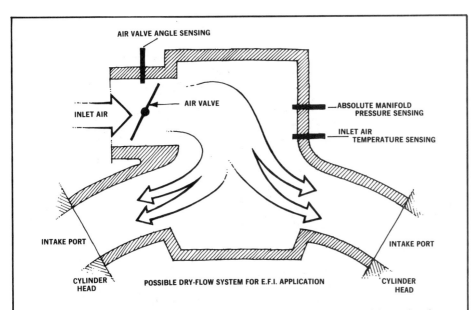

AIR VALVE ANGLE SENSING

INLET AIR

AIR VALVE

ABSOLUTE MANIFOLD PRESSURE SENSING

INLET AIR TEMPERATURE SENSING

INTAKE PORT

INTAKE PORT

CYLINDER HEAD

POSSIBLE DRY-FLOW SYSTEM FOR E.F.I. APPLICATION

CYLINDER HEAD

For those who would like to fabricate their own intake manifold for dry-flow EFI systems, this diagram shows how a side-entry air entry and fundamental flow sensing element locations could be used to accomplish the fuel delivery requirements.

A reduction in the sharpness of these edges helps prevent air-fuel separation within the "dog house" manifold.

METERED AIR & FUEL ENTRY

ROCHESTER F.I.

Runner length tuned for power band of 4500-7200 rpm. Some improvement in manifold performance can be achieved by radiusing of entry sides to each runner (per insert)

Improved air-flow into the runners of the Rochester F.I. system can be achieved by removing the top of the "doghouse" and radiusing the entry portions of each runner. While this may seem of little consequence, the results in terms of air-fuel separation and lost power are not.

typical sample of fuel *within the intake manifold.* This suggests that for fuel injection systems employing wet flow fuel delivery, proper heating of the incoming mixture (with exhaust gas crossover passages or comparable means) can aid in reducing problems associated with air-fuel mixture separation inside the intake manifold. The point being made here is that through the use of exhaust gas (in proper proportion with surface areas over which air-fuel mixtures pass), it is possible to reduce air-fuel ratio variation from cylinder to cylinder. This is especially true in fuel injected engines operating at something less than "race" rpm levels.

Since most "race" engine design is of the V-8 type (primarily domestic engines or variations thereof), less is published about the characteristics of inline 4- and 6-cylinder engines with respect to fuel injection and intake manifold design (remember the latter element is significantly affected by firing order and cylinder arrangement). For example, in an eight-cylinder engine, there is roughly 130 degrees (crankshaft degrees) during which reversion pulsations can be "felt" by other cylinders in the engine. This figure is reduced to about 95 degrees in a six-cylinder engine, and to as little as 40 degrees in a four-cylinder design. You can see that as the number of cylinders in the engine is increased, so is the amount of reversion pressure that must be damped (or absorbed) by adjoining cylinders.

As a side-note, you might consider that in many six- and eight-cylinder engines (due primarily to the time between firing impulses or inlet cycles), there exists bi- or two-directional flow at the air-valve (point at which air or air and fuel is admitted to the intake manifold). This further enhances air-fuel separation and places even more emphasis on the fact that "timed" fuel delivery is important to multi-cylinder engines, insofar as power output efficiency can be improved by the reduction of reversion pressure influence.

As a final note to the so-called "science" of intake manifold tuning for fuel injection systems, the following comments might be made. First, regardless of whether the intake system is flowing dry or wet air flow (fuel admitted upstream of the cylinder or near it), certain flow velocities are critical to the production of "resonant boosts" over a given engine speed range (rpm range). At whatever rpm these velocities are achieved (and there are typically two such velocities on the intake-side of the engine), there will be an attending value of torque output, either side of which there will be a torque value less than that observed at the respective "peak". If the induction system is designed to incorporate individual runners that collect into a given "air cavity" in the vicinity of the air valve (as opposed to runners each of which contain their own throttle valve), there will be two times in the engine's rpm span at which torque "boosts" will be observed.

Should the induction system be designed such that each intake port receives air and fuel from an individual passage (or runner), a single torque peak will result as a function of the cross-sectional area (or area average) of the path leading to each of the engine's cylinders. In this case, there is no chance for a "double resonance" condition and a torque peak based on the critical velocity of the manifold runners only will be all that is available. The point here is that "collected" induction systems for fuel injection (such as the Cadillac and Chevrolet Rochester designs) are particularly sensitive to both port runner cross-sectional area and plenum volumes.

Fuel-injected engines intended for low rpm use respond very well to intake manifold design that includes both port runners and plenum chamber (two torque peak potential and a broad torque curve). Those to be used for race-only applications appear to respond best to carefully-calculated port runner design (including runner length and "ram tube" height) such that major torque gains are a result of runner cross-sectional area exclusive of plenum chamber volume.

More often than not, what you see in terms of race-only fuel injection is a network of individual intake port runners (not connected by any sort of a common volume or plenum chamber) to which some length of "ram tubes" has been added. The purpose of these tubes is to improve the mid-rpm torque output of the engine, which can lead to reductions in power above peak torque. Although you do not yet see such an approach, a more logical design might be to collect these individual runners into some form of plenum chamber (common volume joining all runners) so that low-rpm torque increases could be produced as a function of the plenum and the runner size could be adjusted to provide torque gains at the higher engine speeds. Even though you may never see such a system, there is considerable data to suggest it would be more than just a "pipe dream."

Some Comment on Fuel Injection Systems As Received from the Manufacturer

At the risk of arousing concern on the part of fuel injection system manufacturers, there are some comments that should be made in the interest of consumers.

First, you should accept the fact that some amount of work (modification) will need to be performed on just about any of the currently-available injection systems designed for high-performance applications. Owing in part to the fact that there is a limited number of such manufacturers, there does not appear to be significant demands placed on the manufacturer to provide systems that are free of defects and/or quality control problems. As cast, some of the intake manifolds used in injection systems require both "cleaning up" and re-machining to properly match the engines for which they were designed. Aside from the usual "port match" steps associated with high-performance intake manifolding, you may be faced with such operations as special bushings for throttle shafts, relocation of injector nozzles (possibly a change in the relationship of flow direction and injector nozzle axis), and similar changes to a system otherwise touted to be "ready to install and run" on a given engine.

Please understand that this is not intended to be a criticism of currently-available injection systems. Rather, it is a precaution that you should: 1) be

more than casually aware of both how and what is involved in the operation of the system of your choice before a purchase is made, and 2) an understanding that some amount of modification may be required (not suggested by the manufacturer) just to get the system to perform to expectations. In part, this is a result of mass-produced systems for a wide variety of engine applications. And, it is also a result of not having to do much more than is necessary because, from a consumer's standpoint, there are not that many sources for aftermarket fuel injection systems. Hopefully, this information will be of benefit to you without causing irritation with certain manufacturers who should already know about the problems whereof we speak.

Expanded Discussion About the Rochester F. I. As Offered by Chevrolet

Many people have said the reason Chevrolet discontinued production of its Rochester Division fuel injection system was because "line mechanics" at the dealer level were unable to properly service the unit. While opinion differs among proponents of the

Restored early-60's Rochester F.I. system shows simplicity of intake manifold design and location of such pieces as the fuel meter. Overall doghouse intake manifold design covers up the Tunnel-Ram design of each intake port runner configuration. But the ram-tune concept is still included.

Rochester system, the fact remains that this O.E.M. (original equipment manufacturer) approach to providing a means for improving both fuel economy (if you could keep your foot out of the throttle) and engine performance was one of the best ever offered for domestic production engines. What follows is a rather detailed description of how the system operates and what you might want to examine if something prevents things from working the way they should . . . like a trouble-shooter's guide to making the Rochester system do what it is supposed to do.

Essentially, there are three types of fuel injection units: Timed, Constant-flow, and that characterized by the Rochester system (one that uses a "variable jet" in the fuel return line). Timed injection, of the type used by Mercedes, provides an injection of fuel (gasoline or diesel) into either the combustion chamber, intake manifold, or intake port. Such "timed" fuel deliveries are set to discharge at a precise point before piston top dead center position. Constant-flow systems (as mentioned earlier in this section) use a fixed by-pass for delivered fuel and use a fuel pump for which pumped fuel volume depends upon engine rpm—more rpm, more delivered fuel volume. In systems of this design, air-fuel ratio is determined by the amount of fuel by-passed back into the fuel tank. By changing the size of the by-pass return-line "jets," fuel flow to the injector nozzles can be both varied and

The Rochester fuel injection has undergone a tremendous resurgence in popularity. Today these units may sell for as much as $1000 for a complete system with distributor (from which power is derived for the fuel pump). This highly-modified street unit has been fitted with two air valve assemblies.

controlled. Such systems work well with engines where a relatively constant rpm is required and throttle operation is at or near the wide open position.

The Rochester system, utilizes a so-called variable jet in the return line. By incorporating such a variable fuel metering device, the amount of fuel supplied to the engine is governed by engine speed and load throughout the engine rpm range. This way, air-fuel ratio can be controlled more accurately than if a single jet or flow orifice arrangement was used. Since the Rochester unit is designed to vary the size of the by-pass opening as a function of engine demand for fuel, more constant air-fuel ratio control is provided.

To this end, some input is necessary so that the system knows what fuel requirements the engine has at any particular point in time. Intake manifold vacuum and venturi vacuum (actually measured on the air-valve side of the intake manifold sometimes called the "doghouse" for reasons we never learned) are the two principal inputs to the system with respect to fuel requirements. Intake manifold vacuum is measured in a range of from 0.5-inch of mercury to as much as 21 inches. Venturi vacuum measurements (actually the weaker of the two signals) vary from a maximum of 10 inches of water to a minimum of 0.250-inch of water. Note that inches of water indicate a data base of much less signal strength than that of inches of mercury. By way of comparison, one inch of mercury is just about equal to 13.47 inches of water, so you can see how much more sensitive the intake manifold signals are to change than those metered in the air-valve or air-metering portion of the system.

In terms of which of these two signals does what, the weaker venturi vacuum signal operates on a vacuum diaphragm which controls part of the fuel metering system. This same diaphragm also controls the operation of the by-pass valve which regulates net fuel flow. This valve is sometimes called a "spill plunger," but only if you

CHEVROLET V8 RAMJET FUEL INJECTION

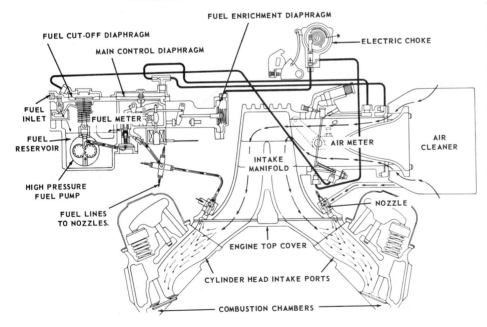

The operation of the Chevrolet Ramjet Fuel Injection system is simple. The accelerator controls the volume of air admitted to the engine. A mechanism continuously measures the volume of incoming air and automatically meters the precise quantity of fuel to be mixed with the air. Other mechanisms enrich the mixture for acceleration, hill climbing and warm-up; and also insure instantaneous delivery of fuel for starting, provide for smooth engine idling, and fuel cut-off when coasting.

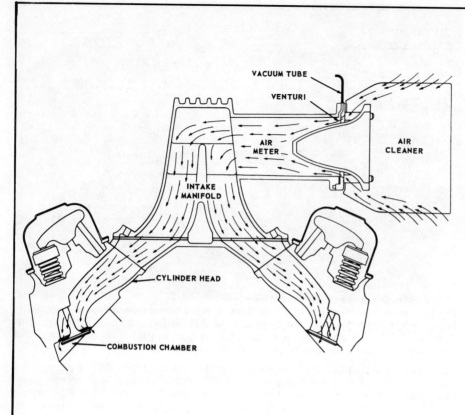

AIR INTAKE

Outside air for the engine is routed through an air cleaner, where dust and foreign matter are filtered out, and then passes into an air meter, the intake manifold, cylinder head, and combustion chamber. The entrance to the air meter is through a venturi or narrow passage. This passage also has a small opening leading to a vacuum tube. As the outside air rushes into the engine through the venturi, it tends to draw the air out of the tube, which creates a vacuum in the tube. The degree of vacuum is an accurate measure of the volume of air being drawn into the engine. A large volume of air creates high vacuum in the tube, while a small volume of air results in low vacuum.

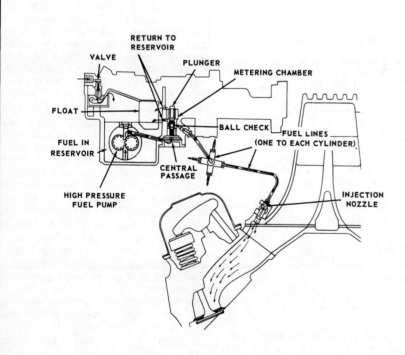

FUEL INTAKE

A fuel meter is used to supply and regulate fuel to the engine. The regular engine fuel pump sends fuel through a fine filter and into a reservoir in the fuel meter housing. The quantity of fuel in the reservoir is maintained at a fixed level by a float-controlled valve. Another fuel pump, submerged in the reservoir fuel, is driven by the ignition distributor through a flexible cable. Fuel under high pressure from this pump passes into a central passage where it must lift a ball check before flowing through a series of small holes into a metering chamber. At this point the fuel can go either to the injection nozzles at the intake ports, or back to the reservoir, depending upon the position of a plunger. When the plunger is raised, fuel flows back to the reservoir. As the plunger is lowered, a portion of the fuel flows to the injection nozzles and the remainder returns to the reservoir. The ball check in the central passage permits fuel to flow from the pump when fuel pressure is about 15 pounds or higher so that any vapors which may have formed are compressed back into a liquid.

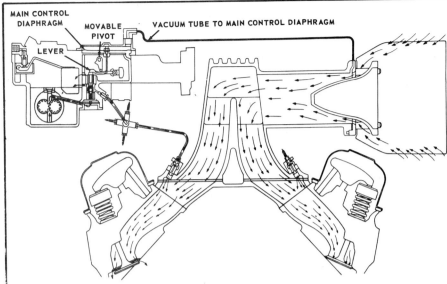

RIGHT AMOUNT OF FUEL TO MATCH AIR FLOW

As the incoming air passes through the venturi and is measured, it sends a vacuum signal to a main control diaphragm in the fuel meter. Depending upon the amount of vacuum, the diaphragm meters fuel by raising or lowering the plunger through a lever, thus delivering with high accuracy the precise quantity of fuel required by the engine for the volume of air being used.

All levers in the fuel metering system are counterbalanced so that their movements are unaffected by their own weight. Lever positions are determined only by forces exerted by the sensing devices.

HIGH AIR FLOW CALLS FOR HIGH FUEL FLOW. **LOW AIR FLOW CALLS FOR LOW FUEL FLOW.**

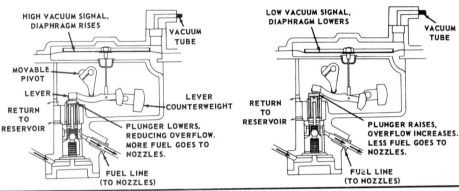

FUEL MIXES WITH AIR AND IS DRAWN THE COMBUSTION CHAMBER

The intake manifold has eight individual passages, called ram pipes, one for each cylinder. The fuel injection nozzles are mounted in plastic insulators in the lower part of the intake manifold, near the cylinder head intake ports. As the inlet valves open, fuel spray from the nozzles, which has mixed with the onrushing air, enters the combustion chamber where it is compressed and ignited in the same manner as in a conventional carburetor system. A throttle valve, controlled by the driver through the accelerator, determines the quantity of air, and as previously explained, the quantity of fuel supplied to the engine.

So that the amount of fuel injected is determined solely by the fuel metering system, and not influenced by variations in vacuum, the nozzles are designed to inject fuel into atmospheric pressure at all times. This is accomplished by supplying air from the air cleaner to a small chamber in each nozzle. The fuel injected from a small orifice passes through this chamber, and out a small opening to the intake port.

The arrangement has the added advantage of assuring a consistently accurate fuel air ratio for idling the engine. The volume of air passing through the chamber, although smaller when compared with the volume flowing through the intake manifold in normal driving, constitutes a major share of the air used by the engine during closed throttle or idling conditions.

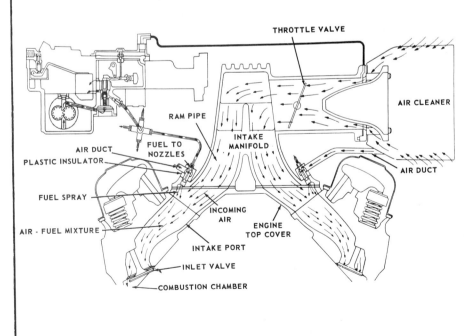

FAST ACCELERATION

The movable pivot in the fuel metering system is connected by a rod to a fuel enrichment diaphragm, and is normally held in a position which provides maximum economy of operation. The enrichment diaphragm is controlled by vacuum created when air rushes past the opening at the throttle valve. When the throttle valve is partially opened, air rushes through the small space of the opening on its way to the engine, and tries to draw air out of the enrichment vacuum tube. The resulting vacuum in the tube is strong enough to hold the diaphragm back against the opposing force of a spring. This holds the movable pivot in the fuel economy position.

When fast acceleration or more power is called for, the driver presses on the accelerator which opens the throttle valve wider. The incoming air now has a larger opening to pass through, and therefore draws less on the enrichment vacuum tube, reducing the vacuum. The spring now overcomes the reduced vacuum force and moves the diaphragm out. As a result, the movable pivot is pushed toward the end of the lever, moving the plunger down. Therefore, fuel return to the reservoir is reduced and fuel flow to the injection nozzles increased. The richer mixture gives increased power for fast acceleration.

EASY COLD STARTING

For fast engine starting, it is necessary to get fuel to the nozzles quickly when the starting motor is turned on. Since it would take from 20 to 30 seconds at cranking speed for the fuel pump to build up enough pressure to unseat the ball check, a solenoid is used to open a direct fuel passage to the nozzles.

When the starting motor is engaged, the solenoid, which is automatically energized at the same time, forces a solenoid link upward. This, in turn, pushes the starting lever which forces the plunger down, unseating the ball check. Fuel then is routed directly from the fuel pump to the nozzles. The solenoid is de-energized when the driver releases the key-turn starting switch.

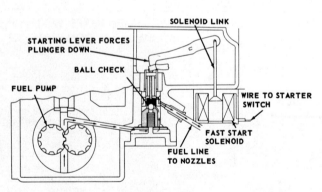

STARTING FUEL

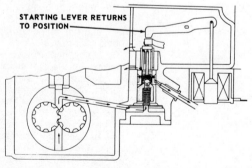

RETURN TO NORMAL

ENGINE WARM-UP

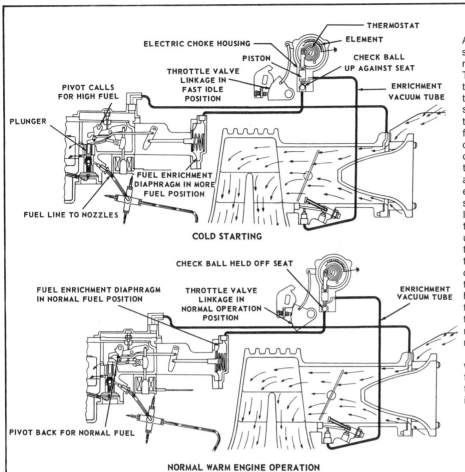

THERMOSTAT
ELECTRIC CHOKE HOUSING
ELEMENT
PISTON
CHECK BALL UP AGAINST SEAT
THROTTLE VALVE LINKAGE IN FAST IDLE POSITION
ENRICHMENT VACUUM TUBE
PIVOT CALLS FOR HIGH FUEL
PLUNGER
FUEL ENRICHMENT DIAPHRAGM IN MORE FUEL POSITION
FUEL LINE TO NOZZLES

COLD STARTING

CHECK BALL HELD OFF SEAT
FUEL ENRICHMENT DIAPHRAGM IN NORMAL FUEL POSITION
THROTTLE VALVE LINKAGE IN NORMAL OPERATION POSITION
ENRICHMENT VACUUM TUBE
PIVOT BACK FOR NORMAL FUEL

NORMAL WARM ENGINE OPERATION

After starting and during warm up, it is desirable to furnish slightly richer fuel mixtures than would normally be supplied. This is accomplished by changing the position of the pivot in the fuel metering system to call for more fuel. The fuel enrichment system and an electric choke are used for this purpose. The enrichment vacuum route from the air meter to the fuel enrichment diaphragm passes through the electric choke housing. On cold starts, vacuum in the housing pulls a check ball upward against a seat, cutting off the vacuum to the enrichment diaphragm. As a result, the spring moves the pivot toward the end of the lever, moving the plunger down, routing fuel to the nozzles. In the choke housing the vacuum is then applied to the bottom of a piston. At the top end, the piston is linked to a thermostat heated by an element which carries electric current whenever the ignition switch is on. As the thermostat is heated, it relaxes and allows vacuum to pull the piston downward. In its lowest position the piston pushes the check ball off its seat, returning the fuel enrichment system to normal operation.

The electric choke also controls linkage which holds the throttle valve slightly open for fast engine idling after cold starts. As the thermostat heats up, the linkage and engine idle speed return to their normal settings.

FUEL IS CUT OFF WHEN COASTING

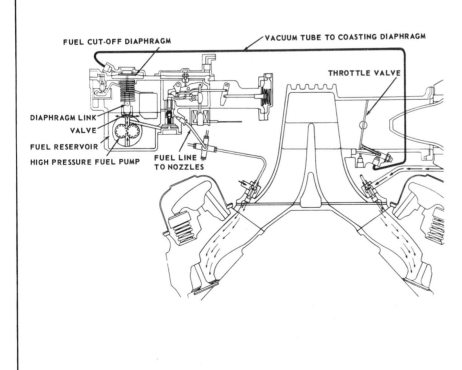

FUEL CUT-OFF DIAPHRAGM
VACUUM TUBE TO COASTING DIAPHRAGM
THROTTLE VALVE
DIAPHRAGM LINK
VALVE
FUEL RESERVOIR
HIGH PRESSURE FUEL PUMP
FUEL LINE TO NOZZLES

When coasting downhill or decelerating from higher engine speeds, an automatic fuel cut-off system stops fuel waste and discharge of exhaust fumes containing unburned fuel. Other gains are quiet engine operation and the elimination of exhaust sputtering.

When going downhill with the foot off the accelerator, the throttle valve is closed, but the engine, being pushed by the vehicle, tries to pull in large quantities of air. This creates an unusually high vacuum at the closed throttle valve. This vacuum is used to send a signal, through a tube, to a diaphragm located above the high pressure fuel pump. The high vacuum raises the diaphragm and a connecting link opens a valve over the fuel pump, and discharges the fuel directly back to the fuel reservoir. As a result, all of the fuel from the pump is discharged in the fuel reservoir, none going to the injection nozzles or engine. The high vacuum diminishes as the vehicle slows down, closing the valve over the fuel pump, and fuel again flows to the nozzles. The transition from coasting fuel cutoff to normal operation is so smooth that the driver and passengers are not aware of the change.

happen to be careless.

The second, and smaller, fuel control diaphragm (identified by its almost vertical positioning in the system) is operated by the much stronger intake manifold vacuum signals. Actually, in real-world operation, the by-pass valve (or spill plunger) becomes the variable by-pass valve, regulating just exactly how much fuel goes to the engine and how much is returned to the fuel tank. A high-pressure fuel pump (driven by the engine's ignition distributor and, therefore, varying fuel delivery as a function of engine rpm) provides fuel to the variable by-pass valve (or spill plunger). During times when the engine is required to produce maximum power (wide open throttle, maximum venturi vacuum and minimum intake manifold vacuum), the spill plunger is closed so that all pumped fuel goes to the engine.

When power demands are low (idle, light-throttle cruise), this situation is turned around to provide much less fuel to the engine, resulting in what many proponents of the Rochester system have claimed to be the reason fuel economy benefits are a part of this method of fuel control. Under such light-load conditions, the spill plunge is at or near its wide open position, returning most of the pumped fuel back into the fuel bowl and not to the engine.

Because engine vacuum (both intake manifold and venturi) is varying constantly with engine operation, both rpm and load, the spill plunger is in a

Early Rochester systems employed longer intake manifold runners inside the doghouse, owing to the fact that more low-rpm torque was a necessity to street-use vehicles.

continuing state of movement. It does, therefore, regulate the amount of fuel delivered to the engine, resulting in what was previously termed a "more constant air-fuel ratio control." But this segment of the Rochester system deals with fuel delivery. On the other "side" of the unit is the air metering device

which deserves some discussion.

Here, in-coming engine air is regulated and it provides a place where both fuel-control vacuum signals are monitored. Much like the throttle blades found in a conventional carburetor, there is a single "blade" located in the air valve which, depending upon the degree to which it is open, governs the amount of air available to the engine. A so-called "diffuser cone" is installed at the mouth of the air valve passage such that a vacuum signal proportional to the volume of air being provided to the engine can be measured. The venturi effect enables the Rochester system to "measure" incoming air much like the pressure transducers of today relate vacuum signals to the volume of air flowing into an engine. While pressure transducers were not commonly available in the mid-1950's, the method employed in the Rochester system was just about as effective.

By way of an annular groove (inside the venturi throat), a varying vacuum signal is sent to the main fuel control diaphragm. Since this is the low-vacuum member of the two-vacuum sensing system, a larger diaphragm is required to provide the necessary sensitivity.

As a review, this description shows how low-vacuum signals are generated by air flowing into the engine. These relatively low vacuum signals cause the fuel control diaphragm to move in direct proportion to the volume of air flow into the engine. Because of the

Later model Rochester fuel injection systems incorporated a removable doghouse "lid" so that alterations to the injector manifold were possible. The removal of sharp radii to each inlet runner was facilitated by this design change.

linkage arrangement that is built into the fuel control diaphragm housing (and below the diaphragm), fuel is delivered to the engine in direct proportion to its air-fuel ratio requirements. High engine speeds generate large amounts of air flow into the engine which, through the fuel delivery mechanisms, causes maximum fuel to be fed to the intake manifold. As engine speed decreases, manifold vacuum is also increased resulting in gradual (or full, depending upon manifold vacuum) opening of the spill plunger so that most of the available fuel is passed back into the fuel bowl.

Actually, the main fuel control diaphragm provides a rough air-fuel ratio for any engine requirements. Finer control or adjustment of the mixture ratios is made by adjustment of the rich-lean limits. For example, the engine can be made more lean by backing off the lean stop limit, which in turn causes a change in the amount of enrichment control lever travel. Within the system, this causes more fuel to be passed by the spill plunger (or bypass), resulting in less that is delivered to the engine. As a function of engine load (therefore manifold vacuum) and throttle position, the system's two vacuum signals are balanced such that the optimum air-fuel ratios are provided.

A variety of methods have been used by Chevrolet to control fuel metering during cold-starting of the engine and warm-up periods. Each method has been a combination of electrical and manually-operated parts, with the most

The Rochester system utilizes a secondary fuel pump to boost fuel delivery pressure to the nozzles. This pump is driven by a cable from the distributor housing. At left is the rare dual-drive unit used to drive both the injection pump and a cable-drive tach. At right is the standard low-performance injection distributor.

All of the injection distributors utilized dual-point plates. On the left is a '58-'65 injection distributor with a vacuum-advance plate. On the right is '58-'66 hi-performance distributor without vacuum plate.

popular approach being that developed for use on the '64-'65 Rochester system. This design incorporates a conventional automatic choke and a microswitch that operates a low-pressure flow of fuel into the injectors for start-up. This valve is actuated when the ignition key is in the "start" position, returning to its closed position whenever the key is switched to the "run" position.

These fuel delivery nozzles, actually mounted in pairs and in plastic blocks, incorporate check valves which are intended to help prevent flash fires in the system if the engine happens to backfire. The nozzles also contain idle air bleeds (tubes) which connect to the inlet air side of the so-called "doghouse."

Of the three types of spill-plungers available for the Rochester system, the one used in the 1958 and 1960-1962 units appears to be the better for throttle response and overall fuel delivery control. In terms of maintenance and general trouble-shooting of the Rochester systems, the following section is offered as a guide. Obtaining one of the factory service manuals, if you're really into the Rochester system, would be of particular help, especially if you decide to "restore" one of these packages.

Early 1960 Rochester FI doghouse and air horn showing location of electric choke and main diaphragm equalizing pressure line.

Here you can see a portion of the injector nozzle fuel "rail", idle speed adjustment screw, and part of the line to the enrichment diaphragm (vacuum line) for the early 1960's Rochester unit.

Early Rochester FI systems incorporated air horn entries much smaller than later versions. Engine displacements were also smaller, accounting for part of the reason for reduced air entry size.

This bottom view of the fuel meter shows the various parts of the Main fuel control "spill valve." Note the main plunger, which meters the fuel delivery as dictated by the sensing mechanisms.

Early Rochester unit (1962 vintage) showing enrichment diaphragm and cranking signal valve.

On the underneath-side of the early 1960 fuel control body, you can see the main fuel control valve housing (1), lean/rich stop adjustment (2), and enrichment diaphragm adjustment (3).

Disassembly of the main fuel control diaphragm should include use of a screwdriver (along with small end-wrench) to prevent shearing of the screw inside the diaphragm.

The so-called "octopus" lines that delivered fuel to the injector nozzles of the Rochester systems. Based on mode of engine operation (starting or running), these fuel delivery lines carried all engine fuel to the port nozzles. Regardless of the type of filter used, clean fuel is a necessity of any FI unit.

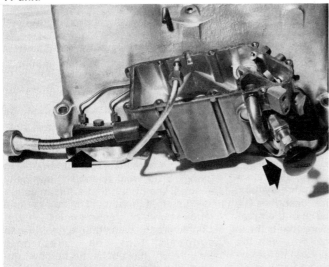

Here the fuel pump drive cable can be seen. Note also a special shut-off valve has been installed in the fuel line to prevent flooding when the system is not in use (a touch added by the owner).

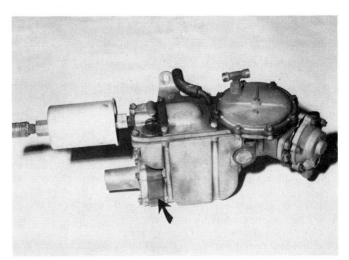

Here's the high-pressure fuel pump portion of the early Rochester FI fuel meters. With these systems, starting fuel was provided by the engine's fuel pump (low pressure), after which a solenoid valve closed, allowing high pressure to be provided for normal engine operation.

There are six different fuel nozzles. They vary in the amount of fuel they will flow. They are designated as W,X,Y,Q,R, and S. The W,X and Y nozzles from the '63-'65 models have the greatest flow. From left to right we have the special racing nozzle with an extended tip (very rare), a mid-'57-'65 nozzle and an early '57 model.

Here you can see the single-blade air-valve of the Rochester air control unit. Idle speed and enrichment adjustments were much like that for conventional carburetion. Single venturi air valve is similar to that used in Edlebrock EFI systems.

ROCHESTER FUEL INJECTION TROUBLE-SHOOTING GUIDE

Preventive Maintenance

Water the float bowl:

This should be checked periodically, even if you use one of the available fuel tank additives designed to reduce the amount of water in the fuel. This is especially a problem in climates of high humidity.

Air filters:

The air filter should be replaced frequently (less than 10,000 miles) or cleaned if it is of this type. Never operate the Rochester system without the air cleaner installed. Dirty cleaner elements will change the fuel meter calibration and affect overall engine performance accordingly.

Fuel filters:

Whether you have the replaceable fuel filter cartridges (as used on pre-1962 Corvettes with F.I.) or in-line filter elements, replacement intervals should be in the 5000-8000 mile range.

Pump-drive cable:

Remove and lubricate (after cleaning with a suitable solvent) this cable every 4000-5000 miles, using a good grade of wheel bearing grease, moly-based grease, or Delco ignition distributor grease. Just about any other type of grease tends to dry out and lose its lubricating properties.

General Troubleshooting

Engine won't start:

Cranking-signal valve not operating. This keeps the main control diaphragm from operating the spill-plunger to the rich level for engine starting. To check the valve, remove it and suck through the threaded end. You should be able to hear air just barely passing through the valve. By sucking through the opposite end of the valve, it should close.

Broken fuel pump drive cable. This prevents fuel from being delivered to the nozzles and, therefore, to the engine for starting.

Ignition not working. Usually, the ballast resistor shorts out or otherwise stops making circuit. What you usually find is that the engine will fire with the ignition key in the "start" position but die when the key goes to "run" position. You can always short across the resistor with a short section of wire just to be sure this is the problem. Just don't run the engine for any length of time with the ballast resistor shorted in this fashion.

Ruptured or leaking main fuel control diaphragm. If this is the case, the spill-plunger will not be operated (due to lost vacuum signal) and there will not be any start fuel to the engine.

And finally, there is a chance that the linkage connecting the main control diaphragm to the spill-plunger is broken. This linkage (sometimes called the axle-linkage assembly, depending upon whose manual you have) when it fails causes the fuel valve to remain in the full-open position, cutting off the supply of fuel to the nozzles.

Engine runs but tends to miss under load (sometimes at idle):

Injector nozzles are plugged if one or more spark plugs shows a lean mixture condition. Other than this, it is difficult to determine plugged nozzles without removing them from the engine and bench-testing. There is also a chance that an ignition analyzer (oscilloscope) will show high electrical resistance in one or more cylinders, suggesting a lean mixture and the possibility of a plugged nozzle.

Burned or broken spark plug wires. This sort of problem (electrical) can even extend to the distributor where cracked rotor or cap can cause the same sort of load-miss.

Poor fuel economy:

Most of the time, the problem here is incorrect calibration of the system. But an important point to remember is that unless the remainder of the engine is in a good state of tune, a companion problem (burned valves, worn piston rings, etc.) could make it very difficult, if even possible, to calibrate the injection system. Factory manuals are available that detail how such calibrations can be made, but the following is offered as a guide when working out calibrations in conjunction with a chassis dynamometer and air-fuel measuring instruments (actually the best method you can use).

At an engine speed of about 4000 (wide open throttle), adjust the rich limit to provide an air-fuel mixture of around 11.5:1. Set the lean mixture limit of about 14.5:1, using a chassis dyno loading of 10 hp at a vehicle speed (on the rolls) of 40 mph. This should put the engine in an rpm range of around 2000-2500.

After these stops are adjusted, the ratio lever should hold on the lean stop at a vacuum of 9 inches of mercury. As the vacuum source is decreased, this ratio lever should contact the rich limit stop at about 3 inches of mercury. At a vacuum source reading of 6 inches of mercury, the ratio lever should be half-way between the rich and lean mixture limits (stops).

Poor fuel economy can also result from a sticking fuel valve or spill plunger. Dirty fuel can cause such a problem. Disassembly of the injection system and a thorough solvent cleaning of all pieces normally cures problems of this nature.

Another fuel consumption problem can result from a ruptured cranking-signal valve. Should the diaphragm be punctured or stuck in the open position, this valve will allow full intake manifold vacuum to operate the main fuel control diaphragm. Consequently, the system will run in its "full rich" condition all the time. You can check this valve by sucking on its inlet end to see if the valve closes. If it does not, you'll need to replace it.

And finally, fuel economy problems can result from a main control diaphragm that has contracted as a result of excessive engine compartment heat. A check for this condition requires removal of the diaphragm housing cover. It should be loose enough that it will "sag" under its own weight. If not, replace it.

Some Summary Bits and Pieces

This section of the book discusses state-of-the-art fuel injection systems not so much from a "here's everything that's on the market" point of view but in a vein to suggest what the fuel injection concept is all about and where such systems may go in the immediate future. Design considerations that influence how a given system performs have been included to show how other areas or parts of a given engine affect both fuel delivery requirements and how these are best accomplished. Emphasis has been placed on the design of intake manifold-ing not because this was just a related area but because overall injection system performance is particularly sensitive to how the intake manifold design problem is handled. From the manufacturer of just about any F.I. system, literature is available that describes the components and operation of their particular package. The purpose in these pages was to familarize you with the objectives and design criteria of fuel injection systems so that personal evaluation of what is good and what is not could be more easily made.

And whether you plan purchase of an injection system or already have one, you hopefully have a better understanding of both what it should do for the engine and where it can get into trouble in trying to do what it should. Ironically enough, the notion that a fuel injection system that really handles all fuel requirements of a given engine is more akin to a carburetor than anything else suggests that the "electronic carburetor" may not be that far down the road. But then again, how much different from such a part is electronic fuel injection . . . in the second place.

CONSTANT-FLOW INJECTION

Though electronically-timed fuel injection systems hold tremendous potential for the future, the constant flow injector is still the king of the race track and drag strip. It is generally held that constant flow systems will not match the fuel flow to engine requirements throughout a wide engine speed range as well as carburetion or a timed injector. On the other hand, these systems are extremely reliable and simple. And, as the saying goes, when the throttle blades are standing on end, nothing works quite like a good constant-flow injector. This may be changed in the years to come but an injected smallblock Chevy is still a very impressive top-end performer.

It is perhaps because of their simplicity that these systems are not suited for day-to-day street performance. However, in bygone days several street rods around the country were fitted with constant-flow injectors. These were probably attempts to impress the local drive-in crowd, but some of these rods were equally as impressive in the performance department. It is said that the success of such a setup depended largely upon the expertise of the mechanic who did the tune-up work. These systems have all but disappeared from the street because of the problems with emissions and fuel economy. Those who had the fortune to see and hear a short-stroke Chevy or Ford with a good injector will not forget how responsive these engines were. We will miss them and lament their passing more than a little.

Among the many manufacturers of fuel injection systems the best known is probably the Hilborn system, designed by Stu Hilborn, and currently sold by Fuel Injection Engineering. Other major suppliers include (or have included): Enderle, Crower, Jackson, Scott and Algon. Most of the description included here is based on the Hilborn system. The other systems operate on roughly the same principles but may differ mechanically from the operation of the Hilborn system. Some of these injectors are no longer available but because of the relative simplicity, even a very old system can be made operative with very little work. About the only parts which cannot be replaced are special gaskets, or O-rings or similar rubber pieces, once supplied by the manufacturer and no longer available. However, it is easy to make your own gaskets and most O-rings are standard in size.

The operation of a constant-flow system is very simple. Air entry to the engine is controlled by a fairly standard butterfly valve arrangement. Usually there is one valve per cylinder, and

The traditional constant-flow injection system is not very sophisticated but its simplicity makes it ideal for drag racing and similar applications where all-out top-end power is the major consideration. Though many systems have been adopted for street use, the lack of accelerator pumps and other sophisticated fuel controls make them somewhat impractical for street use.

each valve is seated inside a separate manifold runner. All of the valves are joined by a linkage assembly that allows them to be controlled in unison. As the throttle pedal is pressed, all of the plates tip open in unison, allowing more air to enter the engine.

The fuel is controlled by a simple delivery system consisting of a fuel pump, a metering valve and individual nozzles located in each manifold runner. As the accompanying diagrams show, there are several variations on these basics to accommodate special requirements. Fuel is supplied from the tank to the fuel pump, usually through some sort of inline filter which is recommended to eliminate the tenant problems that dirt or debris can create. The pump is usually a vane- or gear-type pump that is driven by the crank or camshaft (at one-half crank speed). Fuel is fed under pressure to the metering valve, often called the "barrel value." This valve is directly connected to the throttle butterfly assemblies. As the butterflies open more, the metering valve opens more, delivering an increased quantity of fuel to the nozzles.

As the engine speed goes up, the fuel pump delivers more fuel. However, pump efficiency increases much more quickly than the engine demand. Therefore some means is needed to control the exact amount of fuel and tailor the "fuel curve" to the specific engine and type of racing. This is the function of the by-pass circuit. Excess fuel is bled away from the metering valve and allowed to return to the tank through a separate fuel line. To control the amount of fuel bled from the primary circuit, a small orifice or jet is placed inside the by-pass circuit. This jet is often called the "pill." It is easily replaced and provides a simple means to control fuel delivery. As the by-pass pill is made larger, more fuel will be bled away from the primary circuit and the resultant delivery to the engine will be less (the air-fuel ratio is leaner). As the pill is made larger, less fuel is bled from the main circuit (the engine receives more fuel and the air-fuel ratio is richer).

SPECIAL CIRCUITS

Another problem that must be considered is the extremely high fuel

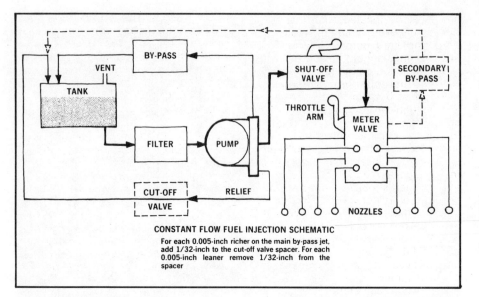

CONSTANT FLOW FUEL INJECTION SCHEMATIC

For each 0.005-inch richer on the main by-pass jet, add 1/32-inch to the cut-off valve spacer. For each 0.005-inch leaner remove 1/32-inch from the spacer

pressures developed at extreme engine speeds. When the pump is driven directly by the engine it will generate tremendous delivery pressures at very high crank speeds. This will be more than the by-pass circuit can handle and more than the engine can use. Therefore, another circuit may be needed in the system. This is the pressure relief circuit. Normally this is controlled by a simple relief valve and spring. When the pressure exeeds 150 lbs. it overcomes the spring pressure behind the valve and the valve opens, allowing excess fuel to be routed back to the fuel tank. This circuit is found only on older systems and has largely been superceded by the fuel cut-off circuit.

As special situations require, there are some additional methods of fuel control that may be added to the standard system. The most common is the secondary by-pass valve. This is yet another fuel by-passing circuit intended to decrease an overly-rich condition when the injector is operated at part throttle and when the throttle is suddenly closed, allowing the car to "coast." It is simply a poppet valve that is controlled by an internal spring. Normally the spring pressure is adjusted at the factory for satisfactory performance, however, it is possible to adjust the spring tension by varying the shim spacer behind the spring. Since the secondary by-pass provides a method to lean the mixture (by returning excess fuel back to the fuel tank) it allows better mid-range fuel control. It usually functions at a relatively small throttle opening position, therefore it will not normally cause excessive leaning at WOT. It is beneficial for drag cars using automatic transmissions (allowing better launching from part throttle) and in circle track cars, such as dirt track and sprint machines that must come off the throttle in the corners.

In certain instances a fuel cut-off valve may also be desirable. This is an additional method to control fuel in one specific engine range, in this case the upper speed ranges. Changing the pill will affect fuel delivery throughout the rpm band, but by installing a fuel cut-off valve it is possible to reduce fuel delivery in the upper ranges, without affecting delivery in the low-and mid-range speeds. This allows a reduction of fuel delivery to compensate for airflow dropoff in normally-aspirated engines. In some cases it can actually increase top-end drag strip performance. The method of operation is again a simple poppet valve. As the fuel pressure approaches the pre-set level (controlled by a spring and shim combinations), the poppet opens and fuel is returned to the tank. Most valves (Hilborn-type) are adjusted to blow off at about 6500-7000 rpm. The action is relatively gradual, by-passing more fuel as the engine rpm and fuel pressure continue to rise. *Normally this valve will not be needed.* However, it may be required in certain engine applications. It is best to obtain maximum engine

performance without using a cut-off. After the best "normal" operation is achieved, a cut-off can be added to gain a better balance between mid-range and absolute top-end performance.

MISCELLANEOUS CONSIDERATIONS

It is recommended that a good fuel filter be used at all times. Injector nozzles are very sensitive to debris that may become lodged inside them. Such a circumstance can be troublesome or expensive, depending upon the conditions. Most manufacturers recommend that a good, high-quality screen-type filter be used. It should be rated to filter at least as many gallons of fuel per hour as will be required under the highest engine demand. Naturally, the filter should be mounted in a secure fashion and the lines leading into and out of the filter must be securely fastened to prevent fuel leaks and to prevent air leakage into the hoses, a situation that may lead to hard starting.

In all-out racing the most common method of driving the fuel pump is with a special aluminum front engine cover that allows the pump to be mounted in front of the camshaft. An intermediate drive assembly of some sort then powers the pump from a takeoff on the cam. This is very adequate for racing. Another method to consider is an accessory Gilmer belt drive, often used to drive something like a dry sump oil pump. These drives are well-suited to power a fuel injection pump and are easily adapted to this purpose. They are normally trouble-free and extremely reliable and offer the added advantage of allowing a normal water pump and fan assembly to be used on the engine (if this is an important consideration for your particular needs). There are also some right-angle distributor drives available to drive the pump from the rear of the

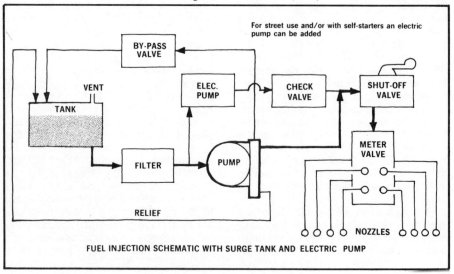

FUEL INJECTION SCHEMATIC WITH SURGE TANK AND ELECTRIC PUMP

For street use and/or with self-starters an electric pump can be added camshaft. Some modification may be required to the distributor but this is relatively simple. This method has been used satisfactorily on many machines.

Fuel-injected engines are very sensitive to "ram tuning" effects. When absolute peak performance is required, considerable experimentation may be necessary in order to determine the best tuned length. This can most easily be accomplished by cutting a normal set of ram tubes in half and using short sections of rubber tubing to vary the length of the stacks until the best overall length is found. Generally, a longer tube will increase low-end performance and a shorter tube will enhance top-end power. In most cases, something about six inches, overall, will be adequate, and most engines will not respond to changes less than one-inch in length, so you may save time by varying the length of the ram tubes in one-inch increments. Remember, also, that the intake tract length will be dependent upon the exhaust length. The best overall performance or the best "specific" power range performance will be gained when the two are properly coordinated (camshaft selection is also important in this "formula" so be aware that a cam change may affect the intake and exhaust tuned lengths).

The key to reliable fuel injection performance is sound fuel "management." It is important that the fuel tank and the fuel lines are carefully attended. The tank should be of sturdy construction, firmly mounted in a protected location. It must be vented to the atmosphere and some sort of control baffling is desirable. The exit line must be located such that it will not be uncovered during acceleration or during hard cornering. The return line openings should be above the fuel levels and should not interfere with the exiting fuel opening or they may induce fuel bubbling in the main line. For an unblown engine the main line should be ½- to ¾-inch, for blown ¾- to 1-inch. On the outlet side of the pump the size should be ⅜- to ½-inch. Of course, all these figures *refer to the inside diameter* and not the o.d. Top quality lines should be used and they should be inspected periodically for interior deterioration. Braided steel lines are not absolutely necessary but they are very popular. If at all possible, no 90° fittings should be used in the lines. These fittings will restrict fuel delivery. Finally, if the engine is to be started with a self starter, the fuel tank must be mounted at a higher level than the fuel pump in order to provide gravity delivery to the suction side of the pump.

A good shut-off valve is important in any constant flow system. This valve controls fuel delivery for start-up and for shut-down. It must be closed to prevent fuel overflow to the engine during long periods of storage. The accepted procedure is to close the valve after initial priming of the system (remember a constant-flow injector does not have an accelerator pump to prime the engine). The throttles are held to WOT until initial firing occurs and the shut-off is immediately opened after the engine lights. When the engine is shut down it is best to close the shut-off and allow the engine to drain the residual fuel in the lines as it stops. If the engine is to be stored for an extended period this will prevent fuel decomposition in the lines (however, if the engine will be stored for very long periods, the lines should be removed, flushed and blown dry with compressed air).

CARE AND MAINTENANCE

Injector maintenance is really very simple. Most injector manufacturers have reliable servicing facilities. It is wise to have the system inspected at least once a year or whenever practical. During the season, the throttle shafts should be oiled as needed, the fuel pump should be oiled occasionally (if it is mounted in such a manner that the rear seal does not receive lubrication during operation), and the nozzles should be inspected for dirt or rubber particles, indicating the fuel lines are beginning to deteriorate. During annual maintenance the manufacturer will check pump bearings and replace important rubber parts and gaskets. It is possible for a competent mechanic to perform this work on his own but he must know exactly what he is doing or performance may suffer. It is often said that poor fuel injection performance is almost always the result of bad "workmanship" by the mechanic.

The enclosed trouble-shooting guide may prove helpful to the novice who has problems. As we said, the greatest beauty of constant-flow fuel injection is its wonderful simplicity. It provides very high performance with a minimum of trouble. If all of the manufacturer's installation and tuning instructions are followed, this can truly be a route to Super Power.

HILBORN CONSTANT-FLOW FUEL PUMP RECOMMENDATIONS

GEAR PUMPS

PG 150A #00 — Used on extremely small engines such as motorcycles, etc.

PG 150A #0 — Medium size engines, 200″ up to 400″, on gas, methanol and moderate amounts of nitro.

PG 150A #1 — Large engines on gas and small percentages of nitro. Also used for blown engines on gas, methanol and small amounts of nitro.

PG 175 #2 — Used for high percentages of nitro with very large unblown engines.

PG 175 #3 — Used for very high percentages of nitro with blown engines.

VANE PUMPS

BL235 — Midget Offenhauser engines and other small such as motorcycles, etc.

BL420 — Medium size engines, 200″ thru 400″, on gas, methanol and small amounts of nitro.

BL630 — Large engines, 400″ and up, on gas, methanol, and small percentages of nitro. Also, can be used on blown engines on gas.

BL1500 — For all out blown fuel engines and special applications where tremendous quantities of fuel are required.

NOZZLE RECOMMENDATIONS FOR NORMALLY-ASPIRATED ENGINES

Engine Size — Cu. In.		Nozzle Size	Engine Size — Cu. In.		Nozzle Size
180″ thru 230″	Gasoline	4A	150″ thru 180″	Methanol	10A
230″ thru 260″	Gasoline	5A	180″ thru 230″	Methanol	12A
260″ thru 315″	Gasoline	6A	230″ thru 266″	Methanol	14A
315″ thru 360″	Gasoline	7A	266″ thru 315″	Methanol	16A
360″ thru 430″	Gasoline	8A	315″ thru 360″	Methanol	18A
430″ thru 480″	Gasoline	9A	360″ thru 430″	Methanol	20A
480″ thru 550″	Gasoline	10A	430″ thru 480″	Methanol	24A
			480″ thru 550″	Methanol	27A

TROUBLE-SHOOTING CONSTANT-FLOW INJECTION SYSTEMS

1. Engine will not start:
   A. Wrong rotation — fuel pump.
   B. Main fuel line loose.
   C. Air leak around fuel filter.
   D. By-pass installed backwards.
   E. By-pass in wrong line.
   F. By-pass poppet stuck in open position.
   G. Secondary poppet stuck open (when used).
   H. Too cold a spark plug.
   I. Improper fuel line hookup.
   J. Too lean an idle mixture.

2. Injector pops back when throttle is opened:
   A. Metering valve adjusted too lean.
   B. Air leak under intake manifold.
   C. Poppet sticking in by-pass body.
   D. Spring missing from by-pass valve.
   E. Faulty fuel pump.

3. Injector will not idle:
   A. Butterflys misadjusted.
   B. Poppet sticking in by-pass valve.
   C. Poppet stuck open in secondary (when used).
   D. Air leak in main fuel line (tank to pump).
   E. Restriction in by-pass line.
   F. Air vent in tank too small.
   G. Throttle stop not adjusted.

4. Injector idles very rich:
   A. Poppet stuck closed in by-pass valve.
   B. Wrong spring in by-pass.
   C. Vent too small in tank.
   D. Metering valve set too rich.
   E. Wrong size nozzles being used.
   F. Restriction in by-pass hose.
   G. Idle mixture too rich.

5. Engine runs lean on bottom end:
   A. Loose fuel line (tank to pump).
   B. Wrong size jet being used.
   C. Pump worn (low volume) faulty pump.
   D. Nozzles too small.
   E. Plugged nozzles.
   F. Plugged nozzle hose.
   G. Idle mixture too lean.

6. Engine runs lean on one bank:
   A. Main cross link adjusted incorrectly.
   B. Air leak in intake manifold.
   C. Plugged nozzles.
   D. Bent butterflys.

7. Engine runs lean on top end:
   A. Air leaks in main fuel line (tank to pump).
   B. Nozzles not flowing properly.
   C. Wrong size nozzles or jet.
   D. Worn fuel pump — low volume.
   E. Shut-off valve too small.
   F. By-pass hose returning fuel directly over outlet hose in fuel tank.

8. Engine runs rich on top end:
   A. Wrong poppet in by-pass valve.
   B. Wrong jet size being used.
   C. Restriction in by-pass hose.
   D. Vent too small in fuel tank.
   E. Wrong size fuel pump being used.
   F. Too cold a spark plug will make engine appear rich.

9. Injector will not start when engine is cold:
   A. Metering valve set too lean.
   B. Fuel tank in wrong location.
   C. Fuel pump weak.
   D. Fuel line loose (tank to pump).
   E. By-pass poppet sticking.
   F. Too cold a spark plug being used.

10. Engine starts, runs for a while, then floods:
    A. Wrong size fuel pump being used.
    B. Restrictions in by-pass valve hose.
    C. Vent in fuel tank too small.
    D. Wrong size nozzles being used.
    E. Wrong spring in by-pass valve.
    F. Pump being driven faster than ½ crank speed.

11. Injector bleeds fuel into engine when not running:
    A. Shut-off valve leaks.
    B. No shut-off valve being used.
    C. Fuel tank mounted too high when not using shut-off.
    D. Secondary poppet sticking open (when used).
    E. Fuel pump seal bad (when cam driven).

12. Injector throttle sticks when engine cold:
    A. This condition is common when running on gas, and all adjustments should be done with engine at operating temperature, cold for methanol.
    B. Bent butterflys.
    C. Butterflys installed backwards.

13. Injector throttle sticks when hot:
    A. Butterflys adjusted incorrectly.
    B. Cross link adjusted incorrectly.
    C. Intake gasket too thick.
    D. Throttle shaft bent.
    E. Rod end bearing worn.
    F. Throttle stops adjusted incorrectly.
    G. Throttle shaft being twisted by drive arm on throttle.
    H. Bent butterflys.
    I. Butterflys installed backwards.

14. Injector throttle closed, yet engine still idles fast:
    A. Idle mixture too lean.
    B. Air leak — intake gasket.
    C. Butterflys bent.
    D. Main cross link adjusted incorrectly.
    E. Worn throttle shaft bores.
    F. Butterflys installed backwards.
    G. Air leak in inlet side of pump.

15. Engine runs, but dies when throttle is closed:
    A. Air leak in main line (tank to pump).
    B. Intake gasket air leak.
    C. Throttle stops adjusted incorrectly.
    D. Metering valve too lean.
    E. Poppet sticking in by-pass valve.
    F. Secondary by-pass valve poppet stuck open (when used).
    G. Wrong size pump being used (too small).

16. One or two cylinders run lean no matter what jet is used when throttle is open:
    A. Nozzles plugged or nozzle hoses plugged.
    B. Blown head gasket gives indication of lean condition.
    C. Nozzle screens removed (faulty nozzles).

17. One or more cylinders run lean at idle:
    A. Nozzles plugged or nozzle hose plugged.
    B. Blown head gaskets.
    C. Nozzle screens removed or faulty nozzles.
    D. Bent butterflys.
    E. Throttle shaft bores worn.

WE'RE INTERESTED IN YOUR OPINION

We would appreciate your opinion of this publication. Please return this portion of the page (or a copy) to the publisher. Mail to:

S-A DESIGN BOOKS
515 West Lambert, Bldg "E"
Brea, CA 92621

How did we cover the subjects?
☐ Covered well ☐ Adequate ☐ Poorly done

On a scale of 1 to 10 (10 being best), I would rate this book:
☐ 1 to 3 ☐ 4 to 6 ☐ 7 to 9 ☐ 10

Other comments (how could we have improved this book, what subjects would you like to read about, etc.).

_____

_____

_____

_____

_____

SUPERPOWER

JOIN THE S-A DESIGN "BOOK USERS GROUP"

As a member of the Users Group, you will receive periodic updates on new books and upcoming supplements, plus special membership discounts. And it's all free! Just mail in the attached post card or use this coupon (or a copy). Mail to:

S-A DESIGN BOOKS
515 West Lambert, Bldg. "E"
Brea, CA 92621

Name _____

Street _____

City _____ State _____ Zip _____

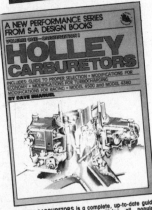

We encourage individuals to purchase books from their local retailers. S-A Design Books are sold internationally in speed shops and book stores. However, if you cannot find our books locally, you may order direct from S-A Design by sending $10.95 plus $1.50 postage and handling per copy to our warehouse (California residents add 66¢ tax each). S-A Design warehouse is located at: 515 West Lambert Blvd., Bldg. "E," Brea, CA 92621.